CONFERENCE INTERPRETING

BENJAMINS TRANSLATION LIBRARY

The Benjamins Translation Library aims to stimulate academic research and training in translation studies, lexicography and terminology. The Library provides a forum for a variety of approaches (which may sometimes be conflicting) in a historical, theoretical, applied and pedagogical context. The Library includes scholarly works, reference books, post-graduate text books and readers in the English language.

Volume 23

Yves Gambier, Daniel Gile and Christopher Taylor (eds)

Conference Interpreting: Current Trends in Research

CONFERENCE INTERPRETING: CURRENT TRENDS IN RESEARCH

PROCEEDINGS OF THE INTERNATIONAL
CONFERENCE ON *INTERPRETING:*
WHAT DO WE KNOW AND HOW?
(Turku, August 25-27, 1994)

Edited by

YVES GAMBIER
University of Turku

DANIEL GILE
Univ. Lumière de Lyon 2 and ISIT, Paris

CHRISTOPHER TAYLOR
SSLMIT, Trieste

JOHN BENJAMINS PUBLISHING COMPANY
AMSTERDAM/PHILADELPHIA

The paper used in this publication meets the minimum requirements of American National Standard for Information Sciences — Permanence of Paper for Printed Library Materials, ANSI Z39.48-1984.

Library of Congress Cataloging-in-Publication Data

International Conference on Interpreting--What Do We Know and How? (1994 : Turku, Finland)
    Conference interpreting : current trends in research : proceedings of the International Conference on Interpreting--What Do We Know and How? : Turku, August 25-27, 1994 / edited by Yves Gambier, Daniel Gile, Christopher Taylor.
    p.   cm. -- (Benjamins translation library, ISSN 0929-7316 ; v. 23)
    Includes bibliographical references and index.
    1. Translating and interpreting--Congresses. 2. Congresses and conventions--Congresses. 3. Communicative competence. I. Gambier, Yves, 1949- . II. Gile, Daniel. III. Taylor, Christopher. IV. title. V. Series.
P306.2.I555   1997
418'.02--dc21   97-16441
ISBN 90 272 1626 6 (Eur.) / 1-55619-707-1 (US) (alk. paper)   CIP

John Benjamins Publishing Co. • P.O.Box 75577 • 1070 AN Amsterdam • The Netherlands
John Benjamins North America • P.O.Box 27519 • Philadelphia PA 19118-0519 • USA

Table of Contents

Foreword

Daniel Gile, *Université Lumière, Lyon 2 & ISIT, Paris*
Yves Gambier, *University of Turku*
Christopher Taylor, *SSLMIT, Trieste*

The conference on interpretation research held in Turku (Finland) from the 25th to the 28th of August 1994 with the aim of finding out "what do we know and how?" was an unusual one; so are these proceedings. The next few pages contain information and pointers to help readers understand and interpret them in the light of the context and objectives of the meeting.

The idea of holding a conference taking stock of developments in interpretation research came from Yves Gambier of the University of Turku's Centre for Translation and Interpreting. The concept was then developed with Daniel Gile, starting shortly after the Fourth Scandinavian symposium on translation theory SSOT IV, in 1992 (Gambier & Tommola 1993). The last 'research conference' on interpreting had been held in Venice in 1977 (Gerver & Sinaiko 1978); another important conference, organized by Trieste in 1986 (Gran & Dodds 1989), though a milestone in the history of interpretation research (see Gile 1995c), was devoted to training issues, not to research. Many translation conferences also included papers on interpretation, but were not focussed and did not give a full picture. The idea was to make this new Conference as interesting and useful to participants as possible. With this aim in mind, a number of ideas were suggested, and two were adopted:
- The conference was to be as *interdisciplinary* as possible, so that interpreters could break away from their own practice-oriented ideas and learn what other disciplines had to offer.
- The conference was to be be as *interactive* as possible, so that participants could have serious, active exchanges, rather than passively listening to a series of papers which, judging by the literature of the past years, would probably not be very innovative.

It was therefore decided to organize the meeting in the following way:
- There would be three keynote speeches by non-interpreters from three relevant disciplines.
- The main thrust of the conference would consist of round tables and workshops rather than paper sessions. The formal distinction between the two was that in round tables, most of the interaction would take place between panelists, and in the workshops, all of the interaction would be with the floor. However, during the conference, most participation materialized in the round table format.
- As far as possible, there would be at least one 'outsider' (i.e. a non-interpreter) on the panel in each workshop/round table.
- There would also be poster sessions allowing participants to present their projects individually.

The meeting was organized by Yves Gambier & Jorma Tommola, who also took care of all the administrative aspects of the conference, Christopher Taylor of the Scuola Superiore di Lingue Moderne per Interpreti e Traduttori (SSLMIT) of the Universita degli Studi di Trieste, and Daniel Gile of the Institut Supérieur d'Interprétation et de Traduction (ISIT) in Paris. The task of enlisting speakers for the plenaries and moderators and rapporteurs for the workshops and round tables was shared between them. Moderators and rapporteurs were asked to organize their workshops and round tables and to recruit panelists.

The themes of the workshops and round tables are as presented in the table of contents. For the three plenaries, the following three speakers were invited:
- From neurophysiology: Franco Fabbro, from Italy, who gave his paper with Laura Gran, an interpreter who has been involved for years in interpretation research related to neurophysiological issues (see Gran 1992).
- From cognitive psychology: Charles Tijus, from France.
- From communication studies: Per Linell, from Sweden.
In addition, twenty one posters were on display.

About 130 persons attended the conference, mostly from Europe, but Canada and the USA were also represented, as well as Israel and Japan in Asia, and Australia. Save for a handful, most were conference interpreters, but there were also a few community interpreters, business interpreters and sign-language interpreters. The vast majority were also interpretation instructors. The conference was therefore neither 'purely' academic, nor purely 'professional', but rather in-between, with a few sessions more pronouncedly on one side or the other. The more academically-minded participants expressed some anxiety over the publication of their contributions in the proceedings of the conference, and were expecting the possibility of publishing full papers in spite of the interactive workshop/roundtable format that had been chosen. The following policy was decided:

- The proceedings would reflect the conference as it was held, that is with three plenary papers and workshop and round table reports, each of which would be prepared under the responsibility of the moderator(s) and rapporteur, either as a general synopsis, or as a sequence of summaries of the panelists' individual contributions. Both formats were produced.

- A separate volume of posters would be published. As a matter of fact some of the posters were expanded into short papers (Tommola 1995).

- Participants who wished to do so were free to publish full papers developing their Turku contributions elsewhere if they felt it appropriate to be more explicit than the synthetic texts included in the reports of their respective workshops and round tables.

These proceedings have taken a long time to prepare for essentially two reasons. While the first is organizational, the second is interesting as a feature of the interpreters' research activities and priorities:

- The three editors were in Finland, France and Italy, the moderators and the rapporteurs spread out over a wider area, including Japan and Israel, and individual contributors were even more scattered. Since a sizable proportion of the participants had to rely on traditional ("snail") mail, sending the contributions, replying with comments and queries and discussing problematic issues required a great deal of time. In retrospect, time could have been saved by asking participants to prepare their written contributions in advance. However, this would have excluded from the proceedings both the interactive part and any corrections brought about in the individual contributions by the interaction.

- Participants whose main activity was academic tended to send in their reports rapidly. However, for other interpreters, the expected added value of the conference seems to have resided mostly in the on-line interaction, and the long and tedious work of producing written texts was lower on the priority list; some contributions were received more than a year after the conference, and responses to queries and comments by the editors were often very slow in coming. Some "academics" understandably expressed anxiety and discontent over the lag time, and the editors considered not publishing those contributions arriving late. However, the conference was a discussion of fundamental research methodology and research policy issues rather than a review of recent results, so that the relevance of the proceedings should not age as rapidly as that of such reviews. Moreover, it was the editors' wish that these proceedings be a faithful reflection of the conference, rather than an academic publication in the usual sense. It was therefore felt that the non-inclusion of significant parts of the total image would be worse than a further delay, however strong the frustration and temptation to inflict capital text punishment upon perpetrators of deadline-violation.

The results of the pre-conference preparation, in-conference interaction and post-conference organisation are finally out in these proceedings. No attempt will be made to introduce the numerous speakers, moderators and panelists because of their large number; an informative profile on some can be found in Pöchhacker 1995, and more generally, in *Target* 7:1, a special issue on interpreting research. On the other hand, a number of features of the *topology* of the interpretation research field can be seen through a meta-analysis of these proceedings:

1. *Interpretation research and interpreter training are inextricably linked*
Almost all contributors and other conference participants were faculty members of interpretation sections of translation and interpretation schools, and whatever their discipline-related approach, their research was predominantly aimed at applications for training. Some constraining implications of this situation are discussed in Gile 1995c. On the other hand, the very fact that participants were heavily involded in interpretation training shows the power of this situation as an incentive for research (see Viaggio's optimistic note in this respect).

2. *For the time being, there are few real applications from interpretation research*
The majority of the reports presented here either refer to basic research or announce *potential* applications; however, in spite of some authors' claims regarding their implications on the practice of interpreting and the training of interpreters, the few findings reported in the conference (also see Tommola 1995) show that we are still a long way from such results (see in particular Dodd's sobering analysis on the lack of effect of research on training). Therefore, while research can be interesting and useful to the career of individual researchers (see Strolz 1995), its *direct* usefulness for the profession has not been demonstrated to this date. As pointed out by Dodds, the one field where some progress may have been made is the neurophysiological one, and   .

possible applications will take a long time to come (see however Riccardi's more optimistic assessment). This should explain the indifference, and sometimes even the animosity of professionals towards interpretation research (as commented upon by Fabbro, a non-interpreter).

3. *Difficulties in establishing real interaction between "central" interpretation research and neighboring disciplines*

This may be one of the most interesting phenomena to become salient in the proceedings of a conference which had been designed with interdisciplinarity in mind (see Moser-Mercer's hopes in this respect). Several authors, in particular Shlesinger, mention the difficulties involved in working transdisciplinarily. Lambert refers to the difference between the foci of interest of cognitive scientists and interpreters. The former prefer the 'clean' 'low' level of cognitive science, in which processes are studied component by component, or small sub-assembly by small sub-assembly, while the latter are interested in the 'high' (holistic) level at which they expect applicable results. Such a holistic level is "as messy as it can get" (Isham) because of the complexity of the assemblies that make up interpretation and of their interaction. Other factors, more sociological in nature, may explain why researchers from other disciplines working on interpretation tend to focus on their own 'native' literature and disregard relevant publications by interpreters - a few such references were added by the editors as editorial comments to give readers a wider perspective of existing research. Interestingly, some interpreters taking up paradigms in established disciplines seemed to behave not unlike non-interpreters in this respect, thus developing an 'immigrant' syndrome leading to identification with the host community and rejection of their native community. Finally, a number of non-interpreters and interpreters apparently tend to be attracted to particular paradigms or tools from such host disciplines, linguistic, sociological and otherwise, proceed to explore their theoretical applicability, and then stop, without actually testing them, adapting them and developing them for actual use on interpretation corpora (again, see Dodd's analysis).

These problematic aspects of interdisciplinary work merit some thought and possibly remedial strategies.

4. *Variability in the writing style*

While the three plenary papers were predictably written in compliance with the usual academic text norms, a striking feature of the reports received is variability in their style. Some are academic, others informal, some rather literary, and others 'dry', some very factual and objective, and some personal and/or normative. No attempt was made to smooth out the differences, since these reflect different 'personalities' who are active in the field and integrated into the interpreting research community, a less frequent social phenomenon in more established disciplines, where the textual dress of activity is more uniform. This heterogeneity can be seen as symptomatic of a lack of institutional maturity in the field of interpretation research, which is not only negative, since the lack of consolidation allows more flexibility and innovation.

5. *Variability on the scale of "scientificity"*
Similarly, while some contributions comply with the major norms of scientific procedure, at least as regards the presentation of their work, and present hypotheses, theories and paradigms, others are anecdotal or descriptive, without any attempt to systematically describe, circumscribe or analyse reality beyond their subjective perception. Again, the fact that such contributions find their way into the interpretation research community is indicative of the lack of maturity of the field as a scholarly discipline.

6. *Variability in the discipline-related approaches*
These proceedings reflect an almost exclusive dominance of the following discipline-related approaches to interpreting research:
a. The cognitive psychology approach (for example in Moser et al.)
b. The neurophysiological approach, which interacts strongly with the cognitive psychology approach (for instance in Fabbro & Gran)
c. The linguistics-centered approach (Taylor-Torsello), which often links up to the cognitive psychology and neurophysiological approach.
d. The sociological approach (for example in Linell)
e. The intercultural approach (for example in Kondo)
f. The holistic approach, in which interpretation is approached at a high aggregate level, for instance in the assessment of interpretation quality by users and in some reflections upon training (for example in Shlesinger).

While in the interpreting research community, the cognitive and neurophysiological approaches are essentially experimental, the linguistics-centered approach is more often observational or 'naturalistic'. So is the sociological approach, with its case studies. The intercultural approach is more ideological and prescriptive. As to holistic studies by interpreters, they tend to be descriptive, experimental or observational.

This discipline-related variability makes the coming together of interpretation research as a unique discipline difficult, as researchers adopting these distinct approaches often have little in common.

7. *Wider horizons*

On the positive side, these proceedings show a definite trend towards a widening of horizons: for the first time, an interpretation conference included not only a significant number of participants and contributions from conference interpreting, but also contributions from liaison interpreting, court interpreting, business interpreting and sign-language interpreting. Moreover, for the first time in Europe, the issue of non intra-European languages and cultures was given a significant share of the available time and attention (Kondo, Mizuno, Setton). While the precise interactions and potential benefits of such multiple approaches remain to be studied and optimized, there can be little doubt that this development amounts to an enriching of the common reservoir of knowledge and mental resources.

What general conclusions can be drawn from the conference as regards the future ?

The quality of interpretation research by the standards of established disciplines, as seen through these proceedings, is highly variable - keeping the theme of the conference in mind, the editors did endeavour to improve the texts with various suggestions and corrections, but did not attempt to change the fundamental nature of the authors' approaches or refuse to publish their contributions, thus affording readers a more representative view of the actual status of the field. Several authors, in particular Isham and Kalina, have noted an improvement over the past, especially in terms of communication and the forming of an actual interpretation research community. Qualitatively speaking, in the literature, there is also an increasing number of solid studies, alongside what still remains a majority of texts which do not comply with generally accepted research norms. In other words, institutionally, the case is far from clear-cut. Will interpretation research develop as a discipline per se (Gran)? Or as a sub-discipline of Translation studies (Pöchhacker)? Will it stabilize temporarily as a fuzzy set of associated activities based on different paradigms? Will it be absorbed by related disciplines? One key to its future is technical, and will depend on the findings both within interpretation research and within related disciplines, especially in the cognitive sciences. Another key is institutional, and will depend on efforts made by academic and extra-academic bodies to promote interpretation research and train interpretation researchers.

Neurolinguistic Research in Simultaneous Interpretation

Franco Fabbro, M.D., *Institute of Physiology*
& Laura Gran, *Scuola Superiore di Lingue Moderne per Interpreti
e Traduttori
University of Trieste, Italy*

The present paper deals with the following five main questions:

1. How does a neurolinguist (who is not an interpreter) see the work of interpreting?
2. How can his field of research shed light on interpretation?
3. What does he expect interpreters and interpretation to bring to research (methodology, way of looking at some processes, interplay between practice and theory)?
4. What is the significance of neurolinguistic studies for interpretation?
5. What are the possible developments in interdisciplinary research?

Items 1 to 3 have been dealt with by Franco Fabbro while Laura Gran has written sections 4 and 5.

1. How does a neurolinguist see the work of interpreting?

With its high level of complexity, simultaneous interpretation (SI) is a cognitive task which also represents an interesting field of research for a neurolinguist. A brief list of the main characteristics which render it interesting for neurolinguistic and neuropsychological research will follow.

1.1 *Language proficiency in interpreters*

The use of conference interpreters as subjects of neuropsychological experiments on bilingualism is a very useful step to overcome one of the main methodological problems of this kind of research. The problem is one of differing levels of proficiency, making for non homogeneous samples (Obler et al. 1982). Professional interpreters as experimental subjects offer the guarantee of knowing at least two languages at a very advanced level.

1.2 *Specific aspects of language production in SI*

Language production in SI has many characteristics in common with everyday language production, but differs in communication "goals". Indeed, in interpretation the actual goals of communication are determined by an external mind, which is not that of the interpreter, but that of the speaker who produces the original message. A neuropsychologist who intends to study the processes of language production can therefore find in interpretation a useful experimental paradigm. As such, it is much more efficient than paraphrasing in that it is by no means artificial to professional interpreters, who engage in it daily.

1.3 *Implicit and explicit aspects of interpretation*

During SI both automatic cognitive components of implicit memory and non-automatic cognitive components linked to explicit memory systems are activated. In particular, the conscious evaluation of the speaker's communication goals, the voluntary monitoring of the interpreter's own production and the self-judging of his/her performance while it is being realized, are all examples of non-automatic, explicit cognitive strategies. On the other hand, the re-organization of auditory and attentive functions during SI, the ability to listen and speak at the same time, and the correct use of two languages at the same time are examples of implicit automatic cognitive strategies (Graf & Mason 1993; Paradis 1994).

In my opinion, identifying and studying implicit and explicit components of SI is fundamental not only for research, but also for teaching SI. While explicit components of the interpretation process can be learned and monitored consciously, implicit components are opaque to introspection and are acquired through repeated exposure and practice. Since implicit and explicit components are part of two separate cognitive systems, subserved by different cerebral structures, they should be regarded separately, also for instance in aptitude testing for SI.

1.4 *Studying SI as a paradigm of divided attention*

Since the 1960's, SI has been considered and studied as a "natural" paradigm of divided attention. Other, albeit more artificial examples of divided attention are: reading aloud a text while writing another text under dictation, or playing the piano while shadowing verbal material, etc.

In the process of acquisition of tasks requiring divided attention, some common phases have been observed: at the beginning, students tend to focus their attention on one task at a time, they make many mistakes and get easily tired; then after a certain period of daily training, which may last about 6 to 12 months, some subjects finally succeed in carrying out two or more tasks concurrently, without necessarily focussing their voluntary attention on either of the tasks. After several concurrent tasks have become automatized, they can use their awareness and attention for the purpose of monitoring their performance in general, or even of thinking of something completely irrelevant to the actual complex task.

Since these studies are still at an initial stage, together with Sylvie Lambert of the University of Ottawa and Valeria Darò of the University of Trieste, I have tried to analyse the effect of focussing attention either on input or output during SI performed by professionals. The data analysis has still to be completed, but according to the first results conscious and constant focussing of attention either on the input or on the output turned out to be detrimental to the whole interpretation performance. The use of conscious strategies in a task which should be highly automatized interferes with the normal course of mental processes (Treisman 1965; Lawson 1967; Spelke et al.1976; Hirst et al. 1980; Lambert et al.1993).

1.5 *SI and memory*

SI can also serve as a useful paradigm for research on memory. During SI, working memory systems and long-term memory systems are activated. Pioneering studies by David Gerver and Sylvie Lambert have revealed reduced recall ability for verbal material after SI as opposed to consecutive interpretation or mere listening. Recent studies conducted independently by Bill

Isham and Valeria Darò (Isham & Lane 1993; Isham 1994; Darò 1994; Darò & Fabbro 1994) suggest that the process of SI implies a reduction in long-term memory attributable to the effect of articulatory suppression on working memory, which is caused by concurrent listening and speaking. Moreover, it is reasonable to suspect that in professional simultaneous interpreters the long-term memory systems undergo a functional re-organization, but this is an intriguing phenomenon that future researchers will have to clarify.

1.6 *Auditory feedback in interpreters*

During language production, several systems of feedback monitoring are activated: peripheral feedback systems (auditory, tactile, and proprioceptive), and internal feedback systems (motor pre-programming circuits, such as the cortico-cerebello-thalamo-cortical loop and the cortico-striato-thalamo-cortical loop). In a recent study (Spiller-Bosatra & Darò 1992; Fabbro & Darò 1994), simultaneous interpreters were found to be highly resistant to the language-disrupting effects of delayed auditory feedback (DAF). This shows that interpreters have or have developed a particular neurophysiological organization for language production, which is mainly based on internal feedback systems, thereby enabling them to curtail the detrimental effects of interference between listening and concurrent speaking and to reduce the execution time of some phases of the whole SI process.

1.7 *The processes of oral translation*

The processes of oral translation can be studied through SI. In the past 10 years Laura Gran and I have tried to investigate the linguistic (left hemispheric) and non-linguistic (right-hemispheric) cerebral structures involved in the process of SI (Fabbro et al. 1990; Spiller-Bosatra et al. 1990; Fabbro et al. 1991; Fabbro 1993; Fabbro & Gran 1994). Since SI affects the verbal components (comprehension, translation, production) and the non-verbal components (assessment of the communication goals, monitoring of the correct register and prosody, etc.) of oral communication, we found a general involvement of both cerebral hemispheres, with a greater activation of the right hemisphere than in normal verbal expression.

The use of far more sophisticated techniques, such as PET, EEG and electromagnetic recording, can possibly shed more light on the respective role of the different cerebral structures subserving oral translation processes.

1.8 *Error analysis*

In my opinion, one of the most important fields of research in interpretation is the analysis of errors made during interpretation performances. Some systems of error classification for SI have been proposed in the past (Oléron & Nanpon 1965; Barik 1975; Gerver 1976), but they are somehow incomplete and insufficient, particularly for the quantitative assessment of mistakes during experimental sessions. In our research on attention focussing with Lambert and Darò (to be published), we have tried to revise and extend previous classification systems. In my opinion, much has yet to be done in order to elaborate an exhaustive linguistic analysis of semantic, syntactic and lexical mistakes made during interpretation. Moreover, in such an analysis it would be extremely useful to take into consideration the language pair(s) used in different interpretation settings.

I am convinced that error analysis would greatly benefit from a comparison between errors produced during SI and those produced by multilingual aphasic patients during oral translation tasks elicited in neuropsychological tests for the assessment of bilingual aphasia. Such a procedure could help us to better understand the role of some specific cerebral structures in the process of oral translation.

2. How can neurolinguistic research shed light on interpretation?

My research field lies within the domain of neurolinguistics, which is a branch of neurology. The main goals of neurolinguistics are: a) the clinical analysis of language disorders for the diagnosis and rehabilitation of aphasias; and b) the study of the cerebral organization of language and languages.

2.1 *Methods*

In order to describe acquired language disorders it is necessary to know and to apply the basic principles of linguistics to the study of aphasic patients. For this purpose, special tests have been developed which help to assess the patient's residual abilities in different linguistic tasks (spontaneous speech, comprehension, production, repetition, reading, and writing) and at various linguistic levels (phonological, morphological, lexical, syntactic and semantic). There are standardized tests for monolingual and also for bilingual aphasic patients (Huber et al. 1983; Paradis 1987).

To give a general idea of the tasks of a neurolinguist, I will briefly explain the most crucial aspects of speech analysis in the way it is performed with M.Paradis' *Bilingual Aphasia Test* (1987). Five minutes of the patient's spontaneous speech in each language he knows are recorded and transcribed and then analysed according to the following parameters: 1. number of utterances; 2. total number of words; 3. mean length of utterance; 4. mean length of the 5 longest utterances; 5. number of different words; 6. type/token ratio; 7. number of neologisms; 8. number of phonemic paraphasias; 9. number of semantic paraphasias; 10. number of verbal paraphasias; 11. number of perseverations; 12. number of paragrammatisms; 13. number of agrammatisms; 14. number of word-order errors; 15. number of verbs per utterance; 16. number of subordinate clauses; 17. number of intraphrasal pauses; 18. number of circumlocutions; 19. number of stereotypic phrases; 20. evidence of word-finding difficulties; 21. detection of foreign accent; 22. number of inappropriate foreign words; 23. number of individual sentences that are semantically deviant.

In neuropsychological and neurolinguistic analysis all the components and subcomponents underlying a cognitive process, such as language, are not thought of or theoretically hypothesized by scholars "a priori", but rather they are the result of direct observations on the spot. The patients themselves with their particular detectable deficits suggest to neurolinguists how a particular cognitive function may possibly be organized. Since the first studies on the cerebral organization of language by P.P. Broca and C. Wernicke it has been possible to deduce that language is not a unitary function, but rather a mosaic of several different interacting functions (Broca 1861; Wernicke 1874; Luria 1976; Caplan 1990). Subsequent studies indicated that language can be considered as being organized on three main levels: i) the main level which includes all the others is called the *general neurofunctional language system*; ii) the intermediate level is made up of several different *subsystems*, such as comprehension, production, writing, reading, etc.; and iii) the lower level, which is formed by different *modules* representing the most elementary cognitive units, that are linked together in order to form a particular language subsystem.

From an epistemological point of view, it is important to underline that these kinds of models hypothesizing *subsystems* and *modules* within a general language system are not a product of the fervent imagination of scholars in the field, but rather the interpretation of real phenomena observed in neurological patients showing so-called "dissociations" and "double dissociations". For example, the description of an aphasic patient who has lost the ability to speak but not to understand language following a cerebral lesion, represents a clear "dissociation" between the subsystems of production and comprehension. The description of another patient with the opposite clinical picture, i.e. with intact language production and impaired comprehension due to a lesion to a different brain area, makes the case for a "double dissociation" between these two language subsystems, thus confirming their reciprocal neurofunctional independence. By observing and reporting several different cases of double dissociations, it was also possible to identify different modules of the general language system: some aphasic patients, for instance, who were requested to write words were only able to write the consonants and systematically dropped all the vowels (Cubelli 1991; Shallice 1988). On the basis of similar observations, the existence of independent modules for vowels and consonants in writing has been hypothesized.

2.2 Neurolinguistics and oral translation

The ability to translate from one language into another is a typical instance of the verbal behaviour of any bilingual person; the ability to translate orally for many hours a day is a professional characteristic of conference interpreters. Neurolinguistic studies on translation have described specific pathological dissociations in bilingual patients, which helped identify some neurofunctional components of the translation system. Following particular brain lesions, some polyglot aphasics have been reported to have lost the ability to *translate in both directions* (Gastaldi 1951). According to Roman Jakobson (1971), translation skills are related to posterior language areas (temporo-parietal regions), which generally account for the paradigmatic level of language. A lesion in these areas in unilingual individuals impairs their ability to shift from one word to its synonyms or to its corresponding circumlocutions, whereas in multilinguals it impairs the ability to translate from one language into another. Jakobson's hypothesis was further corroborated by subsequent studies, though recent observations revealed that posterior structures alone do not account fully for translation abilities. Aglioti and Fabbro (1993) have reported the case of a patient who, following a vascular lesion to the basal ganglia of the left hemisphere, was no longer able to translate "passively", i.e. from her L2 into her mother tongue (L1), whereas she could still translate from L1 into L2. The basal ganglia are a subcortical structure of the so-called *frontal lobe system* subserving relevant functions such as the choice of behaviour, the switching from one behaviour to another, speech motivation and initiation, emotional aspects of verbal communication, etc. More recently, another aphasic patient I have studied together with Paradis, who had a lesion of the left basal ganglia, could not translate words from L3 (English) into L1 (Friulian), whereas she still could translate from L1 into L3 (Fabbro & Paradis 1995). Translation impairments in these patients suggest that the neurofunctional components accounting for the ability to translate in one particular direction are at least partially separate and independent from those subserving the process of translation in the opposite direction; they also indicate that some translation subsystems are organized in the structures of the frontal lobe system of the left hemisphere (Fabbro 1994).

Other multilingual aphasic patients showed particular pathological translation behaviour which has been defined as *spontaneous translation* (Kauders 1929; Perecman 1984; Lebrun 1991). After a left hemisphere lesion these patients were no longer able to utter words or sentences without feeling the urge to translate them immediately into another language, or even into all the languages they knew. Some authors (Green 1986) have thus suggested that during the microgenesis of verbal expression, at some higher levels prior to the final articulation, a multilingual person prepares the expression he/she intends to utter in all the languages he/she knows, and then inhibits all the languages with the exception of the one which is to be selected for the production of that particular utterance. It is thus reasonable to suggest that the cerebral lesion of the patients with spontaneous translation behaviour may have damaged the subsystem which inhibits the non-selected languages, thus revealing a physiological stage of the process of verbal production in multilinguals, which in normal polyglots is regularly suppressed and does not manifest itself overtly.

M. Paradis (Paradis et al. 1982; Paradis 1993) described two bilingual aphasics presenting what he defined as *paradoxical translation*. At one moment in time, these patients could not speak one language (e.g. French) spontaneously, but only the other (e.g. English), though they were still able to translate from English into French, a language that they could not speak spontaneously, but not from French into English, a language that they could use for spontaneous speech. According to Paradis (1984), this kind of double dissociation suggests that in the bilingual brain there must be a series of subsystems accounting for translation skills, which are functionally independent from each other, so that one may work while all the others are impaired, and vice-versa. These subsystems are: 1) a subsystem for the comprehension of language A; 2) a subsystem for the comprehension of language B; 3) and 4) two separate subsystems for expression in language A and B, respectively; 5) a subsystem for the translation from A into B; and 6) a subsystem for the translation from B into A. A particular cerebral lesion in a bilingual individual may selectively impair for a certain period only one of these subsystems, while the others may still work.

Finally, another interesting dissociation in translation behaviour which has been observed in multilingual aphasics is the phenomenon of *translation without comprehension* (Veyrac 1931). The peculiar case of a bilingual aphasic patient has been reported: she was no longer able to understand simple questions or commands expressed in her mother tongue (e.g. "What time is it?" or "Show me your tongue!"), but nevertheless she translated them correctly into her second language. This type of dissociation suggests that at least some aspects of the whole translation process can be accomplished without the involvement of the systems accounting for conscious comprehension.

3. What does a neurolinguist expect interpreters and interpretation to bring to research?

3.1 *The significance of research in interpretation*

For the last 10 years I have been devoting part of my research efforts to interpretation. During this time, I have had the opportunity to meet many professional interpreters and a few researchers in the field. I have been able to talk to them about the results of our research and listen to their opinions concerning research, interpreter training and professional practice. One of the most widespread, and in my opinion anachronistic ideas I have heard lingering on in several universities was that research activities in interpretation were largely or even totally useless. For some people, in fact, only the teachings of a few so-called "Masters of Truth" (Detienne 1967) were necessary and sufficient, i.e. the teachings of people who, given their hierarchical position in the academic world or their seniority in the profession, are always right and hold the key to truth on what interpretation is and how it should be taught. Without intending to underplay the importance of good advice based on long experience, it must nevertheless be admitted that this kind of despotic attitude has always been strongly counterproductive and detrimental in the past. It is therefore a platitude, though a necessary one, to underline once again, also within this context, that scientific research, and therefore also research in the field of interpretation, is not an idle "game", but rather a systematic discussion among people who share an interest in the same topic and want to enlarge and usefully apply their knowledge. I am perfectly aware of the fact that these so-called "Masters of Truth" are not going to change their negative attitudes towards the role of research in interpretation. As suggested by Thomas Kuhn (1970), one will simply have to wait for them to die. But in the meantime it is undoubtedly more useful to devote one's work and energies to more receptive minds and to people who want to be trained in research on interpretation.

3.2 Interpreting as a scientific discipline

I think that conference interpretation has many characteristics in common with other professions, like engineering or medicine, where theoretical knowledge (e.g. language proficiency, knowledge of specific technical jargon, knowledge of mathematics and physics or anatomy, physiology and pharmacology, etc.) are absolutely necessary. However, these are not enough: being an interpreter is something more than simply being bilingual, likewise being a physician is something more than being a biologist.

Medical and engineering sciences defined their basic disciplines long ago: e.g anatomy, physiology and biochemistry for medicine, mathematical analysis and physics for engineering. Conference interpretation is a relatively new branch and probably its basic disciplines have not been properly defined yet. In my opinion these are: applied linguistics, psycholinguistics and neurolinguistics related to studies on multilingualism. However, I would like to stress that I am referring to applied linguistics, psycholinguistics and neurolinguistics as they are considered within the Anglo-American cultural domain, i.e. as prevailingly empirical disciplines.

It goes without saying that at present, given the scant knowledge derived from experimental studies, the practice and teaching of interpretation should be based on tradition, experience and common sense. However, this should be seen as a temporary stage, the same way present therapy against AIDS is only provisional while researchers are trying to develop an efficient remedy. At the same time, the results of experimental research must not be taken as axiomatic truths, but they should be discussed and constantly revised in the light of their theoretical relevance and practical utility.

3.3 *Methodological suggestions for further research*

For those who intend to enter this fascinating field of research, I would like to make a few suggestions. After having identified the relevant basic disciplines, a scholar should first of all try to acquire a sound theoretical and practical background of these disciplines, so as to know how to put the pertinent questions, how to set up and develop a research paradigm, how to analyse the data and how to present, discuss and interpret the results of research. Without this kind of background and attitude towards "literacy" in the field, no reliable research can be initiated.

Moreover, in my opinion the results of this kind of research on interpreting should not be published *only* in specialized journals for translators and interpreters, such as *Meta, Babel, Target, The Journal of Interpretation*, or *The Interpreters' Newsletter*, because the submitted paper could be in fact accepted or rejected for publication without being judged by a board of editors with sufficient knowledge in one of the relevant basic disciplines. Although the whole procedure might be longer and more difficult, research projects in interpretation should *also* be submitted to an international journal related to one of the above-mentioned basic disciplines, such as *Speech & Language, Applied Linguistics, Brain & Language*, etc. The same results could be worked out in another paper with a more practical formulation and didactic purposes, and then be submitted to a journal devoted to interpretation and translation. By following this approach, it will be possible to develop research studies on interpretation which will be open to the problems and the methods of other linguistic and cognitive disciplines. This will also force future researchers in interpretation to interact with a larger and more experienced scientific community. Thus the first stage would be characterized by the fact that boards of editors of related disciplines would have to judge research on interpretation, though this necessary initial phase should only be transient; in my opinion it should last at least a decade.

Finally, it is desirable that future academic evaluation of personal curricula that also include research experience should reward in particular those scholars who have also succeeded in publishing their research studies in international journals related to such disciplines, as opposed to those who only faced the judgement of referees and editors working for translation-related publications.

4. The significance of neurolinguistic studies for interpretation

We will now discuss some aspects of experimental studies carried out at the university of Trieste on neurolinguistic aspects of language acquisition, of cerebral lateralization for L1 and L2 and of simultaneous interpretation. Other investigations conducted by our team of researchers are discussed throughout this volume.

4.1 *Modifications in cerebral lateralization during the acquisition of a second language*

This was the first study on cerebral lateralization during intense training in a foreign language in adult age. Full details on the experiment are not given here, as they are available in the relevant publications (Fabbro et al. 1987; Gran 1992). I shall only point out the findings with greater significance for theoretical, practical and teaching purposes.

A group of first-year SSLMIT (Scuola superiore di lingue moderne per interpreti e traduttori - University of Trieste) students were submitted to a dichotic-listening test where figures in L1 were administered to the right ear (implying greater involvement of the contralateral left cerebral hemisphere) and figures in L2 were simultaneously administered to the left ear (right hemisphere) and vice versa. The overall results in this group of subjects showed, as expected, a better performance of the right ear (left hemisphere) in recalling digits administered in both languages. In fact, the left hemisphere is known to be dominant for verbal functions. A group of fourth-year interpreting students submitted to the same test, however, revealed a more symmetrical involvement of the cerebral hemispheres in recalling figures in L2 (while the left hemisphere remained predominant for the mother tongue), thus suggesting a modification of language organization after a period of intense linguistic training. This interpretation (a shift of language competence for L2 from the left to the right hemisphere during the acquisition of a second language), has been somewhat modified as a result of recent studies on verbal attention strategies (Paradis 1990). It is now believed that there may be modifications in attentive strategies regarding L1 and L2 in students who become accustomed to performing a very complex task such as simultaneous interpreting, which requires the participation of both cerebral hemispheres. These subjects seem to develop a dynamic modification of attention as a result of practising SI.

These observations have important teaching implications. Training in the use of language and in simultaneous interpreting modifies the cerebral organization for these tasks, as will also be seen when discussing other experimental studies. Teachers should realize that not only do students develop linguistic knowledge and skills which will enhance their performance in simultaneous interpreting; they also undergo the unconscious process of a cerebral reorganization of linguistic and attentive strategies. As intuitively pointed out by Van Dam (1989), training should also be focussed on the gradual acquisition of some automatic responses without which simultaneous interpreting would be impossible.

4.2 *Cerebral lateralization in simultaneous interpretation*

This study was carried out by using the verbal-manual interference technique, that is to say the subjects considered were asked to perform a linguistic task (simultaneous interpreting) concurrently with a manual task involving the alternating use of the left and right hand (Fabbro et al. 1990; Gran 1992). The intensive use of one hand in a given task (in this case, pressing a button connected to a counter as fast as possible) is controlled by the contralateral hemisphere, whose participation in the concurrent verbal task is thereby at least partly impaired. In this condition the ipsilateral hemisphere is more involved in the verbal task. Since, as is well known, the left hemisphere is verbal "par excellence" while the right hemisphere is allegedly hardly or not at all involved in verbal tasks in right-handed subjects, it was expected that students' performance would yield better results when the right hand (left hemisphere) was not engaged in the manual task and was therefore not subject to any interference caused by the verbal exercise. It was also expected that the right hemisphere would perform more poorly, especially when involved in the concurrent manual task. Surprisingly, the experiment did not reveal any significant cerebral asymmetry or lateralization in linguistic functions. This finding confirmed the results of the previous study, showing bilateral cerebral involvement in a complex verbal task such as simultaneous interpreting. This is probably due to the activation of considerable non-verbal, as well as verbal, cognitive tasks in SI. Green et al. (1990) repeated the same experiment, including simultaneous paraphrasing among the verbal tasks under investigation. Their subjects showed greater cerebral lateralization to the left hemisphere when paraphrasing in the same language and less lateralization when interpreting, which suggests different strategies when working across languages and when performing verbal exercises in the same language.

This finding also has some teaching implications: paraphrasing is certainly a useful exercise for the acquisition of linguistic rapidity and flexibility, but it requires attention and strategies of a kind different from those involved in switching between languages. One may suggest that paraphrasing exercises should be performed outside the booth, with intervals of reflection between input and output, rather than simultaneous paraphrasing in the booth with overlapping input and output, which may be wrongly perceived as a gradual exercise smoothly leading to interlanguage processing.

Another significant result of this study was evidence of greater fatigue when students were asked to interpret sentences - such as proverbs and sayings - requiring deeper semantic analysis and a complete syntactic and lexical rearrangement in the target language. When word for word transcoding was requested - i.e. the subjects were asked to translate lists of words - hesitations, omissions and disruptions were less frequent.

This study clearly confirms that simultaneous translation is far from being merely a linguistic exercise, and sheds some further light on the many components of the interpreting process. In fact simultaneous interpreting presupposes, among other things, the cognitive processing of the deep message underlying superficial morphosyntax, the constant auditory feedback of language production in the target language as well as of the incoming message, the neurophysiological control of voice emission, modulation and prosody, etc. Some of these tasks are typically performed by the right hemisphere.

These indications imply that the training of students should not be limited to linguistic aspects but should also take into consideration non-verbal factors affecting performance, in particular stress, emotional features (such as lack of self-confidence), insufficient control over all the successive and concomitant stages of simultaneous interpreting, etc. Some of these aspects could be taken care of by paying greater attention to the gradual acquisition of each verbal and non-verbal skill needed to become an interpreter.

In Agosti (1995), a dissertation on the influence of stress over interpreting prepared under our supervision, two significant findings emerged: when a state of psychic relaxation is induced hypnotically before performing simultaneous interpretation, formal features (such as prosody, elocution, quality of voice) are significantly improved if compared to performance produced prior to this mild hypnotic treatment. No one doubts that a calm voice and a fluent and pleasant delivery is an asset for an interpreter, as it conveys an impression of self-confidence and reliability. This result may be partly explained by the hypnotically induced activation of the right hemisphere, which is typically more involved in prosodic functions. The quantity of information delivered in this relaxed condition, on the other hand, is reduced if compared to "normal" conditions. This intriguing phenomenon may suggest new ways of reconciling accuracy with quality of delivery. Some kind of self-induced relaxation of tension would be appropriate in order to achieve the right balance between a calm attitude and mental concentration. This is especially true in the case of students who are particularly tense in the course of exams, while professional interpreters develop skills and strategies enhancing self-confidence and therefore reducing tension. It should be borne in mind, however, that, as is shown by studies on blood pressure levels before, during and after simultaneous interpretation (Klonowicz 1994), even experienced interpreters are subject to considerable stress.

4.3 *Recognition of semantic and syntactic errors among interpreting students and professional interpreters*

Another experimental study was carried out on interpreting students at the SSLMIT using the dichotic listening technique (Fabbro et al. 1991; Gran & Fabbro 1991). On this occasion the subjects received a series of sentences from one ear and, simultaneously, the translation of these sentences from the other ear. Some of the translations were correct, some contained semantic errors and others contained syntactic errors. The order of input according to ear (left, right), language direction (L1 into L2, L2 into L1) and type of translation (correct, semantically or syntactically incorrect) was counterbalanced. The subjects were asked to say whether the translated sentences were correct or contained semantic or syntactic errors. This procedure reproduces some of the linguistic processing required in simultaneous interpretation. The same experiment was repeated a year later with professional interpreters with at least 10 years' experience at the EEC Commission. The study produced the following significant results:

a)   no significant lateralization in the recognition of semantic or syntactic errors among interpreting students;
b)   significant superiority of the right ear (left hemisphere) in the recognition of semantic errors in L1 among professional interpreters;
c)   significant superiority of the left ear (right hemisphere) in the

recognition of semantic errors in L2 among professional interpreters;

d)   significant superiority shown by students in the recognition of syntactic errors;

e)   significant superiority shown by professional interpreters in the recognition of semantic errors.

Once again evidence has been found of the dynamic nature of the strategies developed in verbal and cognitive processing in SI. The typical lateralization for language functions to the left hemisphere, which is normally found in monolinguals, tends to diminish concurrently with greater proficiency in a foreign language and as a result of training in the particularly complex task of simultaneous interpreting. Findings b) and c) were initially interpreted as a "shift" of *linguistic functions* from one hemisphere to the other. Recent studies (Paradis 1990), however, suggest that these are in fact modifications of *attentive strategies* which may involve one cerebral hemisphere more than the other.

The awareness of phenomena such as the modification of cerebral attentive strategies in the course of time may suggest that teachers should pay greater attention to the way in which students wear their headphones. Far from imposing any given position, the teacher should encourage students to try and adjust their headphones in different ways until they find the most satisfactory solution. Teaching experience has shown that such apparently trivial questions as the positioning of headphones, the tuning of the volume of the incoming speech, the monitoring of the volume and quality of one's own voice may improve performance more than might be expected.

The last two findings, i.e. students being more aware of syntax and professionals paying greater attention to semantics, are also of considerable practical interest. As was pointed out on previous occasions, this state of affairs is easily explained: students are afraid of missing parts of the original message and stick to the superficial structure of discourse, while professionals are more familiar with language switching and are flexible, relaxed and detached enough to forget words and concentrate on meaning. But one should not jump too quickly to conclusions in terms of teaching methodology. True enough, we all know that meaning is what matters and this is what we try to instil in our students. But the fact is that learning simultaneous interpreting, as is true for any other skill, is a gradual process. Thus we should always consider the actual level at which our students are working, rather than think in terms of the ideal level we wish them to attain.

A great help in acquiring greater skill is working on *language*, e.g. learning a large number of equivalent expressions and phrases, procedural terminology, etc. as suggested by Ilg (1980). This will make it possible to automate some parts of speech production, leaving room and energy to concentrate on the meaning of the incoming discourse.

Referring to Seleskovitch (1975: 175), who stated "Ce qui doit être respecté, c'est le sens et non les mots, et le respect des mots est souvent contraire au respect du sens", Ilg, though not rejecting this approach, specified: "...s'abstraire du mot est un excellent antidote qui permet d'arracher les étudiants de nos Ecoles à leurs habitudes thème et version, mais c'est n'est pas une raison de condamner sans appel le mot..." (Ilg 1980: 118).

Though not speaking in exactly the same terms, Snelling recommends that students acquire great familiarity with the language structures of their foreign language, thus avoiding the trap of ill-digested expressions and phrases. Referring to the need for a language-based approach to interpretation, he also insists on the need for a conscious effort to find "a specific solution to a specific problem" (Snelling 1992: 4), as "...the target text has to be reformulated not with sense alone, but in words." (Snelling 1992: 5)

The same may be said about the need to master the mother tongue in all its nuances and language registers. The point made here, however, is that, through practice, the initial conscious effort leads to an almost automatic or unconscious use of words to express meaning. This aim, though perhaps easier to achieve when working into one's mother tongue, is essential in any language combination if a confident meaning-based approach is to be achieved. Teachers should not forget, however, as shown by the above-mentioned experiment, that it takes several years - and some considerable modifications in cerebral structures! - before the ideal approach is achieved. This fact should also be borne in mind by officials of international organizations who organize tests for candidate interpreters: a young graduate, no matter how good, cannot be expected to have the same approach as an experienced professional interpreter. The latter is also likely to be able to disguise some failures and omissions with greater ease and confidence.

5. Future developments in interdisciplinary research

As Franco Fabbro rightly pointed out earlier on, it is necessary to identify the basic sciences and disciplines which may be usefully applied to research on interpretation. Our research activity has been mainly devoted to experimental studies on neurolinguistic and neuropsychological aspects of language learning and simultaneous interpretation.

On the basis of our experience I would like to suggest a few ideas for future developments in interpretation research. I hope that these comments will stimulate other participants to put forward their own ideas and that some practical conclusions may emerge from the debate.

Since the Trieste Symposium in 1986 a lot of work has been done, other conferences have been held, some books have been written, new ideas have been expressed about what interpreting is about. We interpreters have got in closer contact with psychologists, linguists, experts in communication etc. Much as we owe to these scholars, however, we shall have to become more and more aware of the specificity of our discipline, identify our own problems, set our own goals and be able to use the tools we need to inquire into the various facets of the interpretation process.

In other words, we have to develop our own research guidelines and our own criteria. Referring back to the early 70's, some psychologists and linguists (Goldman-Eisler 1972; Gerver 1972, 1974; Barik 1972, 1973) started to consider certain aspects of interpreting as a means to study some specific features of memory, attention, language production etc. They found some interesting data but after a while those studies were discontinued and for a considerable amount of time no follow-up was made to some of those ideas. Some of those inquiries, however, were not particularly relevant to interpreting and some were typically inspired by false impressions about the interpreting process. Just to give an example, Barik's classification of interpreting errors, which dates back to 1971 was not revised in more realistic terms until very recently. We should be aware of the fact that, while scholars in other fields may be interested in conference interpretation some of the time, we are - or should be - interested all of the time! That is the reason why we should take research into our own hands and decide what we want to find and how to go about it.

There should be no misunderstanding about our great indebtedness and gratitude to the specialists in other fields with whom we have so happily co-operated. Franco Fabbro has just explained how the study of interpretation has contributed - and can contribute in the future - to the understanding of some cerebral mechanisms involved in language functions. In exactly the same way, we have gained better insight into some aspects of interpreting by finding inspiration in previous studies on aphasic patients and in availing ourselves of the generous, unwavering co-operation offered by our colleagues in the medical field. The same can be said of those linguists, text linguists and other experts whom we have met and to whom we are going to listen with great interest in the next few days. We should bear in mind the dynamic nature of our studies: ours is a new science, some of us have indicated certain lines of research, we have - and will always have - to learn a lot from others and we are breeding a new generation of young researchers who will take the baton from us and continue the work we have started according to their own criteria. All this implies that, luckily, a lot of work remains to be done. So, in reply to one of the questions raised by the organizers of this conference "Is interpretation a science in its own right?" my answer is "yes": not a basic science, but an applied discipline, involving a combination of linguistic and non-linguistic features which make it a unique human skill.

Understanding for Interpreting, Interpreting for Understanding

Charles Albert Tijus
Laboratoire de Psychologie Cognitive, URA CNRS 1297
Université de Paris VIII, France

I am happy to acknowledge the assistance of Elizabeth Hamilton in preparing the final version of this article.

1. Introduction

How might the task of interpreting be analyzed from a cognitive psychologist's point of view? How can we build a repair theory to improve the quality of interpreting?

These questions are questions an interpreter might ask a cognitive psychologist. However, the psychologist will respond that psychologists are really asking the same question about the tasks of the mind, because the mind is an interpreter that most of the time provides correct interpretations, but sometimes misses the point. Let us take an example.

The situation of Berlin when West Germany and East Germany were two different countries: Berlin, a city in East Germany, was divided in two, into West and East Berlin. The Berlin Wall created an enclave for westerners in West Berlin. It was a wall that enclosed half the city. Its main purpose was to prevent East Germans from crossing into West Germany by preventing them from crossing into West Berlin.

But many people imagined and still imagine the Berlin Wall as a short and straight wall which cuts the city in two from North to South! (Tijus, & Santolini, 1995). To misconceive of the Berlin Wall as a short, straight wall is to overlook its essential feature. What this means is that people hearing about the Berlin situation regularly interpret it with a misrepresentation of the wall. If they do talk about it, they might express this misconception. Let us take another example borrowed from the psychology of humour. The story starts as follows :

> "A man is walking along the docks and meets a fisherman. The fisherman says "I just saw your wife go by."

We predict that if someone is just repeating (or interpreting) the story, he or she might repeat the second sentence as "the fisherman says I just saw your wife walk by," because that is the way everyone understands this sentence. But this is only one interpretation, as becomes clear at the end of the joke:

> "The husband says,"If you have just seen my wife go by, than she can't be very far." The fisherman answers "You're right, because the current is not very strong.".

How could the mind's task be analyzed from a cognitive point of view? How can we build a repair theory to improve the quality of interpreting? Research on the task of interpreting by an interpreter and research on the task of interpreting with an information processing system begin with common questions.

I will first define what interpretation is from contemporary cognitive psychology's point of view. Secondly, I will report on some remarks made by interpreters about the kind of research that has developed in and around the task of interpretation. Thirdly, I will present our methodology for task analysis and finally, I will introduce a cognitive model which could be used to study the task of hearing and understanding a speech in order to deliver a corresponding speech in another language. Note that I am taking neither the characteristics of the languages into account nor their SL-TL conversion and the production of acceptable sentences for an audience. The model addresses just one aspect of the cognitive processes underlying the task of interpretation from a source language to a target language.

2. Interpretation as categorization

Comprehension is the foundation on which any translation will be built. Frequently, it is also its most difficult part, while reformulation poses no particular problems. In interpreting, comprehension is made more difficult by a number of constraints, including time pressure and the simultaneousness of several tasks.

What is the source text to be interpreted? Like any text, a speech has a macro-structure that can correspond either to a minimal summary of the speech, or to some message the speaker wants to deliver. This macrostructure finds its way into sentences either when the speech is being written, or at the time of speaking. Between this macrostructure and the words that are actually pronounced, there are many intermediate levels which provide both structure and meaning. This being said, note that the author can produce a very large number of different speeches from the same macrostructure and that structure is relevant to the author's intention. A satisfactory translation would respect all the levels of the text's structure from the choice of words to the message. Secondly, and more crucially, note that a large number of speeches can have similar introductory parts and elements without sharing the same message at all.

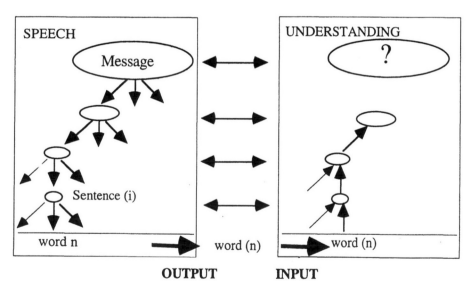

Figure 1.
The source speech (on the left) delivers word-to-word outputs that are inputs for the interpreter's understanding task (on the right). The source speech has a hierarchical structure with many levels that correspond to the way the

speaker delivers his message: this is the macrostructure of the speech. The interpreter has to reconstruct the whole structure in order to have a satisfactory understanding of the task and to provide a correct interpretation. The interpreting task is a task of inductive inferencing.

If the interpreter has the opportunity to read the entire text before starting to translate, he or she has access to the whole structure. Unfortunately, as shown in figure 1, most of the time the interpreter has to reconstruct the structure word by word[1]. The problem at hand is thus one of grasping the structure through inductive inferencing: a problem of interpretation.

In addition, words and sentences are polysemous. Even in word-to-word translation one must understand which meaning of a word is being used in order to choose the correct word in the target language. Consider the following sentences:

"Today, I am going to talk about the bank we decided to buildbased on customer demand. Everything was going well until we discovered a bug in the programme. An economic newspaper made the seashore we had designed public and ecologists protested. The staff was not able to change plans in time and so we lost a great deal of money".

Both "bank" and "bug" are polysemous (financial institution versus seashore, insect versus problem). Here, the meaning of "bank" cannot be ascertained before "seashore" occurs. Fortunately, most of the time, cues are provided by the context to disambiguate polysemous terms. It would, for instance, suffice that the speech be introduced by the phrase "Today, the president of the yachting company will talk about...." Unfortunately, sometimes, cues can reinforce the wrong meaning. Imagine starting the sentence with "Today, I am going to talk about money... uhh... about the bank we decided to build...."

How do polysemy and context affect our understanding? Our theory of understanding provides some explanation. It is a post-Piagetian theory in the Cognitive Sciences that emphasizes Domains, Objects and Properties to model the Human Information Processing System within Semantic Networks of Knowledge. It is also an ecological theory (Anderson, 1991). The mind has to provide an interpretation of the world in order to simplify it, complete it (most of the meaning is literally absent or implicit) and understand it. This understanding is Task-based, goal-oriented (David Marr, 1982) and, in short, proceeds from Physics [e.g. Sounds] to Cognition [Thought, understanding], Information is processed through Language [Syntax / Task-procedure] to

Categories [Semantic Networks].

At every point along the line that goes from perception (hearing speech, for instance) to understanding, the mind deals with a fuzzy, ambiguous and uncertain world by making inferences that are knowledge based (pragmatics included) and goal oriented. Knowledge and goals make inductive decisions possible by using categorization processes. Categorization is the main mechanism that underlies the choice between alternative interpretations, because it helps differentiate between homonyms ("Rose" as "flushed", "a colour", "a girl's name", "a flower" are alternative categories with different meanings) and between meanings of polysemous terms (when the context activates or deactivates categories of connotation: "Red roses for a blue lady", "red roses" as a sign of affection or love, as well as categories of generality or specificity: when John says "roses" is he talking about flowers in general, about roses in general, about white roses as a kind of rose or about the 24 long-stemmed pink roses he's holding in his hand?).

The important role of the context and of the goal is to provide cue-properties that prepare categories that make sense. This priming effect corresponds to the expectations one has about what is going to happen, the direction a speech is taking.

A category is defined by properties and recent studies have shown that three properties suffice to identify one category among six hundred (Mantyla, 1986). This shows that categories can be activated in the memory without being named. Once a term has been assigned to a category, the category will in turn provide cues for further terms to be categorized. For instance the sentence "Paul took the scissors" provides the category of "instrument used to cut" which is a subcategory of "sharp instrument", when preceding cues have provided a "fight" or "dress making" context. The chosen category will in turn provide expectations about the patient object (the object to which something is done, in our example, either cloth or human flesh.) This choice between alternatives is goal oriented and is provided by the macrostructure of the text: understanding emerges from networks of categories and macrostructure from a limited number of more general categories. For instance, "Let's take a look at the mountain" is processed as words (lexicon) in a specific order (syntax) which correspond to a task:

invites [A (an individual, x)],
[B: to look at [[C: some individuals, x, y, z..], [D: mountain]]].

In order to understand this sentence, terms A, B, C & D have to be assigned to categories that will differ according to context (1) if the sentence is extracted from an art book about Cezanne [A: the author; B: look in the book, C: the reader, D: a reproduction of the painting of St Victoire mountain], (2) or if someone says the sentence at a Cezanne exhibition [A: someone; B: come closer by walking, C: someone else, D: the painting of St Victoire mountain], or (3) if someone says it to someone else in a car while visiting Provence in France.

These categories will in turn provide superordinate categories such as (1): [Human] [Art book] [Famous Art work], (2): [Humans] [Museum] [Famous Art work], (3) [Humans], [Car], [Mountain]. Note that the superordinate categories alone provide an understanding of what is going on and a mental representation (mental model) of the situation: if you tell someone "Humans", "Museum", "Famous Art work", he or she can tell you that "people are visiting a museum and are seeing a famous artwork"; it is highly unlikely that the person will respond with "people are living near the museum and a famous art work was stolen".

What are the underlying mechanisms of categorization ?
1. Interpreting occurs by *categorization* in Semantic Networks of categories with *inclusion* of categories and *inheritance* of properties: "Ducks" or "parrots" are kinds of "birds", "birds" are a kind of "animal"; "Ducks" or "parrots" have specific properties, but they inherit "bird" properties as well as "animal" properties (Collins & Quillian, 1969; Collins & Loftus, 1975; Gelman, 1988). The same mechanisms are at work in determining the meaning of verbs :"buying" is a kind of "exchanging" and "exchanging" a kind of "obtaining" (Williams, 1992; Tijus, Legros & Moulin, 1995).

2. Categorizing is either *generalizing* ("he likes flowers": "he likes plants") or *specifying* ("he likes flowers": "he likes roses"), depending on the task at hand (Hunt & McDaniel, 1993).

3. Categorizing is reducing *ambiguity/complexity* by goal "intension" which means understanding objects from the point of view of the selected properties (a flower can be seen from many points of views such as: "needing water", "a present", etc..).

4. Categorizing is *inference making*: the information processed from the text is completed with unseen or unstated properties or cognitive attributes.

5. Categorizing provides an *internal representation* of the situation at hand by creating a temporary semantic network of categories that we construct and

deconstruct until we get coherence. This can be seen as the understanding of the macrostructure of the text.

3. Research on interpreting: some remarks

Before presenting a hypothetical cognitive model for the task of simultaneous interpretation, I would like to express three remarks that will differentiate the present approach from others. After having reviewed David Gerver's article, Empirical Studies of Simultaneous Interpretation (1976), and the recent and fully documented book by Daniel Gile (1995b), I would like to make the following observations.

The first remark has to do with the psychological nature of simultaneous interpretation. Psychologists have used interpreters as subjects (guinea pigs) in psychological studies because the interpreting task provides a good experimental situation in which to study processes, functions or mechanisms that are not specific to the interpreting task. If research on interpretation can profit from these studies, it can also profit from studies based on other tasks that are similar to the interpreting task in one or more ways. I believe that the results of studies on tasks such as on-line text comprehension (Graesser, Singer, & Trabasso, 1994), restructuring in problem solving (Richard, Poitrenaud, & Tijus, 1993), idiom comprehension (Cacciary & Glucksberg, 1991), and so on, may provide information that is useful for interpreting. This is to say that the hypothetical model I am about to present synthesizes the results of experiments in many such areas.

Secondly, the number of syllables or words are not appropriate dependent variables for studies of interpreting. Likewise, counting "errors" can be misleading. I will not elaborate on the use and misuse of error quantification in this context but simply ask: What, after all, is an "error"? If one takes the source text and a final target text and compares them, there will of course be differences (missing words or sentences, for instance). Anyone who systematically calls these "errors" is neglecting the dynamic aspect of the interpretation process. What may look like an error in the final speech, may have been the only or the best possible solution at the time of interpreting. From the minute the interpreter begins translating, he or she is handling a number of different variables not all of which have to do with the meaning of the speech, and is rapidly making decisions that may or may not be conscious. Paraphrasing and omitting words, or even large parts of the source message, and so on, are decisions made under fire at a given point in a constantly changing situation. An interpreter might, for instance, decide to maintain a reasonable ear-voice span rather than translate a particular phrase right away. A true error made earlier may force the interpreter to make decisions that are not errors in themselves but that represent the only reasonable choice. The true error may be undetectable. For instance, the interpreter may at one point have spent too much time formulating a "perfect" translation. This may put him under heavy time pressure and cause him to make mistakes of the kind that can be detected by comparing SL-TL transcriptions. The true error here is a strategic one, it has nothing to do with semantics and understanding the source speech.

My third remark has to do with the need for theoretical models to orient observation and research. At the moment, few existing models of the interpreting task provide this (David Gerver's Information Processing Model and Daniel Gile's Effort Models are exceptions). I think that this inadequacy stems from the level of analysis. Analysis of target texts might provide interesting information, but does not capture the core of the interpreting task.

Interpreting is a Task and has to be studied as such. The relevant domain of analysis seems to be ergonomics, or cognitive ergonomics, including task analysis, which means that the interpreter has a task, a goal, a starting and an end point, a context, as well as operators, procedures and strategies with which to perform the task, and that he or she has some experience, expertise, and some general knowledge to bring to the task, for instance general guidelines or rules of thumb.

4. Task analysis : one method, one model

Reuchlin, a well-known French psychologist, has reflected upon the question of "how to deliver a working knowledge of clinical psychology to students," which is to say, the knowledge of how to provide care to patients. Reuchlin maintains that any scientific activity should be able to explicitly teach students what they need to know to gain expertise. In many professional domains, expertise is not explicitly transmitted to students but acquired through practice. This kind of "learning by doing" is implicit learning: we know how to do it, we can recognize when and how the task is well performed, but we cannot express the procedure that leads to it. Therefore, we cannot teach students how to do it. Task analysis forces us to make it explicit.

My aim here is to provide a word of caution about this first attempt at analyzing the task of translating. Because in recognizing some parts of the hypothetical model I propose, you will wonder why I have gone to the trouble of mentioning something that is so apparent and obvious. But part of modelling cognitive activities is to make explicit what usually remains implicit. Let us take a quick example from the very simple task of doing a subtraction, say, subtracting 17 from 418 with a pencil and paper. If you tell children that they must first subtract 7 from 8, because 8 is at the top of the unit column, the children will find this very evident because the top number is the larger number. Many children think that the procedure consists in subtracting the smaller unit from the larger unit. So, when they have to subtract 18 from 417, they will begin by subtracting 7 from 8 in the unit column because 8, though it is not at the top of the column, is still the larger unit. Here, we have every reason to justify what we do!

Since the development of the Newell and Simon (1972) approach to problem solving, cognitive psychologists have provided methods for describing tasks in many domains, from airplane control to playing chess, with the purpose of facilitating the acquisition of expertise. Today, in what we call "cognitive ergonomics", the problem-solving paradigm has been successfully applied, with new discoveries that have integrated the corpus of knowledge in Psychology and new problems that have led to new explanations.

The first step in analyzing the process of interpretation is to make an ergonomic description of the task, which entails, as for any task, identifying the interpreter's goal, available procedures and strategies (the most important of these strategies being metacognitive ones based on the knowledge of how to deal with specific difficulties: e.g. interpreting rapid speech) as well as identifying the limits of an interpreter's abilities. What we mean here is the ability to evaluate alternative procedures, to elaborate better strategies to improve performance, and to diagnose dead-ends as in problem-solving, and all in short periods of time.

The second step is to model the internal construction of the macro-structure of a speech, something that must be done, as early as possible, starting from a micro-analysis of sentences. Our hypothetized model is based on the construction and deconstruction of the overall intention of the speaker. This is modelled within the constraints of the task, so that the interpreter is able to provide himself with a coherent representation of the content of the source text.

Lastly, we have to address the attentional aspects of interpreting. These are attentional costs both at the task level and at the representation level of the macro-structure of the text, given the attentional limits of the human information processing system.

Let us see what has to be done to analyze the task of translating speeches. We define any task as two states of a microworld (the initial state and the final state) plus a main goal, namely moving from the initial state into the final state, by means of "actions/operations" that become a procedure once the "operator" knows how to perform the task. There are many differences between tasks:

1. "static" versus "dynamic" microworlds
A static microworld is one that does not change unless you perform some actions (e.g. solving a problem on paper); a dynamic microworld is one that changes even if you are not acting (stopping a fire or simultaneously translating a speech)

2. "well defined" goals versus "open-ended" goals
The goal can be either very precise as when the end-state microworld can be described with exactitude and precision ("checkmate" in chess), or it can be open-ended, a goal for which the end-state can only be defined globally, within the limits of a certain number of constraints that define what the microworld must and must not be: for instance designing a building that must have a given number of floors, a parking lot, a given number of spaces with a given surface and so on, or in our case the fact that participants must be able to follow the speech of the speaker in another language.

In the case of dynamic microworlds and open-ended goals, we define two kinds of constraints: first order constraints and second order constraints. First order constraints are constraints that guide actions, or procedures, by providing variables with values that have to be respected (for instance about the dynamic evolution of the speaker's speech; variable: *part of the speaker's sentences to translate*; value: *do not lose too much of it*). Second order constraints are metacognitive constraints that define the values of the first order constraints, when all the constraints are not known before starting the task. Metacognitive constraints supervise the task by diagnosing the first order constraints (for instance, to evaluate the resources that will be necessary; one variable could be: *some problems with unusual professional terms ?*; and another *time to do my best ?*") and by providing constraint values for them (value: *I might have some problems with technical terms*; value: *I will not have time to do my best*).

Task Analysis requires defining first and second order constraints, and making an inventory of all known procedures for solving the problem. This corresponds to a theoretical and formal analysis done at a macro-level where it is not necessary to take into account the human operator who will perform the task (because one might be able at this point to describe any kind of behaviour even if one has no idea of what will in fact be observed when a particular individual performs the task. But this framework makes observation possible).

But how can we know how a given operator will perform the task ? To simulate task performance, we must obtain precise knowledge about (1) the operator's representation of the task, which is the way he describes to himself the first and second order constraints and the available procedures, (2) the content of the task, which is the way the objects of the microworld change through actions or procedures, both from the point of view of the operator and from the point of view of an objective description of the domain, and (3) the way the attentional system (input/output) will deal with processing the constant changes that occur in the microworld, given the results of the operator's actions, the dynamic nature of the domain, and the operator's representation of the task.

In summary, this defines three levels of analysis (figure 2). These three levels are not levels of independent processes, but levels of cognitive processes that interact and must, in the end, be integrated as we will see later on.

5. Ergonomic analysis of the interpreting task

Now, let us see how we might analyze the task of translating by listing all the constraints that could influence the process as a whole.

5.1 Controlling the Task : The Metacognitive System

Remember that metacognitive constraints are second-order constraints stemming from first order constraints. They provide the kind of knowledge about a task that allows people to get ready to meet its demands.

The first of these metacognitive constraints, besides not getting the two languages mixed up, is the knowledge that the translation cannot be perfect, that the interpreter will come to some impasses, that some errors will be made along the way and that remedying these errors will require making further decisions. I am also supposing that the kind of conference, the kind of audience, and the kind of speeches are variables that will define the demands of the task.

Note that, at first glance, treating different kinds of speeches differently might seem to contradict professional ethics, because interpreters are supposed to be equally careful with all of the talks that they have to translate. However, doing one's best with every translation does not mean

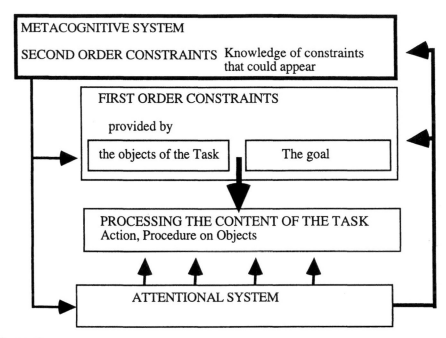

Figure 2.
*The three levels of task analysis: (i) the subject's representation of the task,
which is the way he describes to himself the first and second order constraints
and the available procedures, (ii) the content of the task, (iii) the attentional
system (input/output) which is the way the system will respond to the evolution
of the microworld, given the results of actions, the dynamic nature of the
domain, and the subject's representation of the task.*

treating them in exactly the same way. What we are talking about here is not
the kind of difference in treatment which occurs when, over a long work
period, the interpreter's readiness and interpretation may flag, so that one can
expect a better translation for a keynote address than for the last speech that
takes place just before lunch, when the room is half empty. What we are
talking about is discriminating between different types of speeches, for
instance economic reports. Interpreters will predict that they will have to
translate many numbers. If they are told that transparencies will be used in a
scientific report, then they know that they are going to have to interpret very
quickly, whenever the speaker points out some detail in the figure, and be
prepared not to translate numbers written on the transparencies.

The greater part of the task is, in this case, knowing what to expect, and being ready for it, and this comes from practice (figure 3). These second-order constraints indicate the constraints that must be considered in defining the goal, strategies and procedures. David Gerver (1976: 176) reports that teachers of interpreting at Lomonosov University in Moscow consider that "many of the types of political material interpreted at United Nations meetings are highly redundant both in form and content." This kind of knowledge, and what is implicit in it, that if someone says something new, this will be known all over the world, is what helps to define strategies. The novice interpreter may make errors if he ignores this.

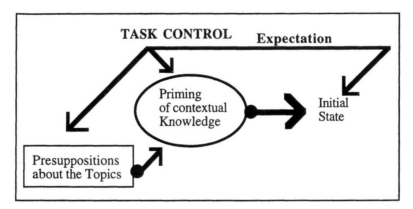

Figure 3.
Effects of Expertise probably come from readiness due to plenty of practice: metacognitive constraints (called "task control") allow interpreters to hypothetize about the topics, to prime compatible knowledge and to get ready to begin interpreting with the right expectations.

A first analysis of the task of interpreting requires making a list of the constraints students do not learn about in school, unless the teacher provides them with many different kinds of simulated conference contexts and evaluates their readiness. These constraints define the constraints that will apply to the goal and the constraints that will apply to strategies and procedures.

5.2 Solving the Task: The Working System

5.2.1 Constraints associated with the goal and subgoals
Choosing a goal allows one to proceed on to choosing the strategies and

procedures that are best suited to its pursuit. The main goal is to arrive at a state where the speech has been translated. Is this sufficient? Interpreters should provide themselves with additional goals: to transmit the speaker's underlying intention (for instance, to discredit the previous speaker, something which may have little or nothing to do with the subject of either speech), to reproduce irony, humour, changes in vocalisation and stress, etc., all of which require a thorough understanding of what is at stake.

Here we have to list not only the usual goals of translation experts, but all the possible constraints that could be used to define a given goal in a given context. When this is done, we have to list the subgoals, as they are a product of the constraints that stem from the main goal. Note that some of the subgoal constraints will be static, which means that they are like steps to be taken in the course of the translation, and some will be dynamic, which means that they provide parameters throughout the translation.

Static subgoal constraints might include, for example, "start translating as soon as possible", "find the structure of the text", "find the intention of the author", and so on. Dynamic constraints might include "do not let the speech get too far ahead of the translation", "report numbers carefully", "make the structure of the text clear", and so on.

Now, supposing we have listed (1) the metacognitive constraints, knowing what to expect from different kinds of conferences, and how these define specific goal constraints for specific kinds of conferences, (2) the usual goal constraints and (3) that we have separated these constraints into static and dynamic ones, this list can be considered as a model for interpreter readiness. We hypothesise that intra-individual differences (quality differences between translations of the same level of difficulty made by the same interpreter), as well as inter-individual differences (quality differences in translations made by different interpreters with the same background in translating), can be predicted from the order in which the interpreter(s) has listed and established a hierarchy among constraints. The list will be more or less functional.

5.2.2. Constraints Provided by Strategies and Procedures
From here on, the actual task of translation can begin. Procedures are what will be done to achieve the subgoals, and can be seen as co-ordinating sub-subgoals applied to the specific objects of the task; here the content of the speech. They are content-based and cannot be analyzed independently of the basic objects of the task. If the main object is the sentence, and not the word, as I suspect, such procedures should be as hypothetized in table 1.

Table 1
List of constraints that could be used to simulate the interpreter's task

- Detect specific grammatical difficulty,
- detect errors as they occur,
- if there are errors, correct.
- When under time pressure,
    · do not correct small errors,
    · summarize,
    · do not spend too much time translating.
- If you cannot hear or understand,
    · guess, aiming at consistency,
    · omit,
    · change the level of speech segmentation
    (part of sentences, word-to-word),
- and so on.

For the purposes of ergonomic description, the procedures are presented here as rules to be applied to object-sentences. This is not the proper description. As described later, in the second section, we will see that these rules are part of the semantic construction of the representation of the speech and of its translation. We will show that the encoding process determines categories of sentences (sentences to be summarized, sentences to be corrected, etc.).

Strategies are meta-rules that guide and supervise the choice between alternative procedures in the course of translation. For instance, under time pressure, procedures will be adapted accordingly.

Now, let us take an interpreter doing his/her job. Note that adapting to the speech with the necessary flexibility involves changing strategies and then selecting suitable procedures. Imagine for instance that the job is relatively easy at first, the speaker is speaking slowly, and suddenly realizes time is running out and begins speaking in a rapid "staccato." The interpreter will have to change strategies.

5.3 Processing the Content of the Task : The Symbolic System

Now let us take a look at the content of the translation. First we must bear in mind that by definition, (1) language is structurally ambiguous, (2) language, like any stimulus, is perceived and represented at a variety of levels of processing, in a continuum from its concrete sensory features through to the abstract, semantic knowledge that is associated with it (Posner & Warren, 1972). This process is hierarchical: from individual phonemes to combined phonemes, from the level of words to the level of sentences, from the level of symbolic units (objects and states plus actions and events) to the level of relations between units, and from the level of automatic inferences to the level of controlled inferences which is conscious thinking. (3) Ambiguity exists at all of these levels.

Secondly, the cognitive system operates mainly by suppressing ambiguity to respond efficiently. Disambiguation is performed through mechanisms that interact. These mechanisms include processing local contextual effects, syntactic effects, parallel activation of hierarchical knowledge in bottom-up and top-down processing, and comprehending the intention of the text as a macro-structure.

The way the cognitive system operates on language and on understanding is well simulated by Connexionist Networks (Rumelhart & McClelland, 1986) with P.D.P. models, where simple groups of nodes represent a given level in the hierarchy of knowledge. I will not describe here how Connexionist Models work, except to say that, in connexionism, the way in which the nodes will combine is impossible to ascertain in advance; the symbolic model we use provides the same kind of functioning. Disambiguation occurs, here again, by bringing to light constraints that are generated by processing the content of the sentence both in extension (words and syntactic structure) and in intension (meaning and semantic structure). Note that both syntactic and semantic structure are embedded in larger and larger structures: linearly or sequentially for the syntactic structures; by abstraction for the semantic structure (see figure 4).

Let us take the French sentence "*Le manger cru pourrait avoir des vertus thérapeutiques*" ("Eating raw food could have therapeutic virtues") as noted by Cori & Marandin (1994). "*Le manger cru*" can either be interpreted as a Nominal Group (ie. "raw food"), introduced by the requisite "*Le*" which we don't need to translate into English, or as a Verbal Sentence in which "*Le*" designates the thing (ie. "it") that could be eaten raw (ie. "eating it raw"). As the sentence occurs in isolation and there is no possibility of anaphor with a pre-existing reference (ie. That's a nice apple. Eating it raw could...), the common syntactic interpretation is to consider "*Le manger cru*" as a Nominal Group (ie."raw food"). But suppose that you hear "*ranger*" (which means "to tidy up, to put things away") instead of "*manger*". "*Ranger cru*" has no immediate meaning, yet "*cru*" will activate everything that could be "raw", and if you then hear "could have therapeutic virtues", this phrase will activate everything that "could have therapeutic virtues". The juxtaposition of the set of everything that can be raw (as opposed to cooked) and the set of everything that can have therapeutic values, makes it obvious that the subject of the sentence is nutrition and thus allows understanding that what was heard as "ranger" ("to tidy up, put something away") must needs be interpreted as "manger" ("to eat"). This, plus the information that "manger cru" has a meaning and that a verb can be used as a noun, transforms *"ranger"* into *"manger"*. These mental operations take place in less than a split second and we are not always aware of them. This example was to show how disambiguating occurs in extension.

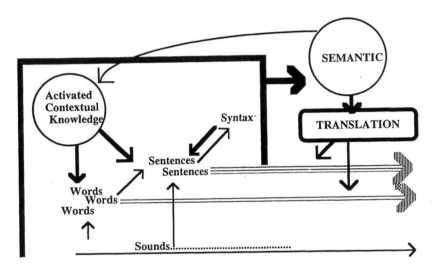

Figure 4.
The effect of meaning on translating. Understanding helps current word-to-word translation, but also helps prepare the interpretation of the sentences to come by activating knowledge that could be relevant in advance. This mechanism has the effect of disambiguating the source content that is provided by sounds.

Another source of ambiguity comes from the categorial representation of objects, actions, and properties. Because symbols denote categories, a symbol has a polyvalent specified meaning that consists of all the subordinate categories of the denoted category and a core meaning whose locus is in the upper level categories. In order to understand "the Berlin Wall situation" [example 1], as given above, one has to choose between different kind of walls (straight walls, enclosing walls, etc..) that can be used to prevent passage (different kinds of walls are a subcategory of "wall"). But, at the same time, one must be able to access the superordinate category to which "wall" belongs. This is the category of all things that separate, isolate, contain or block off (borders, natural boundaries, boxes, cartons and other sorts of packaging, bags, many types of furniture, walls, etc.) This helps to understand that the Berlin Wall (a specific instance) is not just a kind of wall (subcategory of "wall") but also something that has a core meaning (to separate, contain, isolate, block off, etc., a superordinate category). Understanding is capturing the general sense that corresponds to the macrostructure and the specified sense that corresponds to the specific situation at hand. Similarly, in order to understand the joke that contains the sentence "I just saw your wife go by" [example 2], one has to capture the right specified sense (to walk by), and the core meaning (to move), and then attribute a different specified sense (to "float by"). If the sentence was "I just saw your parrot go by", the right specified sense would be "flying", but the core would remain the same. Note that understanding is based on our knowledge of the domain (how properties characterize objects and how objects characterize properties).

5.4 Paying attention: the Attentional System

Much of the attention we pay is under the control of the Metacognitive System, as described above by top-down processing. However, the Human Information Processing System has limited capacities when processing inputs which require specific bottom-up attentional processing. Such limited capacities have been found for immediate memory, and short term memory. Other requirements for a specific low-level attentional process come from the fact that much of the time the signal delivered by the input has to be enhanced by low level mechanisms. Many of the findings reported in psychological literature can be adapted to the translating task (Gerver, 1976; Gile, 1995b); for instance, the discovery that practice enhances the performance of the attentional system. What the reader might find surprising, however, is the role of potentially distracting things in focussing or distracting attention. "Distractors" are only distracting to the extent that we are attracted to them.

There are two kinds of distractors: external and internal distractors. There are external task distractors that can be avoided by focussing on the task, but there are also external distractors that can be used in order to focus on the task. For instance, an interpreter may be distracted by watching another interpreter who is doodling while attentively interpreting. The former might lose part of the speech while the latter will not.

There are internal task distractors that are "false alarms". They contribute to cognitive load because they are fully processed instead of being avoided. When one interprets "bank" as a financial institution [example 4] instead of a seashore, and has thus become confused and given the audience the wrong meaning, the question is how long one will remain attracted to this wrong meaning, because one has to detect the mistake in order to repair it, mainly by adding supplementary sentences (hum, sorry, the speaker was talking about a seashore). And this will cost time and overload memory.

Therefore, I think that the interpreter's most important skill is to be able to detect polysemous phrases very early on in the processing of speech. This ability helps to avoid giving wrong interpretations. In polysemous situations, the best strategy is to wait for additional information to clarify the meaning. Secondly, as wrong interpretation leads us to incoherence in the sentences that follow, I think that another of the interpreter's professional skills might be to detect inconsistency very quickly and to resolve it right away. This requires creativity, something we believe to be the ability to reinterpret the meaning of the material. To do so, the interpreter needs to reconsider the input with exact recall. This requires input memory. The two professional skills that I have mentionned here are very appealing subjects for our research in semantics.

6. Conclusion

Cognitive Psychology has developed theories and models of how the human information processing system can solve many tasks, like problem solving and text understanding. In this article, I have made an attempt to apply what we have actually found in problem solving, task analysis, and text understanding, to an analysis of the task of interpreting a speech from a source language to a target language. Though I do not pretend to offer a correct model here (I hope it is somewhat wrong in order to follow up on it in our research), and though I have not taken into account the production of the interpreted text, nor the double-task situation of the interpreter, the model I have outlined here can be formalized with components of existing computer models.

In order to do this, we will need (i) a data-base containing knowledge in the form of a semantic network, that we will use for activating concepts, (ii) a module that produces meaning by creating temporary semantic networks that correspond to the running situation as it evolves from input sentences, (iii) a module with production rules that executes the first order constraints and the metacognitive constraints as defined above and (iv) an input module to process the word-to-word input sentences that could be provided in real time by typing a text into a computer file. However, as yet, I can see no way of implementing the interpreter's attentional capacities described in the last section. To be of any interest, the simulation has to include the great amount of knowledge that is necessary but not always used. Let us say that such a project may be of interest for research per se, with a very short text to be interpreted and a little knowledge data base. But, I am sure that such a system will avoid making the mistake made by a machine translation product now on the market, which translates "*voler un livre*" by "to fly a book".

Note

1.   I agree that the most interesting problem, which is not within the scope of this paper, but which is encountered in studying the task of interpreting, is the problem of the language in which the macrostructure of the text is represented in the interpreter's mind: is there a single understanding unit for both source and target text or are there two distinct understanding units in the interpreter's mind, one for the source text, another for the target text ? The former solution means that there is no problem of internally translating the macrostructure, while the latter necessitates translating the macrostructure from the source language to the target language. One argument favours the second hypothesis: due to culture differences, a macrostructure from one culture has to be adapted to another culture in order to be acceptable.

Interpreting as Communication

Per Linell
Department of Communication Studies
Linköping University, Sweden

In this paper I will comment on interpreting and, to some extent, on translation from the point of view of Communication Studies.[1] However, this is not an easy task, since Communication Studies is hardly a homogeneous discipline with only one coherent view on its subject matter.[2] On the contrary, there are many different approaches to communication, and I shall bring to the fore some of the controversies, and suggest that they have somewhat different consequences for theories of translation and interpreting. In particular, I shall lay out some features of a so-called dialogical view of cognition and communication, and explore some of its implications. The general plan of this paper is first to deal with language and communication at a general and abstract level, then proceed to some concrete examples of what a dialogue analysis can contribute, and in the end return to some general considerations.

1. Perspectives on language, communication and human action

1.1 Language

In the language sciences, one might distinguish between two main perspectives on language and linguistic phenomena. These research traditions view language in terms of *structure* vs. *discourse*, *system* vs. *use*, or any other similar dichotomy, such as language vs. speech (Bloomfield), langue vs. parole (Saussure), or competence vs. performance (Chomsky). A slightly more elaborate conceptual framework is shown in Figure 1:

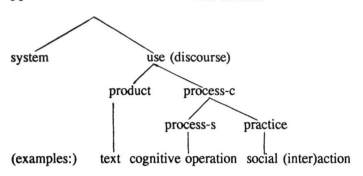

Figure 1.*Perspectives on language*

According to Fig. 1, we may distinguish between three discourse-oriented foci; product, process and practice. The term 'process' is sometimes used in a broad sense (process-c /comprehensive), which subsumes both 'process' in the more specific, or narrow, sense (process-s /specific) and 'practice'. The latter two may be characterized roughly as follows. Process-s refers to the implementation of predefined operations (input-output processing), most often viewed as cognitive, intraindividual processes in real time. Alternatively, we can think of a process-s as a train of causally determined events in which something is transformed or changed. The concept of practice, on the other hand, emphasizes active and interactive problem solving in situational and cultural contexts. A practice is a process-c in which an actor does (or makes) something, transforming some input material into a product. Practice, but not process-c, emphasizes meaningful and purposeful action.

System and use (process/practice) are looked upon in different ways, with opposing priorities, in different approaches to language. Compare Hymes's list of differences between a structuralist, or formalist, and a functionalist perspective on language and linguistic phenomena:

        "Structural"   "Functional"

Structure of language (code) as grammar Structure of speech (act, event)
                                              as ways of speaking

Use merely implements, perhaps limits, may correlate with, what is analyzed as code; analysis of code prior to analysis of use	Analysis of use prior to analysis of code; organization of use discloses additional features and relations; shows code and use in integral (dialectical) relation
Referential function, fully semanticized uses as norm	Gamut of stylistic or social functions
Elements and structures analytically arbitrary (in cross-cultural or historical perspective), or universal (in theoretical perspective)	Elements and structures as ethnographically appropriate ("psychiatrically" in Sapir's sense)
Functional (adaptive) equivalence of languages; all languages essentially (potentially) equal	Functional (adaptive) differentiation of languages, varieties, styles; these being existentially (actually) not necessarily equivalent
Single homogeneous code and community ("replication of uniformity")	Speech community as matrix of code-repertoires, or speech styles ("organization of diversity")
Fundamental concepts, such as speech community, speech act, fluent speaker, functions of speech and of languages, taken for granted or arbitrarily postulated	Fundamental concepts taken as problematic and to be investigated

(Schiffrin 1994: 21, after Hymes 1974a: 79).

The perspective of linguistics (and language sciences in general) has clearly been "formalistic": language system comes before use. Language is seen as an autonomous instrument, rather than as logos, as constituting the appearance and understanding of the world (cf. Nouss 1993:56). The functionalist perspective is the opposite, i.e. communication/practices in actual performances are primary; they are the locus where meanings are constructed and where language and culture are continuously reconstructed, and the system is an abstraction, derived through decontextualization, by disregarding aspects of contexts[3] and thus generalizing across situations.

I shall return to formalist and functionalist perspectives later on, and then discuss the related perspectives on communication (rather than language) as monological and dialogical, respectively. I shall also return to the discourse-oriented concepts of product, process and practice, and relate them to translation and interpretation. Before that, however, I need to sketch some theories of communication.

1.2. Communication

Among theories of human communication, there are naturally many models of the processes and practices involved. However, it makes sense to consider only two basic models as the major alternatives, namely the *transfer* (conduit) model, and the *social-interactionist* model. The former is monological, and assigns prime (or exclusive) importance to the speaker, while his or her partner is just a recipient of what the speaker creates. The social-interactionist model is dialogical; the speaker interacts with his/her physical and social environments, with interlocutors and situational and cultural contexts; messages are co-produced in dialogue.

These models make different assumptions about what communication consists of, and about what resources people put to use in order to achieve communication. According to Taylor (1992), it is a pre-theoretical given in mainstream theories of language that in and through communicating we ordinarily understand each other and what we talk about in the same way; i.e. successful communication yields shared and mutual understanding. There are two main types of theory as to what resources are used in this process:
- code theory; language provides us with signs with fixed meanings, and the proper use of this code will guarantee shared understanding and (possibly) complete intersubjectivity (a tradition comprising thinkers like Condillac, Saussure, and Chomsky).
- relevance theory (Sperber & Wilson 1986); this is "naturalism with a twist" (Taylor op.cit.:133); the combination of a linguistic code and specified contexts (contextual conditions) will enable people to compute shared (relevant) understandings.

The other, very different type of communication theory, social-interactionist, contextualist theory, contends that in communicating we engage in practical problem-solving routines in situated action, yielding understanding for practical purposes, i.e. sufficient understanding of current projects, of what we, you and I, are saying or doing just now, so that we, as parties to the communicative process, can continue and proceed to subsequent communicative projects (and other projects) without any salient problems. Such practices result in only *partial* intersubjectivity; there are good reasons to assume that we don't understand everything, not even everything relevant, precisely in the same way. What is meant by this is that in most situations, say in giving and receiving (using) a route direction, we do not consider whether all words used are fully adequate descriptors of their respective referents, or which exact sense of a word the speaker is driving at, or precisely which aspects of various kinds of background knowledge the speaker presupposes, or is trying to conceal, etc. We do not raise these questions all the time, but if we tried to do so, we would surely discover large fields of only partially shared meanings, of incongruent understandings, etc. Normally, we are content with provisional understandings, and trust that this is enough for current purposes, e.g., in our example, finding our way to a particular destination. But *if*, or when, we encounter problems, we do of course start to probe meanings and explore possible misunderstandings. This is possible, according to the social-interactionist models, due to the ongoing interaction between the sense-maker and his interlocutors and contexts (cf. Linell 1995a).

So, theories of communication within the field of Communication Studies are fundamentally different from one another. Therefore, translation and interpretation (henceforth: T&I) cannot be assessed in only one way. The researcher's adherence to, or affiliation with, one or the other paradigm will have an impact on how T&I will be understood.

1.3. Meaning and action

Theories of communicative processes are correlated with theories of the relation between language and the world:

(A): If communication is thought to be a transfer process, then
- we (usually) also entertain the theory that language *reflects* (selected details of) the world; which also means that:
- linguistic practice is theoretically unproblematic, a question of adequately assembling the right words and linguistic structures.

(B): If, on the other hand, communication is interaction, a complex interplay between discourse, actors and contexts, then
- language *refracts* (rather than reflects) the world; language and the (appearance of the) world mutually constitute each other, and
- linguistic practices are not independent of actors' perspectives, particular cultural frames etc, many of which remain, and must remain, backgrounded.

As comprehensive theoretical frameworks, (A) and (B) may be called monological and dialogical,[4] respectively. These are correlated with formalist vs. functionalist theories of language (Table 1).

Table 1. *Correlated theories of language, communication, and human action and meaning.*

	Correlated set (A)	Correlated set (B)
Theories of:		
1. language:	structuralist (formalist)	functionalist
2. communication:	transfer (conduit)	social-interactionist
3. action and meaning	monological	dialogical

The set of theories (A) clearly constitutes the mainstream perspective on language, cognition and communication in the language sciences. They take speakers, codes, and social structures to be primary, to exist prior to and be causally involved in processes of language use. They assign the whole authority and responsibility for the communicative act to the speaker. They endorse some version of a transfer theory of communication, and basically they regard language as a code, i.e. as a system of symbols with fixed meanings. According to this view, these stable meanings are invoked in language use, which would then explain why people can (allegedly) establish complete intersubjectivity. As one example of a monological model of language use, we may take Searle's theory of speech acts (for some discussion, see Linell and Marková 1993).

A dialogical theory (B), on the other hand, assumes that discourse, activities and contexts (and meanings, understandings) are inextricably interrelated. These concepts (activities, contexts, understandings) are all different ways of capturing aspects of the same complex of interactive sense-making. The overarching activities or communicative games (genres), and their purposes etc., co-determine the acts and processes that are part of the activities. For example, utterances in a court trial are understood in particular ways, partly because you know that the frame is that of a court trial. Accordingly, contexts play a crucial role: everything, every activity, takes place in a matrix of situational as well as socio-cultural contexts. Understanding means, almost by definition, creating coherence and making sense in and through discourse (text) in particular contexts, by connecting discourse with contexts and various kinds of background knowledge. Finally, the content or meaning of the communicative acts are not independent of their forms, and, conversely, activities and processes are not independent of content.

All in all, this means that messages are co-constructed; speakers are not the only authors, but instead interlocutors are often co-responsible, and speakers rely on frames that are presupposed in the socio-cultural contexts involved. Utterances are therefore not the speakers' sole responsibility. Discourse and contexts emerge together (rather than discourse being determined, or even caused, by pre-existing contexts plus speaker intentions). Communication involves interaction on many levels. Language is not a code, but a stock of resources with meaning potentials that interact with contexts to yield situated meanings.

2. A dialogical approach to interpreting

At this point, I shall take time out from the abstract and general topics and allot some space to a few examples of what a dialogical approach can be used to highlight. These examples are drawn from our own research on dialogue interpreting (e.g. Wadensjö 1992; Linell et al. 1992; Linell 1995a).

2.1. First, interpreters, and especially dialogue interpreters, do more than translate! They interact in a peculiar triadic situation, with three (or more) people co-present with each other. In this situation, on the one hand, primary parties do interact with the interpreter and with each other, para- and extralinguistically at least; parties cannot help sensing the moral nature of being together with other human beings, and having to manage a social situation in situ, including, for example, the need for face preservation. At the same time, the interpreter is the only person who (potentially) understands everything said. Apart from being relayers (translators), interpreters must (and do) act as chairpersons and gatekeepers, monitoring the social and discursive situation. This basic assumption is substantially corroborated in Wadensjö's dissertation (1992).

2.2. Communicative accomplishments, understandings as well as misunder-standings, take place in social interaction, and are not the effect of single contributions. This also applies to the interpreter's discursive actions. I shall presently demonstrate this with a few concrete examples (cf. section 3).

2.3. Primary parties (PPs) are not uninfluenced by the process of interpreting. Obviously, we are faced with a peculiar kind of communicative interaction, in which primary parties give little feedback to each other. These and other phenomena were discussed by Linell et al. (1992) in terms of lower degrees of "communicative contact".

2.4. PPs accommodate to the conditions of communicating via an interpreter, and they contribute to discourse in a different way than in non-interpreted (direct) interaction. Jönsson (forthcoming) has studied the linguistic composition of turns by legal professionals in court, as these professionals (judges, prosecutors, lawyers) speak without an interpreter to defendants and witnesses who understand and speak Swedish, and through an interpreter when they address non-Swedish-speaking defendants and witnesses. Among other things, what they do differently in the latter case is:
- give considerably less interactive feedback (as opposed to structuring feedback);
- prefer short, but not very short, utterances (very short turns of 1-4 words are much more common in interaction with Swedish interlocutors, while turns of about 7-12 words (corresponding roughly to full but simple sentences) are typical of dialogue-interpreted originals);
- use fewer elliptical (syntactically incomplete) sentences;
- use fewer pronouns and pronominal adverbs (which express cohesion with prior turns, thus relying on prior co-text) (i.e. they tend to use full nominal heads instead, even if several such expressions are co-referential);
- use fewer requests for clarifications (i.e. initiate repair sequences less often);
- prefer one-question turns to multi-question turns (avoid the funneling question strategy).
   These, and possibly other findings, seem to suggest that legal professionals tailor their contributions to dialogue-interpreted courtroom talk in such a way that the discourse becomes less interactive and more explicit (thereby in fact strengthening features which are already typical of ordinary courtroom talk, as compared to informal conversation). Court trial with an interpreter is not the same as without one; the interpreter is *not*, as it were, just an extra joint mechanically fitted into a communication pipe-line between primary parties (see on this issue Morris 1989a).

2.5. The peculiar turn-taking conditions of a dialogue-interpreted interview have an impact on PPs' opportunities for particular discursive practices, e.g. their chances of telling stories; the non-standard turn-taking conditions lead to fragmentation of discourse (Wadensjö 1992:224). Accordingly, there are indications in our data that narration becomes more difficult.

2.6. Finally, let us point out that dialogue interpreting is different in different contexts, i.e. in situations involving different over-arching activities. Clearly, it is one thing to interpret in a court trial, where particular wordings may carry judicial meanings and need to be closely monitored, and another thing to act as a dialogue interpreter in a health care context, where issues of treatment and therapy, sometimes even a matter of life and death, are perhaps more important than precise wording. Exactly how these and other differences play a role in determining interpreter conduct is a matter for more empirical research.

3. A concrete example

I have just reviewed six points illustrating why dialogue-interpreted conversations must be studied as collective, genre-bound activities. Let me now introduce an example. It is drawn from a police interrogation of an immigrant who applies for a residence permit in Sweden. He and his wife want to join his mother who already lives in Sweden. Where we come in, the police officer (P) has brought up a document, in which a "referee", an uncle of the applicant, has stated that two years ago the applicant (F) had been divorced from his wife.

Excerpt (from Tema K: G 21:20; P=police officer, F=Russian man, D=dialogue interpreter. Rough English translations are given in italics for each utterance in Swedish or Russian.)[5]

1.P: denne man din morbror han skriver nämligen att du är **skild** ((F clears his throat)) från din fru. skild står det.
*this man, your uncle, he writes, you see, that you are **divorced from your wife**. **divorced** it says.*

2.D: e::... и этот ... человек, сказал что...вы разведены e::... с женой.

ah:.. and this...person, said that.. you are/were divorced ah:.... from
your wife.

3.F: мы - мы были в разводе.
      we- we were divorced (lit: in divorce)

4.C: ja vi har **varit** skilda
      yes we have been divorced

5.F: мы были в разводе.
      we were divorced (in divorce)

6.C: vi har **varit** skilda
      we have been divorced

7.P: har **varit** skilda? men numera? vilket förhållande råder just nu?
      have been divorced? but nowadays? what relation is prevailing right
      now?

8.C: а сейчас какие у вас отношения?
      but now what relations do you have?

9.F: с кем?
      with whom?

10.C: med vem?
      with whom?

11.P: med din fru.
      with your wife.

12.C: с вашей женой.
      with your wife.

13.F: ну хорошие, самые нормальные.
      well, fine, the most normal ones.

14.C: ja de e... trevliga dom bästa förhållanden.
      well, it´s ...nice the best relations.

15.P: frågan är, har ni **varit** formellt gifta och hu- hur är **det** förhållandet just
      nu?
      the question is, have you been formally married and ho- how is that
      relation right now?

The excerpt starts with P reviewing some of the contents of the report,
and the dialogue interpreter (D) relays this. We can note two details: P (line
1) uses the present tense ("writes") in Swedish, and D (2) the past tense
("said") in Russian. Furthermore, the lack of a copula in Russian (cf. the
naked participle *razvedeny*, "divorced") renders the temporal relations
somewhat unclear, and (2) is therefore, on this point, something of a

despecification. Irrespective of whether F is aware of the difference between P's original (1) and D's rendition (2), he himself (3) underscores the past in referring to past circumstances (which may seem to imply that these are no longer the case). In (5) he repeats his reply. In her Swedish renditions (4, 6), D uses the perfect tense, which is more specific an interpretation than the Russian original; *byli v razvode* would be either Engl./Sw. preterite "were divorced (then)" (possibly though not very plausibly implicating: "and still are") or Engl./Sw. perfect "have been divorced" (implicating: "and are no longer"). However, the stress on *byli* ("were") in (3) seems to induce the Swedish perfect in (4, 6). P pays attention to the potentiality of understanding (4, 6) as meaning that the state of divorce belongs to the past, and asks (7) about the present circumstances. He ends up selecting a rather abstract formulation (in rough literal translation: "what relation is prevailing right now?") instead of asking, say, "but are you now married again?". D in (8) builds upon P's abstract formulation but shifts from the singular to the plural ("relations"), a change which perhaps influences F's subsequent divergent interpretation of the word "relation" in the local context. Furthermore, D, in her rendition (8), omits those parts of P's original which preceded his abstract formulation. F now requests a clarification (9); he seems to have been mystified by D's (8). After a repair sequence, in which it is made clear that P's question concerned F's relations with his wife, he answers on a rather different level than P intended; F speaks about his social and emotional relations with his wife, not about his marital status according to civil law (13). P totally ignores this answer, going back to his question about civil status (15).

This sequence seems to contain several obstacles to achieving mutual understanding. The question at the outset, the point where P does not understand F, concerns F's marital status, and this issue is left unresolved even as we leave the excerpt. Within the sequence we find a local miscommunication event (ME; cf. Linell 1995a), which is suspected and indicated through F's (9) and is then developed through divergent interpretations of the situated meaning of "relations". The microgenesis of this ME appears, in retrospect, to be quite obvious. If any contribution is the core utterance, it is D's (8); in this rendition, the first two fragmented questions of the original (7) ("have been divorced? but nowadays?") remain unrelayed. Yet these questions constituted parts of the significant context of the final-turn question "what relation is now prevailing?"; within (7) this can be regarded as a reformulation on a more abstract level of the preceding questions. When this context is eliminated in (8), it amounts to an ambiguation or local decontextualization. Another change in (8), with regard to (7), is the use of the plural ("relations"), which seems to guide the interpretation towards something other than the singular question of civil status (married or not?). Note also the discrepancy between the abstract *råder* "is now prevailing" of the Swedish original and the simple "have" (or rather "be (with)") of the Russian rendition.

D's (8) is the core of the local ME in our example. But (8), in its present form, would probably not have been formulated in that way, had not P, in (7), moved expression and interpretation onto "relation(s)", rather than staying on the more concrete level of "are you married now?" (cf. P's new attempt in (15)). In addition, the joint efforts in - more or less unambiguously - relegating the state of divorce to the past (3-6) may (to F and D) have temporarily removed the issue of civil status from the agenda. Anyway, we see a subtle interplay and a collective construction and management of an ME; (8) has its contextual premises in (7) and, to some extent, in the prior discourse.

The ME is undoubtedly a consequence of the discourse being dialogue-interpreted. The interpreter performs a local decontextualization in (8), thereby cutting off P's formulation of "prevailing relations" from its prior semantic context. But again, the opportunities for miscommunication are largely due to P's introduction of a new word (or concept) into the discourse ("relation(s)"). It would seem to be a universal phenomenon, in all kinds of conversation, that the discourse gets channeled into new paths because actors do not agree upon how to interpret newly introduced words in the given context. Such troubles with mutualities are frequently remedied through side-sequences involving local decontextualization followed by clarification, (and such sequences may be somewhat less frequent in dialogue-interpreted conversations).

Our general claim, then, is that a single contribution, such as a rendition by the interpreter, which at first glance may be thought of as engendering miscommunication, must actually be explored in its sequential context.

4. Interpreting: Products, processes and practices

Earlier (Fig. 1), I introduced the "discourse-oriented" concepts of text, process and practice. It seems that these concepts highlight and fit different forms of T&I:

text	translation (of texts, without consideration of time constraints)
process (cognitive, intraindiv.) (human actor/processor, usually taken as a solitary individual,"an asocial information-processing system", often discussed in terms of limitations in human information-processing capacities)	simultaneous interpreting
practice (social practice, interaction) (full-blown communicative interaction)	dialogue (consecutive) interpreting

As regards texts and translated texts, they may, at first sight, be seen as neutral with respect to monologism or dialogism. But there is a strong tendency to reify the text, to see texts as self-contained objects in their own right. Texts are thereby treated as decontextualized, which means that the perspective in practice squares more with monologism than with dialogism. Yet, this decontextualization of texts from their contexts, and of translated texts from the situations which motivate and affect the translation, is conceptually troublesome. If we take such a translation-theoretical concept as translation equivalence (Hietaranta 1993:116), it is not a relation between texts, but a relation between texts-in-contexts (SL text in its contexts, TL text in its different (esp. sociocultural) contexts).

Incidentally, it is obvious that many theoreticians in the field of translation studies stress that translation and translated texts must be viewed within their proper situational and socio-cultural contexts. To take just a few examples, this is assumed, if my understanding is correct, in the *skopos* theory of Vermeer,[6] in Holz-Mänttäri's theory of translatorial action, and in the general theory of T&I proposed by Pöchhacker (cf. Pöchhacker 1993a:89).

If we move to simultaneous interpreting, especially in conference interpreting, this seems to invite a monologistic account quite strongly. Here we have an interpreter who is isolated in a remote booth (rather thaa positioned within the primary interaction itself), and who receives a linguistic input that s/he cannot influence (as opposed to a situation where the primary party's discursive conduct is influenced by the co-presence of the interpreter and her/his contributions). We seem to be faced with a unidirectional line of processes applied to an input already defined and constructed. (Indeed, this is how many textbooks portray communication and speech production in general (sic!). See e.g. Levelt's influential textbook *Speaking*, 1989). Yet, it must be kept in mind that situations of simultaneous interpreting also vary; they too are to some extent situation- and genre-bound. For example, the interpreter may sometimes find that her/his renditions (rather than the originals) may have an impact on what PPs say later in the debate.

Dialogue (consecutive) interpreting naturally makes a dialogical account almost self-evident, and I have already dwelt for a while upon this point. And yet, monologistic accounts abound in the theoretical and normative accounts of interpreting, as if the interpreter's contributions are nothing but translations from PPs' originals. It is an empirical task to research under what conditions they can be truthfully described as such.

5. A unified theory of interpreting?

The opposed theories of monologism and dialogism have several other implications in the field of T&I. Let me speculate on some of these. In doing so, I shall presuppose a definition of "translation" roughly as "the creation of a text (piece of discourse) in one language (called the target language = TL) such that the text expresses the same content or is pragmatically equivalent by fulfilling the same communicative functions as a previously existing text in another language (the source language, = SL)".[7]

We know that translation or interpretation, according to this definition, is a difficult, indeed an unattainable, goal. But *why* is this so? Here, our different theories have different answers. If, according to monologist transfer theories, translation is SL text-to-TL text transfer, under conditions of semantic and pragmatic correspondence (equivalence), it (the translation) is problematic mainly because languages are different; they select the aspects of the world which are to be reflected in linguistic "representations" in different ways. Barring this difficulty (and target languages can be regimented), pure and adequate translation should in principle be possible; what you need for understanding the original, and for translating it, is "there", "in the text". Discrepancies between originals and renditions are due to discrepancies between languages, or to speakers' and translators' mistakes (faults, misrepresentations) or sheer ignorance. These could, in principle, be dealt with.

With a dialogist epistemology, translation can never (or seldom?) be pure. According to this framework, *not* everything is "there in the text". Originals and renditions always occur in their situational and socio-cultural contexts from which they cannot be extracted without some change of meaning, and these contexts are (by definition) not present or fully manifest in the texts themselves. The difficulties are of course a matter of degree; they would seem to be most obvious perhaps for poems, less so for texts on, say, a mathematical topic. By way of conclusion, then, in addition to the problems the monologist recognizes, the dialogist also points to the fact that there is no way that discourse, texts (originals, renditions) or transfer processes can be understood outside of their respective relevant contexts.

Another difference between monologism and dialogism (which assume, basically (as I hinted at above), that languages reflect vs. refract the world, respectively), seems to be that the former takes translation, in some form or another (perhaps something close to the definition suggested above), to be a phenomenon that we can observe in the world. With an abstract model of cognitive processing, it is possible and rather easy to assume translation processes to be a unitary phenomenon; one and the same (type of) translation would occur as a common factor in text translation, simultaneous interpreting, dialogue interpreting etc. The nature of the translation process is then seen as independent of activity types and communicative genres, contexts and contents.

Contrary to this, I would argue that the traditional concepts of translation and interpreting are conceptual tools that we use in our attempts at understanding what people do in certain linguistic activities; to some extent, the same activities might be understood in other terms as well. Moreover, there is a strongly normative component in notions underlying the definition of translation as above; such notions try to account for how we, in many situations, argue that translators and interpreters *should* carry out their tasks. José Lambert (1993) notes that activities of translation and interpreting, as well as our theories about these activities, are part of the "Western institutionalization of language, societies, <and> cultures" (p. 21). He also argues that the idea of translation, as only *one* kind of mental processing, cannot be taken for granted.

According to the competing dialogistic framework, translation is a sociocultural concept, constructed in certain cultural contexts. That is, within some of our cultural traditions, we have a belief in "translation" as a practice or process, with something like the above-mentioned properties. Thinking of dialogue interpreting in terms of translation is a culture-specific way of understanding it. On the one hand, this may impede us from seeing other features of dialogue interpreting practices-in-context (such as those mentioned in section 2). On the other hand, the theory is of course also reflexively related to actual practices; by believing in the possibility of language-to-language transfer, we may make the actual performance move closer to this ideal. I would not deny, in other words, that norms of (what is considered to be) correct or neutral interpreting have an impact on actual conduct, or that interpreters may stay close to the task of "merely" translating, but it is of course entirely an empirical question how far these ideal norms fit actual conduct, and/or vice versa. Likewise, what kinds of variation there are among the activity types in which interpreting occurs is a matter to be empirically researched.

As I have suggested, dialogists take cognitive activities to be socio-culturally situated and subject to cultural variation (cf. Hymes's list, point 5). We know that cognitive activities like reading, learning, remembering, and understanding vary with activities and contexts (there are many different ways, styles and levels of reading, etc.), so why shouldn't there also be variation in translation and interpreting? Harris (1994), for example, gives an impressive list of different modes and functions in interpreting. Naturally, there is *something* common to these different types of T&I, just as there might be something common to different kinds of reading, but there are also many discrepant distinguishing ingredients.

6. Interpreting as decontextualizing practices

I would contend that dialogism (or, in other terms: social-constructionism, interactionism, contextualism) is the appropriate overall framework to be used in the semiotic sciences, i.e. those which deal with human action, meaning, and sense-making. I have also suggested that there are dangers inherent in decontextualizing linguistic formulations, texts, processes etc. from their functions in their embedding activities and contexts. But I now want to complicate the picture: a reasonably sophisticated dialogism must recognize that many human activities in the world involve different kinds of decontextualization, and that monologistic theories have their proper place within many scientific enterprises.

What I therefore suggest is that contextualization and decontextualization co-occur, in different mixtures, in communicative activities. In fact, there are countless examples of decontextualizating practices in our everyday world of language use. Consider, for example, what happens in quotation and citation; a quotation cannot be understood unless one considers the effects of its being de-contextualized from the quoted context and re-contextualized into a quoting context (Tannen 1989; Clark & Gerrig 1990). Or take the case of someone writing a report on the basis of what was said in an interview between him or her and some other person. This involves major de- and re-contextualizations, through which things said in the interview appear selected and seen from a different perspective within a co-text (the report), which is subject to other expectations and relevance criteria than the original spoken interview (e.g. Linell & Jönsson 1991, on police reports of suspects' stories). But all these decontextualizations are themselves context-bound. They occur under certain contextual conditions. We might call them *situated decontextualizing practices* (Linell 1992). Note that this means that an activity is seen as decontextualizing and contextualized at the same time. When we engage in decontextualizing and abstracting, we do so in certain situations and for certain purposes.

Returning now to the phenomenon of interpreting, we find ourselves concerned with decontextualization at (at least) two different levels:
- one is interpreting itself: the interpreter's activities in the world,
- the other is our (i.e. the researchers') theorizing about interpreting.
On the latter point, we may choose to look selectively upon interpreting in a certain way for our specific research purposes. For example, we may wish to look at only the cognitive (mental, neurolinguistic etc.) processes involved, for some purpose and in some research context. Scientific theorizing, prone as it is to looking analytically at one thing at a time, seems to be partly decontextualizing almost by necessity.

First-order (level) decontextualizing activities tend to invite decontextualized (or decontextualizing) theories. In the case of text translation, it is fairly easy to think of it as targeted at creating self-contained texts which obey an autonomous equivalence condition with respect to original source texts. This is a possible approach, but not the *only* one. If we take simultaneous, unidirectional (conference) interpreting, its remotely positioned interpreters work under decontextualizing conditions; they receive a linguistic input that they cannot influence, and are supposed to translate with severely restricted opportunities to interact with their social environment. Yet, the activity takes place in its own particular contexts and concerns specific knowledge domains.

Finally, consider dialogue interpreting. We then find that what the dialogue interpreter does is limited from a communicative point of view. His/her activity too is decontextualizing, largely concentrating on linguistic features. Each contribution by the dialogue interpreter is a small, or local, semi-autonomous communicative project with strongly circumscribed goals; basically, it is a matter of making sense of and relaying a particular original. In other words, the predicaments of the interpreter's utterance *are* in some respects decontextualized. Yet, what would become absurd in my view would be to take an abstract theory of translation (and also a model of linguistic processing where operations are entirely determined by their linguistic input and independent of social context), and then apply these theories to conversational discourse and to dialogue interpreting, thus in effect assuming that the interpreter does nothing but perform oral translation operations in two directions.

8. Conclusion

In summary, there are different theories of communication (and similarly of language, cognition, and human action). I have pointed to a distinction between monological and dialogical theories. The dialogistic framework is of central importance in human semiotic sciences. Contexts are of fundamental importance in theories of communication, and interpreting must be understood in terms of special kinds of context-bound semiotic activities. But we must be more sophisticated than this; decontextualizing practices have also secured their place in the world, and in our theories about the world. Interpreting is a case in point. Like other semiotic activities, it is both socially situated (bound to particular contexts) and decontextualizing, but it is so in peculiar ways. A lot of empirical research remains to be done, if we truly want to understand these ways.

NOTES

1.   Work on this paper was supported in part by grants no. 89/44 by The Bank of Sweden Tercentenary Foundation and F402:87 by the Swedish Research Council of the Humanities and Social Sciences. These projects have focussed on dialogue interpreting, more specifically on community interpreters working in institutional discourse situations, mainly legal contexts (court trials, police interviews) and health

care contexts. See esp. Wadensjö (1992), and also e.g. Linell et al. (1992). For comments on this paper I thank in particular Linda Jönsson and Cecilia Wadensjö.

2.   See e.g. the special issue (Summer, 1993) of *Journal of Communication* 43. 3.

3.   'Contexts' comprise diverse phenomena such as the prior co-text, the surrounding concrete (perceptually accessible) situation, and various kinds of abstract background knowledge, including frames of activity types (situation definitions), models of current topics, and general knowledge of language, culture, and the world. See Linell (1995b) for a full discussion of the dynamics of contexts in discourse.

'Contextualization' means, of course, putting something, e.g. a piece of discourse in a relevant context (or matrix of contexts). By definition, understanding a message amounts to relating it to a relevant context. 'Decontextualization' refers to the extraction of a piece of discourse from some particular contexts, and 'recontextualization' means the transfer of a piece of discourse from one context (or matrix of contexts) to another.

4.   'Monological' and 'dialogical' refer here to 'monologism' and 'dialogism' (as different theoretical frameworks), respectively, rather than to 'monologue' and 'dialogue' (as discourse types with divergent participation structures). If we want to be punctilious, we may therefore prefer the forms 'monologist(ic)' and 'dialogist(ic)'. Alternative terms for 'dialogism' could be social-constructionism, interactionism or contextualism.

5.   This example was discussed in Linell (1995a) (also in Wadensjö 1992:189ff.). In the transcripts, **boldface** denotes emphasis, and <u>underlinings</u> mark the extension of simultaneous events.

6.   Even if perhaps more speech-act theoretical interpretations of Vermeer´s theory are possible, I take *skopos* to mean the purpose for which the translation (or interpretation) is produced. Such purposes are typically entertained by target text users not as individual intentions but as aims inherent in the activities and contexts in which the actions of translation are embedded.

7.   This may be a definition that not everybody, indeed not many, would fully endorse, but it will do as a point of departure. Moreover, translation theorists seem to come up with similar definitions, if they are pressed to be succinct.

Interpretation Research Policy

Jorma Tommola, *University of Turku* (Moderator)
Ivana Cenkova, *Charles University, Prague*
Daniel Gile, *ISIT & INALCO, Paris*
Masaomi Kondo, *Daito Bunka University, Tokyo*
Sylvie Lambert, *University of Ottawa*
Franz Pöchhacker, *University of Vienna*

1. Introduction

In the invitation to the participants in the Research Policy Round Table, two potential themes were suggested as a loose basis for discussion. The first was the content of research: What are the most productive and central research questions, where do they stem from, and what is the status of interpreting studies? From the point of view of research, is interpreting a phenomenon of intercultural communication, or of neuropsychological and psycholinguistic processes, to be studied, as any form of language use, with the methodologies of these areas of research? Or can we speak of interpreting studies as an independent discipline, not only to promote this research in the eyes of university administrators, the general public, or others, but also because research questions, theories and methodologies arise from within the subject area itself? Another question suggested to the participants was what could be done to enhance cooperation and coordination within the community of people interested in looking at interpreting in a scientific way.

The moderator's decision has been not to write a personal synopsis of the discussion of the panel. Instead, each contributor was asked to provide a statement based on his or her introductory turn, and on the brief general discussion that the timetable allowed. The contributions have been slightly edited, but it is the moderator's belief that the local topics of research policy, problems of interpreting research, and the participants' individual views, attitudes and styles are more correctly represented in this way than by a summary provided by an outsider. A brief selection of some central points in the contributions might, however, be useful as an introduction to this composite report.

Cenkova starts the discussion by examining the status of interpreting research policy in the Czech context, and stresses the need to establish interpreting studies formally as an academic discipline. Kondo considers the state of interpreting research in Japan, and emphasizes the point that the nature of interpreting as a task, and also the research questions one may wish to pose, may be affected by cultural and linguistic distance. Lambert's view is that of the cognitive psychologist looking at interpreting as behaviour. One central point in her statement is that even today the interests of researchers and practitioners may not always meet: what may appear theoretically highly interesting to a psychologist may seem irrelevant to practising interpreters. Gile points out that both the quality and quantity of interpreting research should be increased before interpretation research (IR) can be called an academic discipline, and also emphasizes the need for closer contact with the research and practitioner community, and research by non-interpreters from different specialist fields. The need for an institutional framework mentioned by Gile ties in with Cenkova's views. The question of academic "independence" versus the status of IR as an application of existing sciences is also a starting point for Pöchhacker, who sees the development of IR as requiring both a critical mass of research effort and, again, an established position within academic institutions. According to Pöchhacker, what is also necessary is a clear picture of what the relation between IR and translation studies really is.

2. Contributions by panelists

2.1 Ivana Cenkova: The Status of IR in the Czech context

The Institute of Translatology & Interpreting, Faculty of Arts, Charles University, Prague, is the only higher education establishment in the Czech Republic accredited to award M.A. degrees in translation and interpreting. Regular university training of interpreters and translators was launched in this country in 1963; as of September 1, 1993, the Department of Translation Studies & Interpreting was granted the status of an institute and was accordingly renamed the Institute of Translatology & Interpreting. In terms of scientific research priorities, the Institute is divided into four branches (called "seminars"):

Translation Theory and Methodology Seminar
Interpretation Theory and Methodology Seminar
Comparative Translation Studies
History of Translation.

The aim of the reorganization is twofold: to provide more favourable conditions for scientific research in the field of translation studies as well as to advance a state-of-the-art training approach. Instruction is divided according to languages, and each language has its own Director of Studies. Thus, there are Directors for English, French, German, Russian, and Spanish. These members of the Faculty are responsible for the teaching and organizational aspects of courses. The new structuring of the Institute testifies to the fact that translatology has been recognized as an independent scientific discipline by senior academics and officials of our School and University (see also a relevant article by Pöchhacker 1993b). However, the attitude of the Commission for Accreditations (Ministry of Education) to the proposed introduction of postgraduate programmes in translatology is as yet negative; in their view, translatology is not a sufficiently theoretical scientific discipline.

In spite of this rather unhappy circumstance, our research work has been going on continuously since the foundation of the first university-level translation and interpreting unit in 1963. Most of the research has dealt with the communication aspects of interpreting, rate of anticipating, and functional-communicative equivalence in interpreting. Research typically involves the analysis of the interpretation process between specific language pairs. One Ph.D. dissertation was submitted and successfully defended (Cenkova 1988), and a Reader in Interpreting has been appointed. It seems rather odd that one can become a reader in translation studies and interpreting without the discipline being recognized as a scientific (Ph.D.-worthy) one.

Our undergraduate courses last for five years and are divided into two blocks, called cycles. To obtain a degree (usually the M.A. type), all students are required to pass final examinations and write a diploma thesis. Before leaving for this conference, I visited our reference library to find out how many diploma theses have been composed on interpreting; their total number has reached 31. I consider this a momentous accomplishment that can be matched by few other interpretation schools.

When reflecting on research into interpretation, one has to ponder a series of questions; I believe that this conference will assist me in finding answers to at least some of them. Such questions include the following:

- WHEN should one start doing research? I think that the appropriate moment to embark upon scientific investigation is the 3rd-year course of lectures on the theory of interpreting, when students are introduced to what has been done in this field all over the world. This knowledge can subsequently be projected into their diploma theses.

- WHERE should one start doing the research? From what has already been said it is obvious that the most appropriate places where research should be conducted are either universities or professional guilds (in the Czech Republic, the *Association of Conference Interpreters* and *Union of Interpreters & Translators*).

- WHY should the research be done in the first place? Here, a definite answer cannot be found so easily. It is evident that purely theoretical research is essential for advancing the discipline still further; applied research may be even more crucial as its results can be immediately implemented in the methodology and system of individual interpretation courses.

- WHAT kind of research should one carry out? Empirical, pragmatic, experimental, theoretical, etc.? All these options are closely linked with what has been stated above. Research projects should be more specifically defined, focussing on a narrower range of questions; consequently, the resulting analysis could be more profound and versatile. The choice of method is left to your discretion - it is, however, desirable to combine several approaches. I believe that the time of a comprehensive approach to interpreting may be over and that we should turn to more specific issues that can be tackled more effectively even within the framework of international projects conducted with colleagues from other countries.

- WHO is involved in the research? As a rule, it is the teachers of interpreting who are at the same time active conference interpreters. Unfortunately, in this country, no specialists from other disciplines seem to be interested in issues of interpreting (apart from a few phoneticians). That is why one has to spread the word about the usefulness of our research both among practising colleagues and in academic circles. It is often the case that the research is done to obtain a necessary degree or higher academic rank, and it may be that universities do not always provide adequate recognition, time and material support for such research. Practising conference interpreters, on the other hand, are extremely difficult to lure into any scientific projects; what one could expect from them at the most is a willingness to serve as informants who let you record their performance, or answer your queries. In addition, one has to be aware of the fact that some interpreters might not be properly qualified to handle research work.

Hence, I believe that it is time to join forces, to promote exchange of information (bulletins, newsletters, etc.), to set priorities that should be addressed through carefully planned joint projects, to organize customized seminars or workshops for teachers of interpreting and other specialists, and to cooperate in selecting topics for future diploma theses of our students. It is the only way we can further the inspiring scientific discipline of translatology.

2.2 *Masaomi Kondo: Interpretation research and research policy in Japan*

I wish to make essentially three points: 1) the Interpreting Research Association of Japan was established in 1990 to promote research on interpreting in Japan; 2) Japanese researchers need to be more active in order to contribute to the international community of interpreting researchers, if only to draw benefits from studies involving not merely Indo-European (IE) languages but also non-Indo-European languages; and 3) there are few occasions where studies involving non-IE languages seem to offer interesting insights into some aspects of research on interpreting.

Just as simultaneous interpreting got started at the Nuremberg Trials in the West, so it did at the Tokyo War Criminals Trial in Japan in 1946. By the late 1950's, simultaneous interpreting was employed quite widely, in the Hiroshima and Nagasaki peace conferences, in business contacts with the West, and in other general intercultural encounters. Since the Japanese economy took off to a high growth period in the 1960's, there has been a spectacular growth in the interpreting market in Japan. Not only the growing contacts with the rest of the world but also the traditional emphasis on written language learning (and the deliberate de-emphasis on speaking the foreign language) probably helped enhance the need for interpreting.

Strangely, however, no science of interpreting was born out of this growing popularity. Few practicing conference interpreters tried to explain what they were doing in a systematic way until rather recently. No linguists took interest in studying interpreting skills. No psychologists, few brain specialists, and few communications researchers found it worth their while to investigate the interpreters' performances.

When Akira Mizuno and I were asked to review interpreting research in Japan in 1993, we were able to compile a rather extensive collection of literature involving Japanese either as a passive or an active language. We also found that most of these writings lacked scientific rigour, and mainly described the authors' own experiences in essay style, or gave "how-to" advice. Few were aware of the on-going research in the rest of the world.

When the Interpreting Research Association of Japan was formed in 1990 (IRAJ, 1991-1994), it was vaguely realized that we were about 30 years behind the West in interpreting research. Our first task was, and still is, to absorb the research thus far carried out within various disciplines in the West, without, however, accepting the results of past research blindly. Nor can we do so, as we have found, because they deal mainly with intra-Indo-European language combinations.

When I started to read Western writings on conference interpreting, I found myself agreeing with most of what I was reading. Kirchhoff's (1976) three-party two-language model of interpreting was a confirmation of what I had argued. I had little doubt that on most interpreting occasions it was better to try to convey the meaning or the message contained in the original utterance, although many colleagues in Japan opted (and still opt) for closer word-for-word correspondence. But eventually I came across more and more papers that posed this question: While the interpreting theory developed in the West needs small adjustments, fine-tuning and minor revisions, would a qualitatively different theory be needed if one tried to account for the interpreter's work involving non-IE languages?

Let me cite a few examples of specific difficulties:

- In many Japanese sentences, there is no indication of the main verb. The most basic construction of Japanese sentences is said to be not (subject + verb) but (indication of the subject matter of the sentence + its description). The same Japanese sentence could mean for example: *I know you had faith; He knows I had faith; She knows we had faith; They know she had faith*. And yet, when interpreting into English, we must almost always indicate the subject and therefore infer the correct subject of the Japanese sentence.

- One more illustration, this time on the lexical level. Ullmann (1977:149) says in his standard book on semantics that such words as *poetic, oxygen* and *television* are international words of classical origin. He could have said that most of the vocabulary used in political science, sociology, anthropology, economics, law, astronomy, biology, etc. belong to the same group. But outside the IE-linguistic sphere, that does not apply. Would there not be some qualitative difference between a language combination where these international words of classical origin are in abundant use and one where there exists no such co-relation in most of the vocabulary used? Recent entry of newly coined words into the Japanese vocabulary has contributed to a complex psychic anomaly of the Japanese toward Western science (Kondo, 1992).

The list of illustrations could be further extended (see Setton 1993a). But hopefully the point is sufficiently made. Every language is different, but some languages are more different and this may make the nature of interpreting work qualitatively different depending on language combinations. If there is one set of cultures closer to one other than another set, it seems that we as interpreters must travel shorter or longer distances depending on the language combination in order to transfer the meaning to the receiving culture. Mizuno (1993), after examining a number of paradigms depicting simultaneous interpreting, says it cannot be explained unless we recognize some automatic (non-thinking) transposition of individual words and phrases (there would otherwise be overload on the brain's processing capacity). There may be a substantial difference in the importance of these automatic reflexes between intra-IE interpreters and those involving non-IE languages. Considerations such as these may require not merely some shifts of emphasis in the general theory of interpreting but a qualitatively different body of rules, principles, and hypotheses: There may be some qualitative differences between short-distance running and long-distance running. Short-distance runners may not be as lonely as long-distance ones.

However, I am reluctant to advocate the need for a completely different set of theories for J-E and E-J interpreting. If the general theory posits that interpreters deal not with words but with ideas and concepts to be first grasped and then encoded in another code (language), then it is equally relevant to the case of interpreting involving non-IE languages. Also, I wish to avoid being trapped into claiming that everything Japanese is unique.

It must also be pointed out that it is mainly the task of the Japanese interpreters and researchers equipped with non-IE language capabilities to reveal the perspectives obtainable from the studies of IE- and non-IE language combinations. It is naturally assumed that IE-language researchers are sufficiently open-minded not to reject them. Different perspectives that we can mutually bring in from other languages, and more broadly, from other cultures, are of immense value.

Max Weber said that one of the essentials of social science methodology is *value-freeness*. In the West, the common sense interpretation of this phrase is that you must rid yourself of your values in your scientific endeavors, and that social science can become science only when researchers' values are completely eliminated. Many Japanese Weberians offer a different interpretation. They say Max Weber was not so naive. In fact he emphasized the importance of values even in science. What he meant was that in order to make your value-loaded work part of commonly accepted science you must temporarily or theoretically free yourself from your own values so that you may be able to see the subject matter fron someone else's viewpoint, in order that a variety of angles of observation be mobilized to come ever closer to the truth. If these Japanese Weber scholars are right, this is essentially what the professional task of interpreters is about: setting our own views aside temporarily in order first to decode the in-coming message, and then to encode it in a way intelligible to the receiver. Not only that, this methodological requirement should also be valid and useful for interpreting research.

In conclusion, let me cite a few cases where such a methodology of mutual reinforcing between IE- and non-IE perspectives has produced useful insights in interpreting research. They may be an indication of one of the ways it will proceed in coming years.

1)   Wakabayashi (1992), essentially in comparison with English, characterizes the Japanese national style of speech as involving abundant use of phatic language, toleration of repetitiveness and verbosity, preference for indirect expressions, the use of indeterminate sentence final expressions and of self-effacing expressions, and liberal use of hyperbole and rhetorical questions. It is useful to have these points made explicit.

2)   Gile (1992) points out that Japanese has significantly more of what he calls predictable sentence endings than at least either English or German. He showed that 46 percent of the Japanese sentences examined from different source texts have PSEs of five or more syllables, with 9 per cent of the texts having PSEs of 8 or more syllables. Generally it is held that when 5 or more syllables are

predictable, the interpreter's task is considerably facilitated.

3)   One of the important features of English from the perspective of a Japanese speaker is that agentive verbs can take inanimate subjects. In English, inanimate entities, such as pieces of news, ideas, places, time, facts, events, organizations etc. can behave as if they had their own wills to do things. This feature may be too obvious to native English speakers, including grammarians, to deserve careful study. I have argued that one of the important methodological underpinnings of modern economics, pioneered with the use of English as the medium of thinking and communication is precisely this: A greater supply *pushes* down the price, a lower price *encourages* people to buy more of that product, higher value of the yen *makes* Japanese exports more expensive abroad., etc. (Kondo 1986). The difficulty that this feature of English causes to the interpreter recoding in Japanese, as well as how it is handled, seems to be an important aspect of interpreting research (Uchiyama 1990).

2.3 *Sylvie Lambert: A cognitive psychologist's view on interpretation research policy*

In this contribution, I am basing myself on the original premise of the Round Table on research policy in interpretation, namely a look at both the *content* of research policy and the *organization of and cooperation within* interpretation research.

Given that simultaneous interpretation touches upon a multitude of fields such as linguistics, psychology, bilingual education, neuropsychology, translation studies, languages, to name but a few, it goes without saying that the most productive and central research questions will logically stem from a multitude of behaviours. As to whether interpretation research is the application of existing disciplines or whether relevant research questions stem from interpreting itself, one is reminded of the moot question as to whether the egg comes before the chicken or the chicken before the egg.

Ideally, one would hope that researchers like myself, not necessarily practicing conference interpreters, would be able to examine simultaneous interpretation from the point of view of cognitive psychology, which, thanks to the likes of the late David Gerver, happened to be one of the pioneering research fields in early research on simultaneous interpretation. At the time, however, cognitive psychology focussed exclusively on the notion of depth-of-processing (Craik and Lockhart 1972). A decade later, another field of research began looking into the simultaneous interpretation process. This time, the approach emerged from the cross-fertilization of the fields of neurology, physiology and medicine combined with conference interpretation at the University of Trieste in Italy.

As to what are the important areas of research, unfortunately what may appear vital to some researchers (such as whether interpreters perform better when interpreting with the left or the right ear - Lambert 1993) may seem ludicrous to some interpreters. By the same token, what appears to be very important for interpreters, may not appeal to the researcher: for example, when I carried out interviews with interpreters and introduced myself as a psychologist, most interpreters began telling me about their unpleasant experiences with colleagues or with stressful situations, since they may have assumed that I was some sort of clinical psychologist with advice for them on how to cope with the stress they were experiencing at the time. After having had the unique privilege of being able to be present at three of the most watershed conferences on simultaneous interpretation research, namely the conferences held in Venice, Trieste and Turku, I was somewhat disheartened to see that what appeared to be of great concern to professional interpreters present at the Turku conference, were the very same concerns of nearly a decade ago: i.e., whether an interpreter should ever be allowed to interpret into a B language; whether shadowing was really a useful training tool for beginners in interpretation; and whether non-interpreters should be allowed to train interpreters.

A more frightening incident of this nature occurred nearly twenty years ago when I was working as a research assistant for Patricia E. Longley at the Polytechnic of Central London. Since I was also enrolled as David Gerver's PhD student at the University of Stirling, Dr. Gerver had suggested that I observe the students training to become interpreters at the London Polytechnic in order to come up with possible ideas for research for my doctoral dissertation. I also carried out interviews with London-based AIIC interpreters and observed them in the booth. It was during such observations that I noticed that not all professional interpreters placed both headphones directly on both ears. When questioned about this fact, professional interpreters replied either that they felt they heard better with one ear as opposed to the other, or that somehow the headphones felt too tight and that removing one headphone off of one ear simply felt more comfortable. How does a researcher set about explaining this phenomenon?

At the time, the interpreters appeared not to know why they removed one headphone from one ear, and, as a researcher, I knew even less about the neurological aspects of simultaneous interpretation. Following the advice of several psychologists, I decided to carry out a pilot test by sending out a questionnaire to all the London-based AIIC interpreters. Some of the questions that were included in the questionnaire have since been published (Lambert and Lambert 1985). At the time, however, only 30% of the subjects responded. One AIIC interpreter went so far as to write a letter of complaint to both Patricia Longley and the Dean of the Polytechnic of Central London denouncing the frivolity of such research and deploring the waste of government funding on such nonsense. At one point I was informed that I would lose my position as research assistant at the Polytechnic as a result of this incident.

So, when asked once again what and where are the most productive and central research questions in conference interpretation, I am somewhat reluctant to propose any trends of research for the future. I can only examine current trends in the field of cognitive psychology, bring them to light at conferences, discuss them with my research students at the University of Ottawa and then sit back and wait to see if there are any takers.

One recent type of model of human information processing which is receiving a lot of attention at the moment in cognitive psychology is the notion of *executive function*. Executive function entails metacognition, which in simultaneous interpretation is an awareness of the kinds of strategies used and knowing what kinds of strategies are needed for a particular type of simultaneous interpretation, as well as being able to volitionally generate those strategies as needed. In other words, metacognition requires a high level of self-regulation of mental processing strategies which are mainly frontal lobe functions. Such self-regulation refers to the control of employment of attentional processes: the attentional processes involved in simultaneous interpretation, for example, might include sustained attention, selective attention, divided attention, shared attention and shifting attention from the input to the output.

So one interesting line of future research for cognitive psychology might consider examining the relationship between these self-regulatory processes and simultaneous interpretation, if cognitive psychologists wanted to make a significant contribution to the field of simultaneous interpretation. Such research would be extremely valuable if someone actually broke down all the processes involved in simultaneous interpretation and while doing so, referred to a particular model of information processing. The executive function model might be a useful framework for this type of research.

2.4 *Daniel Gile: Improving the status of IR as a multidisciplinary field of study*

After many years during which individual calls for a scientific, multidisciplinary approach to interpreting research by Pinter, Anderson, Stenzl and others were not heard, the IR community has finally reached a point where such an approach is widely advocated. Many suggestions have also been made with a view to helping establish interpretation studies as a discipline (see in particular Pöchhacker below). Unfortunately, while many of these suggestions are very good technically, the history of IR, and sociological and institutional factors suggest that major hurdles must still be overcome before interpretation studies can be established as an academic discipline.

Firstly, the amount of research done in interpreting is still very limited, in particular with no more than a handful of empirical studies every year, far from the minimum 'critical mass' that would make it possible to consider interpreting research a discipline on its own. Qualitatively, many IR projects leave much to be desired, and much of the rather abundant literature on interpreting consists of essays and prescriptive writings rather than actual research reports (see Gile 1995b).

This situation can be traced to the following factors:

1.   *The absence of interaction with the scientific community.* For historical and sociological reasons explained in Gile 1995b, after an initial interest on the part of psychologists and linguists in the sixties and seventies, interpreters took over, and most of the interaction between the IR community and the scientific community at large was cut off in the second half of the seventies. Hence the loss of a valuable potential input in terms of knowledge, knowhow, motivation and material resources.

2.   *The lack of an institutional framework.* There is no specialized research institution dealing with IR, though there are a number of organizations devoted to translation research. Neither are there research training institutions which cater to the needs of interpretation scholars, with the single exception of the Scuola Superiore di Lingue Moderne per

Interpreti e Traduttori of the University of Trieste (see below). The major interpretation schools consider that their function is essentially professional rather than academic, and there are practically no research requirements for teachers of interpreting.

3. *Insufficient motivation.* Interpreters are busy interpreting, and IR activity means much work for no financial or social reward. Since, as mentioned above, there are no institutional requirements for research either, motivation is mostly personal, and often does not outlive the fulfilment of the requirements of an M.A. or Ph.D. degree.

4. *Insufficient research training.* Most interpreters have not had any research training, and very few institutions provide such training to future IR scholars (the SSLMIT in Trieste is an exception, though, setting aside training through projects with the neurophysiologist Franco Fabbro for some students and staff, it is not clear how much and by whom research training is conducted at the Trieste school). It is therefore not particularly surprising that many IR texts suffer from severe methodological weaknesses (see Gile 1995b).

How to remedy the situation? The following steps may help by providing some means and, it is hoped, generating some motivation:

1. *Institutionalize research.* Though it seems premature to seek funding for the setting up of IR institutions per se, some degree of institutionalization could be aimed for in I/T schools. Students could be encouraged to undertake a small research project on interpreting as a graduation requirement. Graduation theses are required in a number of schools, in particular in Trieste, in Heildelberg and in Vienna. Some research requirements could be institutionalized for part of the teaching staff - but not for all positions, lest interpretation schools lose the essential contribution of good teachers who are not interested in research.

2. *Provide research training.* This could be done within the interpretation schools, but also, at least in the beginning, in other academic departments within the behavioural sphere (in particular those specializing in sociology, psychology and education).

3.   *Raise research quality standards*. At the present time, many mediocre
       papers on interpreting are accepted for publication in the only European
       IR periodical, *The Interpreter's Newsletter*. In other I/T periodicals and
       in conference proceedings, the phenomenon is even more striking.
       While a rather lenient editorial policy was probably favourable to the
       initial development of IR, now that the volume and influx of writings
       on interpreting are considerable, a stricter editorial policy, as suggested
       by Fabbro in this volume, might be called for in order to raise the
       overall quality of IR.

4.   *Interact with the scientific community at large*. Such interaction is not
       easy because of the differences between the language and approach of
       the IR community and of the scientific community respectively. The
       knowledge gap between the two communities makes communication
       even more difficult, and requires some knowledge acquisition, in
       particular in the cognitive sciences, by interpreters engaging in
       research. However, in terms of research *policy,* such interaction is
       probably the best way forward.

Past experience is not very conducive to high expectations from the
interpreting side. Student interpreters are eager to become interpreters, and are
likely to devote their time and efforts to interpreting rather than to the
acquisition of knowledge in the cognitive sciences and of research knowhow
which may be largely irrelevant to their future professional needs. Qualified
interpreters are bound to devote their time to professional interpreting, which
is how they earn their living, rather than to research. Only a handful of
professionals may be motivated enough to devote a significant part of their
time and energy to research, or indeed to cross over into full-time academic
research, which is financially less appealing than interpretation. On the other
hand, academics and full-time researchers in a number of disciplines within the
cognitive science field inherently have the motivation, the knowhow and most
of the knowledge required to do IR. Indeed, in the literature, the ratio of
serious, innovative papers to the overall number of papers is much higher in
the population of such "outsiders" than in the population of interpreters, and
many of the initial methodological weaknesses decried in the sixties and
seventies have now disappeared from their writings. The number of such
outsiders is small at the present time, and one of the aims of IR policy should

be to increase their number.

In conclusion, though the mass of IR writings is considerable, the amount of actual research done in interpreting is small. This is due to very fundamental factors that are probably difficult to change within the interpreting community, though interpreting schools might improve the situation to some extent by contributing to the motivation and training for research of their students, and by opting for a policy of small, methodologically simple projects with much replication (see Gile 1995b). The most promising avenue is probably the promotion of IR among non-interpreting researchers, especially in the cognitive sciences.

2.5 *Franz Pöchhacker: Mapping IR as a discipline*

2.5.1 *What IR is or ought to be*
The fact that there is or should be something like a *policy* of interpretation research implies that there are or should be IR *policy-makers*. This in turn poses the question of where, in which *domain* of scholarly endeavour, such individuals or institutions are to be found. The term IR offers little guidance here, since research *on* interpretation has been carried out in the framework of various academic disciplines, such as linguistics and psychology and their respective branches. If there is to be a certain domain within and for which such policy-making by policy-makers is said to take place, it would resemble a mosaic of bits and pieces from other disciplines, rather than an "independent" field of study in the traditional sense. Or would it?

It is my contention here that the assumption of an *interdisciplinary non-discipline* is rather questionable with regard to its practical implications for the future development of IR. The trouble with IR policy, if anyone is really troubled by it, starts precisely with the lack of a broad consensus on the nature and status of this research domain. At one end of the spectrum are those who claim that research activities focussing on the phenomenon of interpreting form an academic field of study or *discipline* in its own right. At the other there are those who regard IR as a result of applying the theories and methods of existing disciplines. It is difficult to see how the latter could serve as a premise for coherent policy-making, let alone who the IR policy-makers might be. Between these two extreme positions there is of course plenty of middle ground, which is mainly covered by those who do acknowledge the existence of an IR *community* but observe that its research output and the level of interaction among individual activities are still insufficient to reach "critical mass", and that in terms of quality and quantity IR is not up to par with accepted disciplines.

My aim here is not to analyze which of the above positions reflects the "true" status of IR. Rather than discuss what the present status of IR is I will say what it *should be* and *why*. Underlying this suggested *policy decision* is the belief that in the academic community the attestation that a field of research has "gone critical" and begun to take on a life of its own has less to do with the laws of physics than with tactics and politics. If we as a discipline - let us call it *Interpreting Studies* - want to be accepted as such by our neighbours in the academic community, we need to show (or at least claim) an identity of our own and have a vision of what we want to be. That vision and the territory we stake out for our subject matter must be our very own. Our neighbors may have suitable implements and equipment, but we know and decide what we want to plant and cultivate. At least we ought to.

A couple of examples may be useful at this point to link up my lofty metaphors with the situation of research in Interpreting Studies:
1) A student recently asked a colleague (with post-doctoral qualifications and several publications on interpreting to her name) to serve as adviser for a diploma thesis on terminology documentation for conference interpreters. The student was told that interpreters relied essentially on their quick-wittedness in the oral mode and had little concern for terminology work in their professional activity. In short: not a relevant topic for a thesis!
2) At Charles University in Prague an associate professor specializing in IR cannot supervise doctoral research in her field because interpreting is not accepted as an academic domain in which one could earn a PhD - non-acceptance having been recommended to the administrative authority in charge by a committee made up mainly of professors from other university departments.

2.5.2 *A map of the discipline*
It is against this background of politics in academia (example 2) that I find it advisable to take tactical policy decisions (such as the claim of our existence as a discipline) first before embarking on any specific policy-making. Developments in IR have reached a point where our claim to disciplinary status could be backed up by the increasing number of publications, conference contributions and journals as well as the existence of information and communication facilities such as the *IRTIN* (Interpretation Research and Theory Information Network) *Bulletin*. However, these quantitative features are not

necessarily indicative of a new quality or coherent force in IR. To achieve this, it is necessary that our claim to disciplinary status rest on a comprehensive vision or *map* of the subject matter to be covered by Interpreting Studies (example 1).

Some such attempts at drawing up a map of Interpreting Studies have recently been made, but it is not clear whether they will suffice to establish a consensus on the full breadth and range of topics and issues for research. In the current landscape of IR, work on conference interpreting tends to overshadow research on court and community interpreting, with such other varieties as media interpreting, sign language interpreting or sight translation hardly entering the picture. In addition, process-oriented experimentation seems to stand tall against product-oriented observation and description, and there is very little, if any, work on more general (basic) issues such as the factors governing the use or non-use of interpreting in a given socio-cultural environment or the impact of different modes of interpreting on communication processes, while there is a wealth of literature in the applied branch of (conference) interpreter training.

A good "map of the discipline" must derive from a very broad conception of interpreting, giving room to the full diversity of interpreting activities with (some degree of) professional standing. Based on such a consensus regarding the subject matter as such, the map would show that the field of Interpreting Studies is "wide open" and serve as an orientation towards various landmarks and lacunae. It could help the discipline of Interpreting Studies fulfil its principal task, namely that of defining problems and generating research questions. Once it is clear how much and what there is to find out, the search for answers can be conducted with any methods available, i.e. within any conceptual framework or paradigm and on the basis of any theory and methodology considered useful. As much as the methodological approach may (have to) be inter- or multidisciplinary, it is essential that the relative position of a certain parcel of research on the map remain clear and connections to the rest of the ground to be covered be kept in view.

2.5.3 *Teaming up*
Up to this point Interpreting Studies has been advertised here as an independent discipline intent on close interaction with other disciplines. As indicated in example 2, it is to have its own infrastructure within the academic system, with professors and junior researchers on the diploma and/or doctoral levels. So much for the dream. In order to bring it closer to reality, another tactical

policy decision seems to be called for. Rather than going it alone, Interpreting Studies ought to team up with a better established partner. The obvious choice there would seem to be Translation Studies, which has already at least gained a foothold in the academic system. Among interpreting researchers, though, there has been surprising reluctance to actively seek out the common theoretical and methodological ground shared by the two basic types of translational activity. The situation seems to be changing in recent years, for instance by attempts to focus research on forms of translation/interpreting which cut across the oral and literate media, but more often than not translation and interpreting appear to be bound up within completely separate paradigms. While I would agree that there is no absolute need for Interpreting Studies to try and rely on translation theories and vice versa, in the interest of efficiency a good case could probably be made for every stretch of common ground to be sought out and worked on jointly. In economic terms, there is no need to push for a merger, but much more joint-venturing would seem to be desirable.

2.5.4 *Policy-making*

It is on this basic consensus on the nature and status of Interpreting Studies, namely as a *(sub)discipline* (of Translation-cum-Interpreting Studies) in its own right, that specific policy-making efforts could build. The larger academic infrastructure of Translation-cum-Interpreting Studies offers new channels of communication and interaction which are indispensable for progress in key policy areas. One of these is providing research training in Interpreting Studies, another is developing standards for refereed publications, and a third might be fostering and coordinating cooperative research projects.

In all these areas the feasibility of policy-making and implementation in Interpreting Studies crucially depends on the infrastructure available. It is here that one has to admit that the discipline of Interpreting Studies is anything but fully fledged. With networks such as EST, the European Society for Translation (i.e. Translation - cum - Interpreting) Studies, becoming fully operational, there is at least some reason to hope that policy-making in such key areas as research training, publishing standards and multi-center cooperation will progress beyond isolated suggestions and proposals by more or less prominent figures and reach the stage of widely supported cooperative plans or projects, coordinated by democratic leadership structures and implemented with institutional (and financial) backing by international authorities and organizations.

Speaking frankly among "ourselves", there is no denying the fact that such progress is only slowly getting under way; for quite some time to come the choice of projects and methods in Interpreting Studies is likely to remain subject to coincidental personal and institutional circumstances rather than result from coherent policies and research priorities defined by the Interpreting Studies community at large. An overly self-conscious attitude would be defeatist, however, in our relations with the rest of the academic community, within which we claim to have a rightful place. The more we press on in our work, drawing up a *comprehensive map* of what there is to be studied, defining relevant research problems, and, most importantly, building up our own academic infrastructure (in partnership with like-minded scholars in Translation Studies), the better our chances of convincing those in doubt that if the discipline of Interpreting Studies did not exist, if would be necessary to invent it.

3. Concluding remarks

In sum, then, where should IR policy-makers direct their attention? One direction seems clear from the above contributions: where it has not yet been possible to do so, interpreting studies should be raised, via serious research and training efforts, accompanied by "tactical" policy decisions, to a higher academic status.

Connected with this is a fact of policy which appeared in some of the contributions: the development of research by students, and attention to the connection between training and research is important. In "translation-cum-interpreting" education, students will in all likelihood benefit from an approach that values systematic examination of the task being learned through limited-range research tasks in the form of a university thesis. This particular aspect of training was debated for example in Finland slightly more than a decade ago, when the status of translation and interpretation studies was being decided upon. Although opposing comments are still voiced every now and then in the heat of university-internal financial politics, it seems clear in retrospect that the transfer of translation and interpretation training to university level and the establishment of a thesis requirement was the right decision. The result has so far been over 840 MA-level theses and several licentiates and doctorates from the four Finnish university centres which specialize in translation and interpretation training. Educationalists speak of the *formal* aims of university study: the development of independent and critical thinking through identification of problems, attempts to solve them, and adequate reporting of these attempts. Such aims are important even in areas where the primary goal of instruction is the development of practical skills; and they are particularly important in our field since the processes of interpreting and translation are characterised by constant problem-solving.

Judging from the contributions, another primary aim of interpreting research policy is to raise the quality and broaden the scope of research. This means that researchers, unless they already are specialists in a certain field, should familiarize themselves with the approaches and methods of a variety of sciences. It remains to be seen whether the advancement of the formal academic status of IR eventually leads to a situation where one can really speak of a more or less autonomous "science of interpreting", whose methods, for example, would be internally generated. So far, interpreting seems rather to remain a phenomenon of intercultural communication or of language use, which can and should be approached from various angles of study, and through the methods of several established fields of research. While some research will directly benefit the practicing interpreter, much of it may not be directly applicable in this way. Whatever the case, interpreting research will increase our understanding of what happens when we use languages, and how understanding between different cultures can be achieved.

The Interaction Between Research and Training

John M. Dodds, *SSLMIT, University of Trieste* (Moderator)
D. Katan, *SSLMIT* (Rapporteur)
Hanne Aarup, *Copenhagen Business School*
A. Gringiani, *SSLMIT*
A. Riccardi, *SSLMIT*
Nancy Schweda Nicholson, *University of Delaware*
Sergio Viaggio, *United Nations, Vienna*

1. Introduction

I would like, by way of introduction to the debate on the interaction that exists (if indeed it exists at all) between interpretation research and the training of would-be interpreters, (a) to refer you, with a perhaps timely reminder, that it was Daniel Gile himself who recognised the importance of interaction between theory and practice when he said that all and any research "est susceptible de contribuer à l'enseignement, ne serait-ce qu'indirectement" (1989: 33) and (b) to quote from Catherine Stenzl's excellent paper that she presented on the same occasion at the international conference on the teaching of interpretation, held in Trieste almost ten years ago:

> (...) there must be genuine interaction between theory and practice if we want to see sound and constructive developments in both areas. The reason why I am labouring the point is my impression that we have tended to take that interaction too much for granted and that in our field the relationship between theory and practice has often been one of co-existence rather than interaction" (1989:23).

However, in her concluding remarks Ms. Stenzl expressed serious doubts as to the genuineness of our intentions when she very aptly posed the billion dollar question, which was then and still is now whether we, as professional interpreters, researchers and teachers, "are willing and able to make it [research] interact with our practice" (1989: 26) and consequently with what we hand down to the younger generation in the classroom.

My own personal impression gained from the Turku conference, was that participants were not very interested in the applications of research to teaching or the interaction between the two. Or, to be a little fairer, interest was not made very explicit, in that the words "students" or "trainees" were uttered three or four times at most over the two days up to the beginning of the present discussion.

However, to be even fairer, I must openly give due recognition to the fact that strides have indeed been made since the 1986 Trieste Conference when we were still debating as to whether there was any point to doing research in a field that is so empirical by definition. But, funnily enough, strides seem to have been made in those very areas where evidence of any interaction with the teaching of conference interpretation is probably the most tenuous. I am referring, of course, to those "purely scientific", neurophysiological and neurolinguistic aspects of interpretation activity, seen in terms of describable cerebral phenomena or processes, being admirably studied by Gran, Fabbro, Moser, Lambert and Darò, to name only a few. But clearly here, as we are all well aware, the applications of this kind of study to the teaching of student interpreters in the classroom may, and I repeat, *may* only become apparent after many, many more years of intense research in these areas, even though Gran in her recent book on the cerebral organisation of language applied to simultaneous interpretation suggests in a small chapter (1992: 252-262) a whole series of possible didactic applications of this kind of work. Nevertheless, she does add, by way of conclusion (1992: 262), that if nothing more "a greater understanding of the way linguistic competence develops will lead to the identification of more efficient teaching techniques".[1]

I would also add the identification and improvement of more efficient aptitude testing methods which clearly have direct as well as indirect repercussions on teaching activity too. But, unfortunately, to date, the initial proposals of shadowing and other techniques as possible testing devices have hardly if at all been verified scientifically. And let not their detractors smirk, for they have not been falsified either!

What seems to be happening is that having reached the Moon, nobody is any longer that interested in it. Its exploration and colonisation are of secondary importance, forms of life there have become irrelevant because it seems we must proceed at all costs with great leaps and bounds. Trieste was the Moon but that's now behind us, today in Turku it must be Mars, tomorrow the solar system and the day after the whole galaxy. So what about that little old Moon of ours?

Well, it has been discovered but it certainly has not been explored! Shadowing as an aptitude test, as already mentioned, has not been either verified or falsified scientifically. No adequate replication tests have been carried out to this end. We are as much in doubt today as we were ten years ago in Trieste about its validity either as a testing device or as a teaching technique. And yet the testing of aptitude is surely of fundamental importance as the very basis of successful teaching.

Text and discourse analysis too have been talked about for decades now. It used to be the Kintsch/van Dijk model (1978) whereas today it tends to be Halliday (1973, 1985). But, although the areas of possible research are identified, we prefer to move on to identify new unexplored areas rather than consolidate what has already been identified.

If in the pages that follow in this discussion on research and teaching the topics might appear simple or even simplistic, and if members of the panel may seem somewhat less adventurous than some of our "discoverer" colleagues, this is because we are merely trying to find out what is usable in the classroom, to translate it into simple terms so that both non-specialised teachers and students alike may understand how advanced research may become a clear teaching technique. An example is the simple but not for that any less important preparation of an elementary text such as Nancy Schweda Nicholson has done, or the questions posed by Hanne Aarup regarding course design.

Of course, when university careers or research funding or indeed personal or collective reputations are involved, it is extremely difficult to convince researchers to do the dog-work: firstly the practical, experimental application in the classroom of what has been proposed theoretically, and secondly its replication in other teaching environments. Both Daniel Gile and I have been stressing the need for this for many years now (Dodds 1989: 20; Gile 1990a: 230) but I appeal to you all once again, as professional teachers and for the sake of improved teaching in the classroom with consequent improved performance in the booth later on, not to lose sight of the small, the simple, the practical and the replicable, unexciting as these may be, so that we may consolidate what we have already discovered and to let others, in need of funding, reputations or chairs, go on to where no interpreter has gone before.

The following papers have been edited and rearranged to give a coherent perspective. The first two contain an overview of research development and its influence on training, and current attitudes towards the interaction (or lack of interaction) between the two worlds. The second two are devoted to training the interpreter, concentrating on two specific points: note taking and text selection. Finally, two conclusions. One intentionally individual viewpoint from Sergio Viaggio, a professional interpreter and trainer at the United Nations, and the other, an intentionally objective rapporteur's conclusion to the roundtable discussion encompassing the question session.

2. Conference interpreting: the background to research and training
- A. Riccardi, SSLMIT, University of Trieste

The many and various definitions of conference interpreting (consecutive and simultaneous) are essentially a matter of different perspectives. While the description of conference interpreting in linguistic terms will place special emphasis on the linguistic components, a description of the sociolinguistic variables of interpreting will stress the communicative aspect of message production and reception. Within these descriptions it will be difficult, furthermore, to take the cognitive, psychological and neuropsychological processes fully into account.

According to Salevsky (1993: 148), for example, interpreting is:

> not merely a matter of reproduction [...].The communicative realisation of the target text is only the final link in a chain of mental operations involving a variety of interactions between analysis as recognition and sense attribution, planning, drawing comparisons, probability considerations and the formation of hypotheses involving examination procedures for alternative objectives and means, problem-solving and decision-making techniques, feedback, and mechanisms for control and evaluation.

From the cognitive psychology point of view, simultaneous interpretation is a "complex human information processing activity composed of a series of interdependent skills [...]" (Lambert, 1992: 16-17). Clearly, conference interpreting is still a young and complex discipline and its research borders cannot yet be clearly drawn.

In the '70s, studies into conference interpreting centred more on personal theorising than on scientific investigation. However, the basic ideas (such as Seleskovitch's *théorie du sens*) were developed in those years and formed the foundation for interpreter training. As stated by Gile, after the initial results of Personal Theorising, investigation has been dominated by "assertions and counter-assertions" (1990b: 34). It is clear that still more time will pass before enough is known to formulate an accepted empirically based general theory.

What we do have now is an overall framework which, "even though [...] not complete, is wide enough to accommodate a vast range of variables [...]. It is a dynamic framework that can account for the interaction between different variables." (Stenzl, 1989: 26).

With regard to research, there is a great variety in the activity taking place at Trieste's SSLMIT. While this diversity has been criticised, it is only the logical consequence of enquiry into a young discipline with so many interrelated fields.

There is a broad division of interests and research in conference interpretation, from the investigation of general human cognitive processes such as memory, attention, speech reception and production, information processing (the *conditio sine qua non* of interpretation), to the investigation of translation problems (equivalence, communication factors, surface and deep structure), and text and contrastive linguistics.

Research is already beginning to influence training. Gran (1992), for example, as a result of research on the cerebral organisation of language, has put forward separate teaching strategies for *compound* and *coordinate* bilinguals. Further research in the field of hemispheric specialisation for bilinguals and polyglots, focussing patterns and stages of second language acquisition, will permit greater insight into the interpretation-specific problems of bilinguals. These results should then lead to improved teaching strategies.

Studies and theories in cognitive psychology, neurolinguistics, psycholinguistics and cognitive linguistics have already been applied to research on aptitude testing for interpretation and the linguistic abilities required (recall tests, tests on associational fluency, expressional fluency). Lambert (1989b) has given a detailed account of pedagogical techniques based on "a gradual approach" specifically devised for this purpose. The various cognitive elements and skills of interpretation have been analysed and divided into sub-skills to be taught separately before being combined to form a global ability.

Linguistic models and theories have often been applied to the subject of conference interpreting. Text linguistics has helped build the framework within which source-text and target-text may be analysed for better comprehension. Trainers need to have a background in a variety of research areas if they are to be effective in dealing with individual student problems. The areas include: sociolinguistics, psycholinguistics, neurolinguistics, text linguistics, translation studies, cognitive linguistics and sciences, neurophysiology, semantics, pragmatics and communication theory.

So, basic research is needed which can then be applied to training and be used to develop and test didactic tools. Ideally, research would be carried out jointly by interpreters and researchers from other fields to ensure the interdisciplinarity needed in interpreting studies.

Of paramount importance, first, is a thorough understanding of the cognitive processes involved in interpreting. With this basis, we may look for more specific insights into language combinations and constraints, and those expectations and goals of the receptor which are liable to influence interpreting. Research focus can move from the transfer of cognitive content to the transfer of formal linguistic features. These are of the utmost importance when the text under consideration contains specialised linguistic features. As Nida (1976: 51-52) says, " The greater the significance of the form for the comprehension and appreciation of the message, the more difficult it is to find appropriate formal equivalences in the receptor language," and content often cannot be separated completely from form.

In the future, with specific knowledge gradually acquired from the related disciplines, the advanced student of conference interpreting should be able to consider and understand the interpreting process within the context of the entire communication process. And through the variety of pure and applied research it should be possible to work out a predictive theory for interpretation.

3. Research and training today: two separate worlds?
- A. Gringiani, SSLMIT, University of Trieste

There often seems to be no interaction between research in the interpretation field and teaching and professional practice. The blame, it seems, can be equally attributed to both researchers and teachers. On the one hand, research appears fragmentary, at times even incoherent: its subjects range from neurology to psycholinguistic models of interpretation processes, from aptitude testing to bilingualism, from introductory courses to simultaneous and consecutive interpretation to text analysis.

The application of a rigorous scientific method does not necessarily imply that, in the end, it will be possible to develop a "purely scientific theory for interpreting whereby results are predictable in terms of absolute certainty", as Dodds (1989: 19) points out. Nevertheless, only a scientific approach can validate, or disprove, what personal experience and intuition have led us to believe in our daily practice.

In this sense, observation and descriptive studies are of the utmost importance, since they represent the foundations of any theory. Catherine Stenzl (1989: 24) notes that "it is striking that practically no systematic descriptive studies have been published, so that we have no data based on systematic observation of what interpreters really do".

I believe that it is from the observation of languages and interpreters at work that we have to start studying the interpretation phenomenon. The comparison of source-text language and target-text language has always been somewhat neglected. In particular, interpreters have tended to minimise the importance of "words" in favour of "sense" thereby forgetting about the raw material and the final product of their effort.

Despite the fact that interpretation cannot be defined as the mechanical "transcodage" of one language into another, the observation of interpreters at work, in a real situation, is one of the most promising fields in terms of interplay between research and training. It can reveal the presence and, most important, the recurrence of certain syntactic or semantic strategies that might be profitably taught as technical tools to our students. And the more tools available to the student/interpreter, the less demanding her/his job.

Interesting suggestions have been formulated in this sense by various authors and, though some of them require further empirical validation, others could already be usefully drawn upon in the classroom. The hypothesis put forward by Gile (1985) in his Effort Models means that the more accessible the knowledge of the language and the subject matter, the smaller the global effort the student will have to make, though clearly we cannot expect to provide candidate interpreters with every specific piece of terminology they will need in their future work.

However, as Ilg (1989: 147) points out, "les assemblées delibérantes sont fortement ritualisées et se déroulent d'après des codes stricts" which can be taught to our students. In particular, he refers to major categories like yes-no, for-against, positive-negative, agreement-disagreement, good-bad and to the linguistic expressions used for each of them in different language registers. As regards the use of these expressions, he maintains that "pour dire oui/non, on dispose d'automatismes verbaux de la conversation", and it is this kind of automatic response which should be extended to other categories that are likely to be encountered within a conference. Thanks to these automatisms, the candidate as well as the professional interpreter will be able to concentrate their attention on more demanding tasks in terms of listening, processing and production of a text.

The importance of knowledge has been widely recognised, even if a systematic approach to its organisation is often lacking. What meets a greater reluctance on the part of teachers is a separate kind of automatism whose existence has been suggested by Nowak-Lehmann (1989). She distinguishes between two different cognitive processes: "actes cognitifs internalisés qui ne demandent guère d'énergie cognitive consciente" and "actes cognitifs non-automatisables, complexes, qui demandent de la 'présence d'esprit cognitive'". She then maintains that it would be useful:

> [...] d'automatiser autant d'opérations automatisables que possibles, car le nombre de processus cognitifs conscients qui peuvent être exécutés simultanément est limité; l'internalisation fait en sorte que les capacités cognitives conscientes puissent être utilisées pour l'accomplissement des processus non automatisables. (1989: 153)

This assumption would seem to justify the need to develop a wide range of strategic tools readily available to the interpreter, tools that can only be identified with certainty through the accurate observation of the interpreter's performance. These strategies are observed whenever the interpreter is confronted with a dissymmetry between the target and the source language, and, according to Wilss (1978), when they are language-pair specific. Language combination[2] is certainly an important variable in the interpretation process and its significance is obvious for teaching purposes. It is also true that there are general strategies applicable to all language pairs - greater use of coordination, fewer embeddings, omission of modifiers and generalisations. However, my students working from Dutch into Italian also ask for more specific instruments when confronted with long sentences where the second part of the verbal phrase only comes at the end of the sentence. Hence the need for specific exercises to enable students to practise and improve the skills they will need most when working with a given language combination.

The responsibility for the lack of interaction between research and teaching also lies with the teachers, who trust their intuition and experience and are generally reluctant (myself included) to reconsider their methods. The issue of introductory courses can be best used to exemplify this attitude. A wide range of exercises has been devised and applied over the years: shadowing, sight translation, summarising, paraphrasing, cloze tests, to mention but the most popular ones. Applied research, however, is only now starting to study the validity of these exercises and, since no systematic study has as yet been devoted to them, the results achieved so far can only be considered partial. It would therefore be unreasonable to take up extreme positions on the usefulness of a given exercise as a specific training method in interpretation. Still, most of the controversy around shadowing, an issue that has been dividing trainers for years, is based - once again - on personal experience and intuition, and on very limited objective data.

It is undoubtedly difficult to question what we have been doing for years, especially when no new instruments have yet been found to replace the old ones. Applied research has not provided us with any definitive conclusion that may radically change our teaching practice. However, the first result of interaction between these two worlds should lead us to be more flexible, and at least reconsider our approach.

4. Training the interpreter: Note-taking strategies.
- H. Aarup, Copenhagen Business School, Centre for Interpreting

People who are both teachers and interpreters often ask themselves the question whether interpreting can be taught at all or whether those students who are naturally gifted would have become interpreters even if they had not received any training. I realise that this is largely a rhetorical question since training programmes obviously provide interpreters with skills and knowledge that are invaluable in their professional work.

At the same time it is also necessary for every teacher to reappraise constantly the relevance and appropriateness of their teaching methods. I shall concentrate on some of the components in interpreter training from the point of view of theory, of professional experience, and of current teaching practice, in particular, at the Copenhagen Business School.

Consecutive and simultaneous interpreting are described by several authors as a three-phase process. The three phases are, according to Seleskovitch:

1.   listening to a linguistically meaningful signal that is perceived,
      analysed and understood at an intellectual level;
2.   the signal is then deliberately forgotten leaving only the mental
      image;
3.   a new linguistic signal is created in another language.

These three phases take place simultaneously in such a way that different
messages are present in each phase of the process at the same time. And the
whole process is characterised by being instantaneous as well as irretrievable
in simultaneous interpreting. However, does this, or even should this, apply
to consecutive interpreting?

At first glance, it seems as though consecutive interpreting would offer
a good opportunity for analysis of the source language message before the rest
of the process takes place. In consecutive, the interpreter is under no obligation
to formulate the final message, i.e. move to phase 3, while taking notes. The
notes can therefore relate solely to the utterance in the source language, and
consequently so can the analysis. In short, it would seem that the interpreter's
concern here would be with the source language only.

Also, it is possible for the interpreter to correct the interpretation of the
message in the source language while taking notes. There is, then, time to
produce the general outline of the text, which will form the basis of the new
linguistic signal in the target language. Finally, being able to speak freely and
fluently in the target language, the interpreter should be able to interpret well.

However, when professional interpreters do take language-bound notes
in the *target* language, they seem to overcome most of the barriers that the
notes create at the earliest possible stage in the process. This method provides
good results: a fluent, natural and convincing rendering in the target language.
By and large, there is therefore no basic difference between the two types of
interpreting in professional work.

However, with beginners, the phases do not coincide. The third phase,
reproduction, normally occurs after the other two. Since it is a new skill which
must be learned, beginners usually have trouble in reaching the point where the
message in the target language is simultaneous and irretrievable. The
acquisition of this skill is therefore a key element in the teaching of
interpreting. Instruction must therefore focus on the three phases with a view
to their simultaneity.

Translation also involves the same three phases but without the orality,
immediacy or simultaneity. The crucial difference is the time factor. At the

beginning of the training programme, consecutive students tend to apply a process of translation to interpreting. It is natural, and easier to take notes in the source language. This implies that students only listen to the source speech, but defer the analysis until later or even omit it altogether. This procedure of merely translating notes is exactly the opposite of the essential character of simultaneous interpreting, the mastery of which is the primary objective of the training programmes geared towards modern conference interpreting.

Applicants for an interpreting study programme must have, first of all, an excellent knowledge of their foreign languages, a perfect command of their mother tongue, and broad general knowledge. Without these pre-requisites it is hard to imagine a satisfactory analysis of the source message. In consecutive interpreting, this analysis should be reflected in the notes. So, in terms of pedagogic instruction students should be taught a system whereby they can read the results of their analysis directly from their notes.

Ideally, the students create their own systems for note-taking. If they have at their disposal a set of basic symbols as well as the other pre-requisites, they should be able to make notes that are clear, logical, and easily comprehended.

By the end of the training programme, the importance of notes in consecutive interpreting should be considerably minimised, thus reducing the risk of literal translation, and of taking notes as an end in itself. Ideally, users should be unable to detect any trace of the source language from the interpreter. The ideal interpreter, in fact, will have removed all hindrances to the transmission of the message early in the process.

In conclusion, decoding, analysis, memory, and reproduction must take place at the same time. Analysis of the source speech is the key component in both types of interpreting, and good interpreting is inconceivable without analysis.

Experience shows that students who postpone simultaneous interpreting training until late in their studies are often frightened of simultaneous interpreting, which may even be "mystical" in their eyes. It is therefore pointless to spend time teaching consecutive interpreting before teaching simultaneous.

5. Training the interpreter: text selection for consecutive interpreting
- N. Schweda Nicholson, University of Delaware, Department of Linguistics

Choosing texts for interpreting practice is a task which faces every instructor. The text certainly must be of graduated difficulty and the trainer must constantly strive to create a balance between challenging her/his students and giving them confidence. This is especially true at the introductory stages.

I will give examples from a good type of text to use for beginner students from a videotaped extract of a speech from a university seminar.[3] When choosing materials, both the text itself and how it is presented should be considered.

A. *The Text*

5.1 *Topic*

The topic should be general and familiar to the students. One good example is a paper on democracy in Latin America, originally aimed at giving a historical perspective and a current situation review of democracy in America to a group of 12 Panamanian teachers. The extract used is 2,5 minutes long, which is appropriate for beginning long consecutive.

5.2 *Terminology*

The text should not be specialised, and problematic words should not appear regularly. The sample text presented during the workshop included such words as "dictatorship" and "ousted", but also contained many synonyms such as "military government", "thrown out" and "overthrown".

5.3 *Argument Development*

The speech should follow logic, and, when relevant, chronology - in this case, the historical background of democracy in Latin America.

5.4 *Contextualized versus Non-Contextualized Information*

Contextualization (Schweda Nicholson 1990a) essentially implies relative predictability due to the logical integration of each speech segment. Non-contextualized information includes dates, statistics and numbers which are largely unpredictable. Appropriate texts are typically highly contextualized but with some non-contextualized information. In the text presented at the workshop, reference is made to "the 1950s" and "the 1960s", and some (familiar) proper names such as "the US", "the Caribbean" and "Haiti" are included.

B. *Delivery Format*

5.5 *Voice*

Speakers in video extracts should have a clear voice and preferably be native speakers so as to avoid the added difficulty of foreign accents in the comprehension of the speech.

5.6 *Speaker's Style*

A good example would be that of a speaker speaking extemporaneously with notes, excellent eye contact, and a delivery speed of approximately 130 words per minute. If the text is read, ideation and message planning are virtually eliminated (See Déjean Le Féal 1978 and Schweda Nicholson 1989b).

Delivery should be smooth with normal pauses, no false starts, and no significant hesitations that might confuse. Repetitions should reduce the processing load. For instance, in the following 2,47 min. extract of speech used for training:

> During the last 10 years though, during the past decade, we have seen military governments, dictatorial governments fall in just about every Latin American country so that at the present time civilian power is just about in every Latin American country and even in Haiti where the situation is confused, there is a very strong effort underway [...].

there are many repetitions, including "democracy/democratic" (10 times), "tradition" (6 times), "military governments" (4 times) and "dictatorships/ dictatorial" (3 times). As the students are not continuously receiving new input, they have more time for analysis and to try out their fledgling note-taking skills. They already know the topic of the talk, so they can decide on D for "democracy" or "democratic" and LA for "Latin America". Clearly they will have to choose another symbol for "dictatorship". Essentially, students have to be oriented towards achieving the delicate balance of listening, analysing and, of course, taking notes.

It is also a challenge for beginning consecutive interpretation students to stand up in front of an audience, as many of them have had no experience at all in public speaking. This is another factor that makes things more difficult. They also have to work towards strengthening their short-term memory, while they are developing their note-taking system. This type of text, which uses a 'graduated difficulty' approach helps novices build their confidence in effectively dealing with the attentional demands inherent in the interaction of SL listening, analysing, note-taking, and formulation of TL output.

6. The interaction between research and the profession: Training
- Sergio Viaggio, United Nations, Vienna

I believe the interpreting profession is only beginning to reap the benefits of about 20 years of very hard, individual and late night work. We interpreters still do not believe each other but we are already *listening* to each other. And that is, I think, an important development. I am as recalcitrant as the next man, even if I have not given that impression so far. But the point is that we still have not managed - I think - to establish a real, effective network between ourselves so that we can develop upon the work of experiments that have been done elsewhere. And we invent and re-invent the wheel again and again.

An idea came to my mind regarding Hanne Aarup's analysis of note-taking. There is a very interesting experiment which has been carried out by Daniel Gile. He had two groups listen to a speech for consecutive. One was instructed to take notes, as usual, and the other not to. It turned out that the latter was able to catch a higher proportion of names in the speech than the group of 'note-takers' (Gile 1991c). I did not replicate this experiment because I do not teach consecutive, being dismally inept at it. But I think that once the experiment is there, perhaps three or four applications in different settings should be enough to teach us that right from the beginning note-taking is self-defeating. It creates vices that then are much more difficult to eradicate. Is this a heavy experiment with a capital H? No, it is a very small tentative experiment. Now, let us assume that someone replicates this experiment and comes up with different results. Then let us investigate further to see the reason. And much has been, and will be achieved following this line.

For example, I myself carried out an experiment at the SSLMIT with an exercise that I called "cognitive clozing". It was a cloze text that contained a bare 30% of the lexical material on the page. The students had to come up with the sense behind the text. It was then progressively filled in, and, of course, as more lexical elements became apparent, so their hypotheses were tested, disproved or corroborated.

In itself it was a useful exercise. However, and this tallies with Daniel Gile's experiment, the result showed systematically that the more words the original text had, the less usable the interpretation became. The reason is the text distracted the students away from discourse analysis, and from sense understanding into language extraction. So, let us try experimentally to discover whether understanding the language itself is that important, and whether being able to hear the sounds of every single word in our A language means that we are, in fact, in a much better position to interpret into the B language. This is a line of research that should be pursued.

Unfortunately, we still do not have a regular research network, though we meet again and again. Many of us met in 1994 in Las Palmas, in 1993 in Elsinore, or in 1992 in Vienna, and we always come up with the same questions, the same proto-answers and the same Personal Theorising despite Daniel Gile's speech of ten years in the desert. Of course, there are honourable exceptions. But I submit that it could not be otherwise. How long did it take physicians to have their first conference ?

Professional interpretation exists as a profession. People make a living out of interpreting. But for how long now? Forty years? And here we are at the nth conference. I think that we have had great foresight. The point is that whenever we think of trying a particular experiment or writing a paper and preparing one for a conference, we should ask ourselves whether this really is something new, and whether we will really shed a tiny ray of light upon a corner that had hitherto not been illuminated, or at least not exactly from that angle?

I think it is hopeless even to dream of professional interpreters or translators being suddenly converted by theory or into reading about translation and interpretation - and thus improving their practice. I think that the link is precisely through didactics.

The professional, for the time being, at this stage of development of practice and theory, can afford to be blissfully ignorant of theoretical developments. But he who purports to form those generations that are supposed to inherit our legacy must know. Because unless experience becomes awareness, unless experience can be verbalised and therefore criticised and developed, it cannot be imparted and communicated effectively. So didactics should be this melting pot where theory and practice come together. And I believe that this is the extraordinary responsibility of didacticians: to know and to pass on Hallidayan linguistics, discourse analysis and all those other little black boxes, echoic and iconic memory and so on, together with the big black box.

This is what conferences are for. Of course it would be fantastic if out of 50 presentations each one of them developed a new theory of relativity. It is not going to work that way. But if I take stock of what is said at this conference, I already have in my pocket quite a few things that were not there when I came. A few little things I knew but I did not know I knew. They became concepts that now I can use both in my practise as an interpreter and also in judging the interpreters I am responsible for. Even more important, these new concepts will help in teaching people who I hope will be better than I. Because now I know a lot of things that I should not do and I am too old to stop doing. This is our responsibility and I think this is the meaning of this conference.

7. Research and training: A conclusion?
- D. M. Katan, SSMLIT, University of Trieste

For ease of reference the many points raised during the round table have been organised in terms of the interpreter, the trainer, the researcher, the classroom and teaching methods, which, as mentioned by Viaggio, are the link between them all.

7.1 *The interpreter*

The participants agreed that today we know something about what is going on in the brain but we still do not know what makes an interpreter, at least not empirically. Fortunately there was agreement on what a bad interpretation is, and Viaggio suggested that this be "the bottom line" for what must be a normative approach for interpreting standards.

7.2 *The Trainer*

There is still much healthy disagreement over who should be qualified to teach interpreting students. Basically, university researchers do the teaching. Some, however, argued that being a researcher was not enough, and felt, along with Aarup that "teaching can only be done by professional active interpreters but can be assisted by helpful people".

It also appeared that there was little space for the university trained academic interpreter, though Dodds did bravely point out that, though not an interpreter, he had, in fact, taught interpreting.

7.3 *The Research*

If who should be training was still debatable, there does seem to be much more agreement over research. Professional interpreters are too individualistic to get involved in research projects (Viaggio), so the lot does seem to fall on the shoulders of the trainers and possibly the students themselves. In fact, at Trieste "we teach students to do research" (Dodds). The best and the most motivated are selected and then encouraged to do their own research.

But does a trainer *have to* do research? Certainly, the idea of basing one's teaching purely on personal intuition is suspect, particularly if the Personal Theorising then becomes dogma (Déjean Le Féal).

The basic answer is that a trainer does not *have* to conduct his or her own original research but does have to be open to it and keep abreast of current research findings. The main reason is that this will help trainers to "pinpoint student's problems and find potential solutions" (Moser). An excellent way to keep up-to-date with current research is to read journals, such as *Brain and Language*, *Cognitive Psychology* and *Psycholinguistic Research*; and it should also be remembered that research outside the interpretation field is often "totally relevant" to interpreting (Schweda-Nicholson).

Most importantly "ideas do not belong to those that have them, but to those that use them" (Viaggio), and "scavenging" both ideas and results is what a trainer should be skilled at. If, of course, research is to be carried out by trainers, it does not have to be large-scale either. For example, a mini analysis of repetition in a classroom text for interpreting students should be considered a useful piece of research (Schweda-Nicholson).

However, should research only be applied and centred on teaching methodology? Moser was convinced that "research comes from interest in training: it has to be applied". Van Dam felt that as the profession is not a discipline (echoing Riccardi and Gringiani), then perhaps there was no reason to limit research. In the meantime in Trieste, pure, if not universally approved, research continues.

7.4 *The classroom*

Given that research needs to be carried out, and that it is up to those motivated trainers and students, interest focused on the unique opportunities available to trainers to do the research. Alexieva made the comparison with research on second language acquisition in the classroom. SLA has taught us about languages and by the same means we could learn about the interpreting process by studying the acquisition of interpreting skills in the classroom. One important aspect of doing personal research in the classroom is that, by doing so, unique insight is gained into specific student problems.

     However, Gringiani stressed that one should balance one's research interests and experiments with the needs of the students, and not forget that the principal job of a trainer is to train students.

7.5 *Teaching methods*

There is still much controversy around the subject of shadowing, as noted elsewhere. It is supported by Schweda-Nicholson and rejected by Gringiani. By others it is seen as "a gimmick or doctrine" (Setton) foisted on teachers because there is very little else of substance to teach. However, both support and rejection were qualified. The "non-belief" rather than outright rejection was qualified by the fact that it was based on personal intuition rather than any convincing data on the matter. This led, naturally, to the call for research on shadowing to be conducted in the classroom. The fact that the same unanswered call was raised eight years ago in Trieste, only highlights the state of interpretation research today (Dodds).

     The main objection to shadowing is that it is thought to increase the risk of interference (Setton). So, why not teach the same mechanical skill of listening and talking at the same time when teaching SI, which always involves listening? Another alternative is "on line chunking/paraphrasing". Students begin to paraphrase what they hear only when the teacher gives them the go-ahead. Then, before they finish, the teacher starts reading the next part.

     Support for shadowing was qualified by the fact that though "phonemic is fine - even better are dual and triple exercises" (Schweda-Nicholson), where the student shadows and speaks, writes or does some other activity at the same time: e.g., shadowing and writing numbers, or preparing a summary in L1 or in L2. "Writing", she stressed is "excellent for reinterpretation exercises". The supporters and the detractors were, in fact, suggesting broadly the same thing: an adaptation of the shadowing technique is a valid tool.

With regard to other traditional techniques, it was note-taking which came in for most criticism. There was general agreement that "Gile was right: note taking doesn't help at the beginning". (Déjean Le Féal).

In fact, at the Antwerp school a "no-notes" regime has been in practice since 1977. Gile mentioned that this regime was also in operation at the Paris schools, at least at the beginning of consecutive. The general feeling, supporting Aarup, was that note-taking only slows beginners down, and that students become too dependent on them.

Doubt was also raised (Van Essen) over the conventional wisdom that consecutive should be taught before simultaneous. This and all the other doubts underlined the tone of the round table: both trainers and students of interpretation are seriously questioning received wisdom. At the same time it is becoming increasingly clear that it is also up to the trainers and the students themselves to create the new wisdom.

NOTES

1.   Dodds' translation of the original Italian which reads as follows: "La migliore conoscenza delle modalità di sviluppo delle competenze linguistiche consente di individuare metodi didattici più efficaci".

2.   Language-pair specificity has also been shown by Viezzi (1989, 1990), Giambagli (1990) and Snelling (1992).

3.   The Delaware - Panama partners of the Americas Organization Democracy Education Seminar was held at the University of Delaware November 2-9 1991. The speech was given by Prof. John Deiner, a professor of Political Science.

Methodology

Daniel Gile, *Université Lumière, Lyon 2 & ISIT, Paris*
& Ingrid Kurz, *University of Vienna* (Convenors)
Bistra Alexieva, *University of Sofia*
Sylvia Kalina, *University of Heidelberg*
Bill Isham, *University of New Mexico*
Heidemarie Salevsky, *Humboldt University, Berlin*
Sonja Tirkkonen-Condit, *University of Joensuu*

1. Introduction

This workshop was designed to raise fundamental issues about interpreting research methodology. The idea was neither to make a comprehensive list of any sort, nor to provide solutions, but to make participants aware of the common body of methodological issues that the interpreting research community is tackling and to start a debate, with the hope that such discussions could become more systematic in the future. For that purpose, a group of experienced participants was convened by the two moderators, Ingrid Kurz of Vienna, a conference interpreter and psychologist who wrote the first PhD dissertation on interpreting by an interpreter (Pinter 1969), and Daniel Gile of Paris, a conference interpreter with a special interest in interpretation research (Gile 1995b, *Target* 7(1),1995). The panelists were:
-   Bistra Alexieva, from St. Kliment Ohridski University of Sofia, Bulgaria,
- Bill Isham, an American Sign Language Interpreter and cognitive psychologist currently at the University of New Mexico in Albuquerque,
- Sylvia Kalina, a conference interpreter and teacher of conference interpretation from the Institut für Übersetzen und Dolmetschen of the Ruprechts-Karls-Universität in Heidelberg,
- Heidemarie Salevsky, a scholar and teacher of interpretation from the Department of Translation Studies, Institut für Slawistik, Humboldt-Universität

zu Berlin,

- Sonja Tirkkonen-Condit, the non-interpreting "outsider", from the University of Savonlinna, Finland, who has been very active in the promotion of empirical research into translation (see for example Tirkkonen-Condit 1991). Prior to the workshop, six *leading* and *orienteering* questions were sent to panelists for preparation:

1. How are we (the interpretation research community) doing in research methodology ?
2. What are the advantages and limitations of theory vs. empirical research ?
3. What are the relative advantages and disadvantages of observational vs. experimental research ?
4. What are the technical problems involved in interpretation research? What solutions can be suggested ?
5. How important is it to undertake interdisciplinary research ? With what disciplines ? How to go about it ?
5. How could the situation be improved ?
6. What other relevant questions on interpretation research methodology should be stressed during the workshop ?

The panelists were asked to restrict their presentations to a few minutes, so that there could be ample time for the discussion to be opened to the floor. The following is a synopsis of their written responses to the moderators, of their oral presentations, and of complementary comments and explanations received after the conference.

2. Individual presentations

As can be seen from the report which follows, there was wide agreement on the complementarity of theoretical and empirical research. However, in our view, the points made by each speaker were varied and interesting enough to justify their individual presentation as opposed to a general synopsis. Verbatim quotations of the speakers' contributions are marked with quotation marks, as opposed to the moderators' summaries and comments. The authors of this report have edited to some extent the language and layout of the speakers' contributions, but essentially act as rapporteurs and have not changed their substance.

2.1 *Bistra Alexieva*

"Some of the most serious problems in interpretation research arise from the difficulty in finding the optimum balance between theoretical and empirical components, in finding out the way they delimit each other, in prescribing the boundaries of what can be achieved by employing the first or the second course of action. The reason for this lies mainly in that:
- On the one hand, researchers can analyse tangible data, i.e. SL and TL texts (the products), which can be heard or even seen, if written down on paper. The factthat they are accessible to direct observation often misleads us and makes us overemphasize the importance of the empirical approach.
- On the other hand, the tangibility of the data cannot by itself solve research problems about *processes* involved in SL text comprehension and/or TL text production, as these cannot be seen or heard. And the study of what is not accessible to direct observation has to be based on hypotheses, i.e. on theoretical models, the validity and power of which may or may not be confirmed by the empirical part of the exercise.

It follows that a discussion of theoretical vs. empirical research as an antonomy in the strict sense of the word can hardly be beneficial to the further development of interpreting research. Due to the nature of our object of analysis:
- Theoretical studies are an indispensable part of interpreting research. The more the hypotheses and predictions they generate match the empirical data, the better their approximation of reality.
- Empirical studies can be successfully conducted only if they are based on adequate theoretical models corresponding to the nature of the object of research. If we compare the (theoretical) world of ideas and the real (empirical) world with the two long pieces of wood in a ladder, it is the links (the agreement) between them, i.e. the steps, that are the real landmarks in the progress of one or another branch of human knowledge, and not the length of one pole or the other.

A number of problems may arise due to:
- Inadequate choice of a theory,
- Lack of distinction, within the empirical domain, between:
  * Systemic observation of a corpus of data (real interpreting events),
  * The experiential component, (the interpreter's individual experience),
  * Experimenting, i.e. the *simulation* of an interpreting event.

Overestimating the role of the one or the other may lead to inaccurate (one-sided) conclusions. Relying excessively on experimentation can be particularly risky. Unlike physics and chemistry, in interpreting research, it is impossible to perfectly replicate a conference in laboratory conditions: the only thing one can do is simulate *portions* of a conference.

A felicitous combination of the theoretical and the empirical is a sine qua non condition in solving even what is usually labelled a purely technical problem, namely sampling:
- Sampling in interpreting research cannot be carried out in the same way as in written translation, or in any other branch of the sciences and the humanities, due to the heterogeneity of the macro-text of a conference,
- A more reliable procedure can be developed if all three sub-components of the empirical approach are made use of. The idea is to go through three or four stages of sample selection. A pre-sampling stage, a main sampling stage, a weighted sampling stage and a "cluster sampling" or "large excerpt sampling" stage. It is only on the basis of sampling procedures that cover both the theoretical and the empirical components that a proper selection of reliable samples to be used in an experiment can be achieved."

2.2 *Bill Isham*

"The situation in interpreting research is definitely improving, if only because now some research is actually being done: after a brief flurry of activity by a few researchers in the late sixties and early seventies, interpreting research went through a long, cold, dry spell. The recent upswing is due to many factors, but perhaps two can be named that are of particular importance: the efforts of the faculty and students at the Scuola Superiore di Lingue Moderne per Interpreti e Traduttori at the University of Trieste, Italy, and the efforts of Daniel Gile and IRTIN, which is playing the crucial role of helping those doing research become aware of each other's work.

Empirical research can be categorized into two basic groups: "theory-driven" and "data-driven". In the latter, the researcher simply thinks of an interesting experimental paradigm, and conducts it to "see what happens". From the data obtained, s/he then thinks of an explanation, and so in the end comes upon a theory. There are several problems with this approach. First, it is terribly inefficient and haphazard: it is essentially "trial and error". It is quite possible for no result of interest to be obtained, and as studies are time consuming and can be expensive, this is a waste of resources. Secondly, such studies can only be considered "successful" if a significant result is obtained. Without a theory, there is no way to know whether a null result is in itself of interest. In contrast, if a theory clearly predicts a significant difference of some sort and no such difference is found, the experiment can be considered of great value.

Theories can also be divided into two basic categories: "strong" and "weak". A strong theory is testable: it makes clear predictions for which evidence can be gathered, for or against. This is why Freud's theory of human behavior is considered a weak theory, despite its great detail, thoroughness, and intuitive appeal. It cannot be tested.

Most theoretical claims about interpretation are "strong" claims, in that they are testable. The problem comes when a theorist is resistant to attempts to do that testing. Although theories belong to the world of ideas, we must never forget that they attempt to explain reality. A theorist must be willing to examine experimental results with a detached eye, and amend his or her theory as required. More often than not, the theory will become improved, that is, a step closer to explaining reality. If a theorist refuses to rethink his/her ideas in the face of strong counter-evidence, then the theory strays farther and farther away from the real world, and then its raison d'être will disappear.

A strong theory will lead to good research, and good research will improve the theory. Both are needed.

On the comparative advantages and drawbacks of observational vs. empirical research, both are necessary because they complement each other. The most important advantage of each is obvious to everyone. Observational studies are conducted in natural settings, where all the variables that influence interpretation are at play. If a particular phenomenon is observed in the field, one knows that it is not an artifact of the experiment itself. Experimental research, on the other hand, can isolate a variable for testing. This enables the researcher to untangle the web of variables, and to choose from alternative explanations by testing each of them individually. The weakness of each is the strength of the other: confounds will be rife in any natural setting, and any result observed in the laboratory may be an artifact of the experiment itself. Therefore, both types of research are essential. Observations made in the field can be tested in the laboratory, and results obtained there can be confirmed by observations in the field."

Methodology is in part determined by the question being asked. Isham is interested in processes beyond conscious introspection such as occur in interpretation, which is extremely complicated, and in which variables are hard to isolate. Processes range from low-level perception of speech sounds, through lexical access and syntactic parsing, to higher level processes which have to do with meaning. In general, lower-level issues are "cleaner" (easier) to investigate, and each higher level becomes more difficult because it necessarily contains all the levels below it. Thus, there are more variables to account for, more possible explanations for any result, and so on.

"Interpretation is about as "messy" as it gets. It involves all stages of language processing from low to high levels, and for processing both input and output. And if this were not complicated enough, the input and output processes involve different languages, which of course requires that one understand the nature of bilingualism (or multi-lingualism). Indeed, few questions in language processing research can claim to be more convoluted than interpreting.

Several papers have tried to tackle this problem statistically. That is, many variables were included in the experimental design so that the proportion of variance due to each can be tracked. This approach has its own problems. First, the interpretation of the data becomes more complex; explanations for a given result become as convoluted as the problem itself. There are other, more practical issues, too. Each independent variable added to the design requires a greater number of subjects for the statistics to be reliable. Subjects (interpreters) are difficult enough to come by, and it is unreasonable to expect any study to include them in large numbers.

The solution is to design studies that control for most variables physically, rather than statistically. Any independent variables should be directly related to the hypotheses being tested; others should be held constant (or, in certain cases, counterbalanced). As a simple example, we know that rate of speech has an effect on interpreter performance. If rate of speech is not at issue in the study at hand, then all subjects should be presented texts delivered at the same rate of speech, so that any result cannot be attributable to speech rate. This is a far more elegant method than having different rates of speech and then tracking them statistically. It is true that controlling irrelevant factors in this way does lead to highly artificial experiences for the subjects. To reiterate, that is why observational studies are needed."

Isham used data from his recall experiments to demonstrate one way in which it is possible to get a glimpse of such processing, via the inferences that can be made from an epiphenomenon of the processing itself, in this case recall. In the experiment he described, subjects were interrupted at specific points when listening to or interpreting a speech, and their recall of the last sentence was investigated. The sentences were organized in a particular way that made the features of the recall of the last 13 words meaningful. A comparison was then carried out between interpreter-subjects and listener-subjects.

Among the problems arising in such a set-up is its "off-line" nature, that is one in which the dependent variable is measured not during the processing, but after the fact. This has particular implications on the capacity to discriminate between processes and strategies.

After one member of the audience criticized experiments that did not measure interpreter performance and called them "worthless", Isham explained that sometimes experimentalists are interested in phenomena not directly related to the interpreting process itself. For example, experiments using interpreters as subjects may have much to teach about the nature of bilingualism. Such studies may or may not benefit interpreting studies, but this is not a major problem per se.

Isham also stressed that the "artificial" nature of laboratory experiments may well affect interpreter performance in some ways, but probably would not affect other dependent variables (such as lexical access). In fact, the "artificiality problem" might be viewed as a reason not to measure performance itself in the lab, and particularly not in studies investigating quality directy, without taking special care to reduce or eliminate the "unnaturalness" of lab settings.

2.3 *Heidemarie Salevsky*

The background to Salevsky's large empirical research project presented below was the quest for strategies for SI training in the Russian-German combination. One problem which was identified in students was a significant frequency of incorrect beginnings, repetitions and filled and unfilled hesitation pauses. This was linked with the following hypotheses:
- Working Memory Capacity limitation: According to Kirchhoff 1974 (see also Gile 1995a,b), when working memory is saturated, information loss will inevitably occur unless summarizing strategies are used. Preventive strategies include anticipation, which entails a risk of error leading to incorrect syntactic planning or information distortion.
- Hesitation pauses correspond to the points of greatest statistical indeterminacy, in particular at the beginning of codification units and of transition from high-redundancy to low-redundancy segments (Goldman-Eisler

1958, 1964, Chernov 1978, Shiryaev 1979).

An analysis of SI performance was decided for the purpose of devising strategies aimed at overcoming such hesitation pauses and incorrect beginnings.

Five professional interpreters having Russian as their mother tongue were asked to interpret into German 35 Russian speeches delivered in various United Nations Committees. Recordings of the Source speeches and the Target speeches were made on double track tapes. Time lag and possible reasons for hesitation pauses were analysed.

Salevsky notes that it is problematic to establish a connection between the world of ideas and the world of experience, that is to find the reason, in a concrete setting, for a particular hesitation pause. In her view, it is nearly impossible to avoid misinterpretations in view of the large number of variables involved (the source and target language, the subject matter, the function of the particular speech, the history of the act of communication taking place, the identity of the communication actors, the identity of the interpreter, working conditions etc.) It is therefore difficult to find rules offering a universal coverage of problems. Nevertheless, learning requires practice, and practice requires insight into some concrete obstacles. The idea was therefore that in spite of the limitations of such a study, it could help devise strategies for some specific obstacles, but also some fallback strategies. Findings of the study are described in Salevsky 1986.

2.4 *Sonja Tirkkonen-Condit*

"Theoretical and empirical studies should not be juxtaposed as if they were mutually exclusive. Our knowledge and understanding of translation as a psycholinguistic process, as a crosscultural and crosslinguistic operation, as a profession etc., will not increase if we do not subject theoretical statements to empirical testing. Thus in order to understand a complex phenomenon such as translation we need both theoretical and empirical studies.

Practicing translators have implicit theories of translation even if they have never read theoretical statements about translation. These implicit theories are to some extent revealed by the way they translate and by the way they talk about their work. Another way of eliciting information about implicit theories are think-aloud experiments in which the aim is to get a glimpse of the "on-line" processes of translation and, among other things, insights into the theories and principles which guide the translators' decision-making. This is one way of acquiring knowledge about existing professionalism in translation. We should know what goes on in existing professional thinking and behaviour before we take measures towards changing it. It might be worthwhile, for example, checking empirically the hypothesis recently put forward by Anthony Pym that translators feel guilty because there are always things in their work they know they could have done better had they had more time, energy, interest, money, etc. Pym's thesis is that translators should get training in negotiation theory so they could help their employers decide how much of the translator's time, effort and pay each intercultural communication task is worth investing in (see Pym 1995).

Translation theorists, i.e. people who write about translation, presumably have practical experience in translation, on the basis of which they make generalizations and hypotheses as to what translation is or should be. There may even be a consensus among these writers, and such a consensus might often provide a good starting point for empirical research. In order to qualify for empirical testing, however, a theory and its concepts may need a radical redefinition - perhaps to such an extent that the concepts and terms to be used in the empirical treatment are no longer recognized by those who first suggested the theories. This is what happened to the term "translation problem" shortly after Hans Krings used it as an operationalized technical term in his dissertation. What followed was a futile "discussion" about how this particular term should or should not be used (cf. Hönig 1988, Kring 1986). A juxtaposition between theoretical and empirical studies is as artificial as one between qualitative and quantitative studies. Without theoretical and qualitative analysis we do not know what it is that we are supposed to study empirically or to measure quantitatively. And without empirical testing we will not have accurate knowledge about the phenomena we are interested in. On the other hand, there are aspects of translation that do not lend themselves to quantitative empirical investigation in such a way that the results are meaningful or relevant to the questions we asked. Thus hermeneutic approaches should not be shunned despite the fact that they tend to result in mere terminological squabbles."

2.5 *Sylvia Kalina*

"It is now possible to speak of an interpretation research community, which I think did not exist until some time ago, as everyone was pursuing his or her specific kind of theory, not paying too much attention to what others did.

Exchanging research results seems to me to be of the utmost importance if one wants to make further progress, and as far as I can judge, a spirit has now developed in which such exchanges can take place.

Speaking of "a methodology" is perhaps somewhat premature. But occasions such as Turku (and others before and hopefully after) may provide an opportunity to confront methodological approaches which can then be tested and either developed further or disproved.

Important theoretical studies have been conduted in the past, but sufficient empirical evidence could not always be provided to match them. So although there is much empirical work to be done, as it is progressing, theories may have to be modified, extended and so on. It would be most unfortunate if those engaging in theory as such and those who, like myself, try to provide the data to confirm or disprove theories, could not get together and benefit from each other's approach.

Observational studies should prepare the ground for experimental work, as sets of ideas to be further investigated must be identified. Those of us who have found their way from practical interpreting to the higher spheres of theoretical considerations of the subject will, in most cases, base their initial approaches on individual experience, and it is only when they become more acquainted with research methodology that they can think in terms of real empirical investigations. And there are not too many around who will be getting that far, or are prepared to do so."

As an illustration of her own work, Kalina explained that she implemented a new concept of Thinking Aloud Protocol, which immediately followed the process as opposed to the usual TAPs, which take place *during* the process: information was elicited from interpreters right after interpretation, when traces of short-term memory/storage were still accessible. Kalina used a 7-minute video excerpt of the Queen of England's Christmas Speech. Immediately after interpreting, subjects were invited to listen to the recording of their own TL speech and recall and verbalize whatever they had been thinking. The experimenters expected not so much to obtain information about the subjects' assessment of their own performance, but indications on how they felt during the process, which possible alternatives they had in mind, and data about their expectations and their associations. "It goes without saying that the method is not unproblematic. Firstly, only such cognitive processes or strategic decisions that are consciously experienced by the subjects can be remembered and verbalised. Processes that have become automatic will not leave enough traces in memory to be verbalised at all (cf.

Ericsson & Simon 1980). Secondly, there is a quantitative problem in that even among those processes that are conscious, some may have been forgotten before verbalisation, or may not become verbalised for other reasons. Thirdly, the reliability of the verbal data has to be ascertained with methods that meet the standards of socio-empirical research. After all, the status of those involved in the experiment may affect the truth value of the verbal data, as subjects might be tempted to give judgements or offer justifications of their performance after the event, or might not be willing to disclose all of their personal coping techniques. Non-strategic behaviour may therefore be reported as it if were strategic and thus distort or bias results.

Another significant drawback of the method is that data collected from informants are an amalgam of uncontrolled (spontaneous), partly controlled and fully analysed comments.

They need further treatment to filter out unanalysed think-aloud verbalisations before they are interpreted. The experimenter may have to make use of validation techniques enabling him/her to either make sure that what has been verbalised is in fact related to cognition during the process, or to check with the informant whether there is agreement on the way in which the verbal data are to be interpreted. Further experiments will therefore be needed to overcome at least some of these difficulties.

However, preliminary results seem to indicate that some valuable information about processes can be obtained with the method. The experiments showed that some characteristic phenomena were remembered more easily, as more attention had to be directed towards them during the process. These mainly included problems encountered during the interpreters' performance (whether unsolved or coped with successfully), unexpected turns in the source text (which may result in an interruption of automatic processing) and such source text passages that subjects felt to be conspicuous or otherwise peculiar. Another result is that with a sound balance between intervention and non-intervention on the part of the experimenter, the ratio of reliable information and "truly think-aloud", i.e. unanalyzed data, can be improved. It therefore seems advisable for experimenters to receive proper instructions or even some training prior to the experiment, and it would even be beneficial for subjects to practice retrospective verbalisation before going into the experiment proper."

In conclusion, Kalina emphasizes that "the method can only serve as a supplementary instrument and is not to be regarded as a research method in its own right. It is naturally fraught with errors, due in part to faulty memory or unwillingness to reveal one's problems or a weakness in verbalisation capability. The methodological problem is how to validate the results of such experiments. We had carried out a number of similar experiments prior to the one known as 'Queen' and had established a number of criteria for analysis. From what we have found so far, we think that the validation problem can be overcome to a certain extent. If so, the method - which we call the retrospective think-aloud method may perhaps add one small piece of information to the mosaic of what we think goes on during interpreting, especially in SI processes, a question which has not yet been answered conclusively by any of the existing methods of analysis."

3. Discussion

The discussion centered around five topics.

1. *Experimental vs. observational research*
Since not all participants were acquainted with the terminology, it was explained that both rely on systematic observation, but observational studies are based on phenomena as they occur "naturally" in the field, and experimental studies are phenomena generated in a controlled environment (or "laboratory"). Once this was made clear, as was also pointed out by the panelists, there was a definite consensus to the effect that the two are complementary and necessary. Dieter Huber (Johannes Gutenberg University, Mainz) added that a third method, computer simulation, could also be very useful in checking out theories.

2. *Access to interpreters for studies*
It was pointed out that difficulty of access to subjects was due in particular to the fact that interpreters did not know what interpreting research was all about (Monique Corvington, UN). Isham added that interpreters often seem to think that they are being assessed for quality, whereas this is not the case. Kondo (Daito Bunka University, Tokyo) indicated that the stress of the situation may reflect on their performance. Kalina and Lambert (University of Ottawa) said that once their students had been introduced to interpreting research, they were more willing to cooperate.

3. *Quality*

On the issue of quality (see above), Isham stressed that while as a teacher and a practitioner, he was interested in quality, in his present research, he was not concerned with this aspect of interpretation, and did not make any claims on quality on the basis of his laboratory experiments. Several participants (in particular Karla Déjean Le Féal of ESIT, Paris, and Hans Hönig of Johannes Gutenberg Universität Mainz) argued that research on processes cannot be dissociated from quality. There was not enough time to go into a detailed discussion on that issue.

4. *Students and professionals*

In connection with the higher availability for research of students vs. professional interpreters, several participants (Déjean-Le Féal, Laura Gran of SSLMIT Trieste, Kalina, Salevsky) underlined the differences between the two categories: students tend to focus on language, and experienced professionals on meaning, there is more automation in professionals than in students, etc. Hence, it is important to be careful in generalizing from one category to the other.

5. *Corpus sharing*

In view of such problems, as well as the labour-intensive nature of data processing (Miriam Shlesinger - Bar llan University, Ramat-Gan), several participants (Anne Gringiani of SSLMIT Trieste, Robin Setton of GITIS, Taipei, Shlesinger) expressed the wish to establish a system allowing for a shared corpus and common research protocols. Gile pointed out that one project involving corpus sharing was already in existence (Shlesinger 1995 is one publication which resulted from the use of this corpus).

4. Conclusions

1. There was much agreement between the panelists on basic issues, in spite of their rather varied background.

2. On the whole, the discussion remained very general and focussed on research *principles* rather than on research *methods*.

3. From comments made by the audience and from allusions made by speakers

between the lines, it appears that while the number of people in the interpreting community who are willing to listen to interpretation researchers has grown over the years, the attractiveness and potential usefulness of interpreting research are still viewed as very low.

In particular, while panelists all presented a *balanced* view of issues from the *research* perspective, it was clear from the reactions that some of the participants found it difficult to dissociate research from the quest for practical results. They only seem to view applied research as legitimate, and within applied research, they only accept studies directly linked to interpretation quality.

4. Many of the participants in the audience, including some who have published several papers themselves, appeared to lack familiarity with fundamental concepts of research, which shows the need to offer some kind of methodological guidance to beginning scholars, the more so since no such guidance is available in most I/T schools.

5. Some of the major issues and disagreements that have plagued interpretation research since its beginnings, for instance regarding the validity of experimental research and of research on interpretation *students,* are still very much on the agenda.

Quality in Simultaneous Interpreting

Miriam Shlesinger, *Tel Aviv* (Convenor)
Karla Déjean le Féal, *ESIT, Paris*
Ingrid Kurz, *University of Vienna*
Gabriele Mack and Lorella Cattaruzza, *University of Bologna*
Anna-Lena Nilsson, *University of Stockholm*
Helge Niska, *University of Stockholm*
Franz Pöchhacker, *University of Vienna*
Maurizio Viezzi, *SSLMIT, Trieste*

1. Introduction

Quality is an elusive concept, if ever there was one. Situated at the interface between theory and practice (Marrone 1993), this area of research evokes strong reactions from customers and practitioners alike. Quality according to what criteria? Quality for whom? In an era marked by a plethora of Total Quality Management experts and quality assessment models, the simultaneous interpreting community is also trying to join the mainstream, and to find out just what it is that makes for excellence in our profession.

Thus, for example, in a paper published in the *AIIC bulletin* after the International Conference on Interpretation in Turku, but cited here as an indication of the growing interest in quality assurance, Mackintosh (1995) focusses on quality as one of the basic themes which "constitute the backbone of the Association's current activities and which will be taken into account in any possible restructuring". As the AIIC report (submitted to the Council by a member from the Asia-Pacific region) indicates, while the organization prides itself on excellence and while its Basic Texts "have inherent in them the concept of quality", AIIC is still groping both to define it and especially to devise ways of maintaining it.

Definitions of quality by those in the profession are apt to mirror whatever norms have been internalized by most practitioners, such as the "honest spokesperson" norm, requiring interpreters to "re-express the original speakers' ideas and the manner of expressing them as accurately as possible" (Harris 1990). Beyond such vague formulations, however, it is unclear to what extent one can speak of norms which most interpreters - or even most interpreters for a given language combination - would agree upon, even if only intuitively.

Unlike the translator of a literary text, who has presumably been exposed to a wealth of texts translated in a given target language and target system, the simultaneous interpreter has rarely been exposed to the work of more than a handful of colleagues. Thus, although amply exposed to (original) texts in the spoken mode in his particular target language, and perhaps even in a similar setting (e.g., international conferences), the interpreter does not necessarily relate (consciously or unconsciously) his own output to a body of interpreted texts.

Moreover, the extremely limited number of interpreters for any given language combination in many places in the world and the relatively short history of interpretation have not been conducive to the development of either synchronic or diachronic norms. Thus, while anyone interested in gaining a better understanding of interpretation norms does perhaps have a (rather limited) corpus of pre-systematic formulations (often in the form of "dos and don'ts" or "manuals" for the would-be interpreter), the individual interpreter has only limited access to established norms, i.e. to the "values or ideas shared by a certain community as to what is right and wrong, adequate and inadequate" (Toury 1980:51).

The situation is somewhat different at the few well-known centers where interpreting is used extensively, chief among them Brussels, Geneva, New York and Paris. It stands to reason that exposure to fellow-practitioners in such places does generate a fairly clear shared sense of "good", "not-so-good" and "bad". Another group which is likely to internalize some shared notions of quality consists of graduates of interpreting schools, though it is unclear to what extent different schools tend to inculcate similar norms.

It is therefore particularly interesting to observe the gradual change in how interpreters themselves have chosen to characterize their profession, and in their perception of quality in actual practice. The early writings on interpreting often manifested intuitive, and even self-congratulatory references to an impossible job well done. The following is a representative selection of such comments as they appear in the literature:

- "Translators and interpreters are in general the only people who consistently bridge and build bridges between societies [...] a daunting sociocultural competence [...]" (Criomhthain 1985:142);
- "The Secretary General was so impressed that he provided us with a special room" (Herbert 1978:7);
- "How does [the interpreter] achieve this miraculous feat?" (Gravier 1978:vii);
- "On several occasions, high-ranking members of the staff of the United Nations came to Nuremberg in order to see with their own eyes how the 'miraculous' system of simultaneous interpreting was functioning" (Roditi, s.d.: 14);
- "When we consider information input speed, density, structure and complexity together, it can be seen that conference interpreters are required - nay expected - to translate often highly convoluted written sentences virtually instantaneously, in the process performing a task that would tax the capacity of many a large computer system" (Jumpelt 1985: 83).

As time went on, however, publications began moving away from such sweeping statements towards both macro- and microanalysis. Examples of the former are the attempts to formulate models of the interpreter's task, including parameters of quality (e.g., Bühler 1989; Alexieva 1992; Schweda-Nicholson 1993; Gile 1995a). The latter include observations concerning specific features of the interpreter's performance (e.g., intonation, cohesion, use of terminology, omissions etc.) and the way s/he is perceived by listeners (e.g., Kurz 1993, 1994; Shlesinger 1994).

These more recent treatments of quality have also underlined its context-boundedness and pragmatic implications; i.e., the situational variables that might call for different priorities in different situations (Stenzl 1989:24). As Kopczyński (1994) points out, any definition of quality must take into account such variables as:

"- the speaker, his status and the status of his receptors,
- the speaker's intention in issuing the message,
- the speaker's attitude toward the message and the receptors,
- the receptors' attitude toward the message and the speaker,
- the interpreter, his/her competence, judgments, attitudes and strategies,
- the form of the message,

- the illocutionary force of the message,
- the existing norms of interaction and interpretation of a speech community,
- the setting."

2. The Workshop

As experienced professionals who have regular opportunities to observe and monitor the performance of fellow-professionals, the workshop participants were asked to consider what aspects of simultaneous interpreting strike them as particularly relevant to quality. Moreover, knowing how far we have come in our attempts at self-analysis - and how much farther we should still try to go - they decided not to confine themselves to the practitioners' own perspective, but rather to discuss the following three perspectives as well:

The market perspective
Do our clients know what's good for them? What do they expect, and what will make them happy with the service and product we provide?

The research perspective
What kinds of research should we devise in order to gain a better appreciation of the strengths and weaknesses of our own performance?

The didactic perspective
What aspects of an interpreter's performance should be stressed by those of us who teach it? How can the skills which add up to quality be taught more effectively?

Our workshop followed the loose ormat of an open discussion, preceded by a brief presentation (5 minutes) by each of the seven participants (six individuals and one two-woman team). The following is an attempt to integrate the many points made in the course of the discussion and during the rather substantial Q&A session which followed, and to pull together some of the main threads, while highlighting some points of disagreement.

Two main issues emerged as the most controversial, and drew comments both from the panelists and from many of the participants in the Q&A session: (1) *Quality for whom* - Of the potential participants in the interaction involving an interpreter, who should be the ultimate judge of its quality? (2) *Methodologies for studying quality-related issues* - What are the best methodologies for quality assessment?

2.1 Quality for Whom?

If quality is a function of the attainment of goals, and if the goal of interpreting is to satisfy the requirements of both speakers and listeners, then the attainment of these goals amounts to quality. But this still leaves us with an inbuilt circularity, which the participants tried to explain, and which was brought up again later by Sergio Viaggio. He noted that for the Chinese delegation to the UN, for example, the demand for a rather literal rendering supersedes style and fluency. Thus, the way quality is understood by the Chinese delegates is very different from the way it is seen by many professional interpreters. Ingrid Kurz too noted that different user groups have different expectations, and cited media interpreting as a case in point: TV audiences are very demanding; yet, for them, completeness is less of an issue than smooth delivery and clarity.

Maurizio Viezzi referred to simultaneous interpreting as a communicative event in which not only the listener, but the speaker too - the one who provides the raw material for the event - must be served. In fact, satisfying the speaker's requirements could be a more constructive goal than adopting the listener's perspective. For one thing, quality is a feature of an interpreter's performance even when nobody is listening. Moreover, listeners can hardly qualify as the sole judges of quality; they are not homogeneous in their priorities, tastes and comprehension abilities. In addition, the listener is lacking one of the most crucial means of assessing quality: an understanding of the source message. Thus, for example, smooth delivery may create the false impression of high quality when much of the message may in fact be distorted or even missing. On the other hand, a listener may misjudge a very faithful rendering as flawed when in fact it is the source that accounts for its shortcomings. Anna-Lena Nilsson noted that the same holds true for sign language interpreting; the message may be incomplete, and yet the performance may be judged as being of a high quality, since the customer has no means of telling what has been omitted.

2.2 Methodologies for Studying Quality-Related Issues

All of the participants seemed to agree that we cannot make do with subjective evaluations of quality. A broader and more valid perspective would entail attention to the situation and to the nature of the conference. The target text should be examined on three levels:

- *Intertextually* - a comparison of the source text and the target text, based on similarities and differences.
- *Intratextually* - as a product in its own right, based on its acoustical, linguistic and logical features.
- *Instrumentally* - as a customer service, based on the target text's usefulness and comprehensibility. (E.g., a text that is overly rapid may be judged as lacking in quality in instrumental terms, even though it is inter- and intratextually adequate).

With respect to methodology, two approaches emerged: those who would use questionnaires (often combined with fieldwork (Vuorikoski 1993)) as the key form of evaluation, and those who would focus on other means.

2.2.1 Questionnaires

Notwithstanding the importance of other types of empirical research, the most common means of attempting to define quality remains the questionnaire. Some also regard it as "the most straightforward scientific way of collecting data on actual quality perception by delegates" (Gile 1991a: 163-164). Quality questionnaires, moreover, need not be restricted to end-users or to practitioners. In the case of courtroom interpreting, for example, questionnaires have been introduced as a form of expert opinion; outside consultants were asked to rate an entire cadre of interpreters by observing each of them at work. Thus, the Supreme Court Task Force on Interpreter and Translation Services (see reference below), examining interpreting services in the New Jersey court system, based its conclusions on an evaluation questionnaire comprising twenty-seven questions, incorporating such diverse criteria as: "pronunciation", "retains emphasis of speaker", "presents appropriate physical appearance" (!), "grasps and conveys speakers' meaning accurately" and "uses interpreting techniques appropriately".

While at least four of the workshop panelists had themselves been involved in the use and analysis of questionnaires, all of them seemed to agree about the shortcomings of this methodology as a reliable tool for evaluating quality. The questionnaires which have been circulated to date (e.g., Bühler 1986; Meak 1990; Gile 1990c; Vuorikoski 1993; Marrone 1993; Moser 1993;

Kopczynski 1994; Ng 1994; Kurz 1993, 1994) have focussed, broadly speaking, on the rcspondents' opinions as to the relative importance of different criteria for assessing quality. However, as long as each questionnaire focusses on different· variables, is formulated along different lines and is administered to different types of target audiences, comparisons of the results will be difficult.

Ambiguous wording of the questions may also account for differences in the responses. A case in point, cited by Karla Déjean le Féal, is that of attempting to determine the relative importance of voice quality: based on the AIIC questionnaire results, members of the AIIC admission committee cited voice quality as a relatively unimportant parameter, but noted that some interpreters had rated it elsewhere as "quite significant" (Bühler 1986). The difference may have to do with the vagueness of the term "pleasant voice": does this refer to a voice that is particularly pleasant, or to one which is not so unpleasant as to irritate the listener (Kurz 1994:5)? When different respondents have different things in mind, any comparison of their assessments is liable to be misleading (Seleskovitch 1986; Gile 1991a).

By the same token, a question aimed at evaluating one parameter may lead to unwarranted conclusions about another. Take, for instance, a question aimed at assessing the acceptability of interpreting into a B language focussed on foreign accent acceptability. The fact that most respondents regarded a foreign accent as acceptable, however, should not necessarily be taken as a sweeping legitimization of interpreting into one's B language (a longstanding bone of contention in professional circles).

The questionnaire used in a study by Gabriele Mack and Laurella Cattaruzza (1995) revealed that users have neither the inclination nor the means to provide a careful breakdown of what makes for "good" interpretation. Their approach is more holistic, and it is up to the researcher to infer what factors are involved. The lack of uniformity in the questionnaires was a recurrent theme, which Mack and Cattaruzza saw as pointing to the more basic problem: the lack of a common definition of quality.

Even among the participants themselves, there seemed to be a lack of clarity about the difference between quality criteria and ingrained norms. Thus, for example, one of the participants took it for granted that a quality-conscious interpreter would always finish a sentence, and would never repeat a speaker's mistake (cf. van Dam 1989:170); others took exception to this, and noted that there may well be situations in which either the user or the speaker would prefer a more exact duplication of the original style, warts and all.

2.2.2 Other possibilities
Helge Niska reported on the notion of Meaning Carrying Elements (MCEs) used on the Swedish government's certification tests: the words or phrases in the text that carry the actual message. To pass this test, an interpreter must have conveyed 90% of the MCEs. Whatever its merits as a convenient and objective criterion, the MCE may be a rather simplistic point of departure. Helge's own reservations were mirrored in the remarks of Carol Taylor during the Q&A session, concerning the importance of connectives, anaphora, citations etc. in the creation of meaning.

Another approach to quality assessment was described by Bill Isham, also during the Q&A session: The Registry of Interpreters for the Deaf (RID) in the US, as part of its efforts to revise its certification exam in the '80s, decided to formulate a definition of "good interpreting". During a convention of the RID, all attendees were asked to meet in a plenary session during which the concept of "minimal skill level" (i.e., the minimum which can be expected of every certified interpreter) was explained. The participants were then shown a series of videotapes in which interpreters of varying levels of skill interpreted the same passage. The group simply voted on whether or not each interpreter fit their image of what a certified member should look or sound like. The interpreters were judged on a *gestalt* - in terms of the overall acceptability of their performance. An analysis after the event was revealing in terms of trying to understand what factors made some interpreters more "acceptable" than others.

Franz Pöchhacker called for quality assessment based on investigating the cognitive end-result; i.e., how well the listener had understood the message conveyed. Towards this end, he mentioned many of the variables which might be studied in terms of their effect on the end-user; e.g. speed, pauses, hesitations, intonation patterns, fluency, speech errors, repairs, register and style, cohesion, structure of individual propositions, etc. While all agreed in principle with Franz's pitch for some form of cooperative research, the practical implications remained challenging. This was reiterated during the Q&A portion of the workshop by Daniel Gile, who dealt with such nitty gritty issues as the need for funding, organization, coordination and the like.

Other participants suggested some specific techniques - not so much for evaluating quality as for improving it on an ongoing basis. Karla Déjean le Féal stressed that interpreters do not monitor themselves sufficiently and urged for more emphasis on the value of recording oneself and listening to the output, as a means of increasing self-awareness. In the Q&A session, Sergio

Viaggio too noted that many good interpreters have never listened to themselves, and are blissfully unaware of many readily correctible flaws. It takes a position of strength to subject oneself to such an analysis.

3. Conclusion

The discussion underlined once again the virtual absence of any fruitful exchange between SI research and experimentation conducted in neighboring fields (e.g., discourse analysis, textlinguistics, cognitive psychology, pragmatics). Without belittling either the questionnaire or any of the other methodologies mentioned, it would seem that SI research in general, and the definition of quality standards in particular, might benefit from rigorous analyses of output, in its own right (intratextually), of comparisons with the input (intertextually) and of the effect on users (instrumentally). The methodological difficulties are daunting (Viezzi 1993; Kalina 1994; Pöchhacker 1994). And yet, this is clearly "a necessary part, an indispensable step towards a 'vision' of quality assurance both in the relationship between interpreters and clients in a professional conference assignment and in the joint efforts of trainers and students in the interpreting classroom" (Pöchhacker 1994). Only thus can we hope to continue the move away from the impressionistic to the empirically tested, and from the subjective to the objective.

Karla Déjean le Féal summed this up by pointing out that at a time when English is steadily gaining ground as the *lingua franca* - making interpreting more and more of a luxury item - high quality standards have become a *sine qua non*. Whether they prefer eliciting quality criteria through questionnaires, real-time recordings of professional performance, or replicable experiments - all of the participants highlighted the need to find out more about quality, in the interest of teaching and providing simultaneous interpreting at its best.

Skill Components in Simultaneous Interpreting

Barbara Moser-Mercer, *University of Geneva* &
Sylvie Lambert, *University of Ottawa* (Convenors)
Valeria Darò, *SSLMIT, Trieste*
Sarah Williams, *University of Stockholm*

1. Introduction

The contributors to this workshop consider skill components to be part of a model of the interpreting process that should not be confused with the actual process itself. The reason for considering skill components lies in the conviction that research is incremental, that we cannot look at entire processes, but must decompose them into specific sub-processes. The ensuing problems are faced by all disciplines and are thus not unique to interpreting research. The study of skill components has the potential for becoming a productive research paradigm, yet certain initial considerations are in order.

1.1 *Levels of inquiry*

In psychological research one generally assumes three different levels of inquiry (Massaro 1989): a) a *lower or neural level*; b) a *middle or psychological level*; and c) an *upper or conscious level*. The *lower* physiological level has attracted much attention in recent years as models were developed that supposedly resemble neural processing. It is also the most natural level of explanation because the brain is necessary for mental functioning. The *upper* level is open to introspection, but as very little of everyday activity is open to conscious introspective analysis, because consciousness is involved at only the most general level of our thinking and action, inquiry at this level has not been a focus of experimental research in psychology. In interpreting research a common fallacy has been that there is no need to study a phenomenon unless one was aware of it. The *middle* level, not open to introspection, allows researchers to provide theoretical descriptions and models of the human mind. Various research paradigms have been developed such as the neural-net approach in artificial intelligence and the information processing approach, which is still very productive in trying to come to terms with very complex human behavior.

1.2 *Information processing*

The central thesis of the information processing approach is that complex behavior results from a large number of simpler processes. These *component processes* are assumed to be fairly modular, which is where we can begin to draw parallels with the *skill components* under discussion in this workshop. It is assumed that the functions of one component are relatively independent of the functions of other processes, thus allowing the researcher to study and describe the nature of a component process independently of the other components of the complex process. One must make sure, however, that the conclusions drawn refer to the component under study, and not to the entire process.

The human information processor, the big black box, is now decomposed into several smaller black boxes that communicate with one another. Each black box can be considered a stage of processing, whereby each stage has a memory component holding information, and a process component transforming this information from one store to another. Each processing stage takes time. It is precisely this *temporal aspect* that allows us to isolate one processing stage from another. The big black box approach would not allow for the development of testable hypotheses as in such a molar view no possibility exists for identifying which part of the process contributed to the results, and only general conclusions could be drawn.

Within the information processing framework the goal is then to determine how many boxes there are, how each of them works, and how they interact. The models are formal representations of our knowledge of the mental processes under study and thus allow for consistency in research results and in their interpretation; they also ensure comparability with results from research in other disciplines pursuing the same approach and thus lay the foundation of interdisciplinary inquiry. No model is meant to correspond to the phenomena exactly. If it did, it would no longer be a model but reality itself (Massaro 1989).

The skill components isolated vary from one researcher to another, although some general consensus about major components exists. The smaller the component, the more varied the definitions become.

In information processing one generally distinguishes between detection, recognition, and response selection. Other categories such as perception, comprehension, retrieval, production, and memory have also been adopted and are represented in this workshop. Most research in simultaneous interpreting has focussed on response selection with reaction time and/or error rates being used as central measures in the data analysis. Not always have the two been used together, despite the fact that they are assumed to be converging measures of performance.

1.3 *Methodological research issues based on skill components*

On the whole there are distinct problems associated with research based on skill components, such as the confusion between *structure* and *process*, or between *information* and *processing of information*, or between *performance* and *processing* itself.

Structure and process are tied up together and are easily confounded: only the ingenious experimenter will be able to pull them apart. The same is true for information and information processing as information differences can lead to performance differences, which in turn could easily be taken for processing differences. We know that the quality of the incoming message, which includes all aspects such as sound quality, pitch, accent, prosody, volume, topic, information density, etc., varies greatly from one speaker to the next. If studies in interpreting do not take account of this variety then it may be easy to conclude that any kind of performance difference on the part of the interpreter reflects a processing difference, which would be a misleading conclusion indeed.

Such issues can be resolved only if SI research moves explicitly into the direction of model construction. Such models must provide sufficient detail and should take account of relevant research in neighboring disciplines so that testable hypotheses can be generated. These will in turn allow for partial verification, as we can only extrapolate from specific experiments and never cover all instances of the entire interpreting process. Experimental designs that are not based on specific theories or models are liable to generate non-testable hypotheses. Close collaboration with researchers in related fields will allow us to draw on research results obtained and to extend existing models to the SI situation; the skill components approach sketched in this workshop could allow us to compare our research results with those obtained in other disciplines.

For this workshop the notion of skill components will be viewed from two research perspectives: *How research in bilingualism relates to issues in interpreting,* presented by Sarah Williams, and *The role of memory in interpreting,* discussed by Valeria Darò.

2. How research in bilingualism relates to issues in interpreting

2.1 *Bilingualism*

Within the field of research on bilingualism, a bilingual is generally defined as a person who is able to use two languages, for some or all of the skills of comprehension and production. The technical term for a person who is able to use three or more languages is *polyglot*, although polyglots are often also included in references to *bilinguals*, which is also true for this section.

There are various kinds of bilingualism, depending on whether the languages are native (L1) or "second languages" (L2). L1 is traditionally defined as a language learnt before a critical period, which used to be regarded as being at around puberty. Recent research shows, however, that there are different critical periods for different modules of language (phonetic, syntactic, semantic, etc.), and that at least some of these critical periods take place much earlier than puberty. Bilinguals are thus referred to in the literature simply as either *early bilinguals* (those who learnt their languages during early childhood), or *late bilinguals* (those who learnt one of their languages after early childhood). Early bilinguals are generally regarded as being native speakers of both of their languages, while late bilinguals are not; in cases where late bilinguals have a high level of proficiency in their L2s, they are referred to as *near-native speakers*. Generally speaking, however, when those working in the field of interpreting refer to someone as being a *true* bilingual, it is likely they are referring to someone who is an early bilingual[1]. Determining whether a person's language is L1 or L2 is important in that it has been clearly shown in the literature that different perception and production strategies are used for L1 and L2 (Williams 1994). This has obvious consequences for research on interpreting.

The areas of research on bilingualism presented here are cognitive research on bilingualism, and research on Second Language Acquisition (SLA).

Cognitive research on bilingualism as referred to in this section concerns the relationship of two or more languages to each other within a framework of shared storage and processing capacity; SLA research in this section concerns mainly the differences in the nature and use of L1 and L2 systems, and the effect these can have on each other.

Issues within cognitive research on bilingualism which are relevant to interpreting include language dominance, perception and production, switching and language activation and suppression. Issues within SLA research relevant to interpreting include transfer-related issues, as evidenced in both on-line processing and as inherent parts of a language system, and variability under stress, in terms of register, grammatical features and automaticity. In the last few years there has been a surge of interest in *near-native speakers*, and SLA research has also expanded to include more studies on perception and comprehension (cf. Bates & MacWhinney 1989), and how L2 influences L1 (Seliger & Vago 1991), all aspects that link SLA research to interpreting research.

2.2 *Cognitive research on bilingualism*

A key question from cognitive research on bilingualism which has direct relevance for interpreting is how a bilingual can keep languages separate. Various hypotheses and models have been put forward (see Romaine 1989 for an overview). In 1959, Penfield and Roberts proposed a switch mechanism allowing the bilingual to switch from one language to another. This was later refined by Macnamara (1967), who pointed out that there must be both an input and an output switch, since bilinguals can speak in one language while comprehending another. Macnamara also suggested that the output switch is under conscious control, while the input switch is data-driven, i.e. not under conscious control but triggered by the input. Paradis (1977: 91), however, put forward the idea that the capacity to switch need not be a faculty peculiar to the polyglot, suggesting that there is no need to postulate a particular switch mechanism "other than that which every speaker already possesses and which allows him, among other things, to switch registers within the same language." Albert & Obler (1978) were among the first to dismiss the idea of a single switch mechanism in favor of a continually operating monitor system, in which choices of language, word, phrase, etc., are continually being tested against other competing forms. This has paved the way for later models of activation and suppression, such as that of Green (1986), who proposes a model in which a bilingual's languages can be in one of three possible states: selected, activated or dormant. Separation of the languages is thought to be an issue of successful suppression of the non-selected language(s).

If one accepts the existence of a mechanism which suppresses competing items, both in monolinguals (as regards register) and bilinguals (as regards language and presumably also register), then the situation of the interpreter is necessarily more complicated; presumably, due to the simultaneity of perception and production, interpreters must simultaneously suppress different modules in each language, so that the production module is suppressed in the incoming language, while the perception module is partly suppressed in the outgoing language. However, the perception model in the outgoing language cannot be wholly suppressed, since the interpreter's output serves at the same time as an audial control which modifies further output (Spiller & Bosatra 1989). This means that interpreters have at least one additional burden of suppression, i.e. suppressing part of the perception mode in the output language, which obviously must take its toll on processing capacity (see figure below). This may explain why not all fluent bilinguals can be good interpreters; i.e. it may be possible to be fluent in several languages and thus be able to cope with dual suppression, but not with triple suppression or more (see Williams 1995a).

Monolingual: register

Bilingual: register + language

Interpreter: register + language + production in incoming
                      language + some of perception in outgoing language
                      (some needed for monitoring)

Figure 1. *Areas of control in monolinguals, bilinguals, and simultaneous interpreters*

Considerations such as those put forward in Fig. 1 may be a good starting point for process models ofinterpreting. Indeed, some of the problems encountered by some interpreting students are, for example, lapsing into a simplified register during simultaneous interpreting, or failing to monitor their output, both of which would indicate a problem with suppression. Another (at present tentative) example of how such a model of activation and suppression may be of help is the problem of anomalous prosody in simultaneous interpreting (Shlesinger 1994, Williams, 1995b). It has been suggested that anomalous stress in the interpreter's output may mirror or be triggered by salient but semantically unrelated stress in the input (Williams, 1995b). If this is the case, then this may be a question of mixing incoming signals so that it is the speaker's input, and not the interpreter's own production, which is partially acting as audial control for the interpreter's output. This may then be a case of an incorrect level of perceptual suppression of the output language (i.e. if too much of it has been suppressed, then the speaker's input will totally dominate, thus taking over the function of audial control).

2.3 Second language acquisition research

A key area from SLA research which has direct relevance for interpreting is that of variability in language. Initial work in this area (Tarone 1983, 1985) concentrated on variability in connection with different tasks and different levels of attention to form, and was viewed within a sociolinguistic framework, i.e. focussing largely on the acquisition and use of different registers. Subsequent work has taken up the issue of psycholinguistic variability, i.e. variability in performance (both perception and production) under conditions of stress or limited processing capacity. Here, the concept of variability is used as a new approach towards gaining insights into interlanguage instability, i.e. the tendency of even advanced interlanguage to sometimes revert to an earlier stage of interlanguage under stress (cf. Selinker's 1972 *backsliding*). This is referred to by Bialystock & Sharwood/Smith (1985) as *control variability* and has consequences for the use of, among other things, register, grammatical features and automaticity. Variability in language processing under conditions of stress has obvious relevance for interpreting.

The study of simultaneous interpreting provides a good opportunity to look at two central issues within SLA research. The first concerns the status of L1 and L2. Given that L2 production can regress in certain ways under stress (e.g. interpreting), what happens to L1 ? (see Gile 1987 for an empirical study on the subject). Does it display similar phenomena ?[2] What would this say about the status of L1 and L2? Can we speak of an L1 interlanguage? The second has to do with perception. It seems reasonable to suppose that if production suffers under limited processing capacity, so does perception. Interpreting may provide an opportunity to research the issue that an early strategy used in L2 perception relies on the selective processing of stressed words in the input (Tarone 1974). If L2 production regresses under limited processing capacity to an earlier stage, might this not also apply to L2 perception? If so, then this may mean that during these moments, the interpreter may be extra sensitive to stress in the input as a perceptual strategy *if the input is L2.* This may constitute a factor in the occurrence of anomalous stress, although obviously, this must remain mere speculation until relevant work has been carried out. At the risk of being controversial, SLA literature on L1 and L2 perception and production may revive the discussion on the direction of interpreting.

Cognitive research on bilingualism and SLA research has developed various ways of studying the many components involved in language use. These could usefully be applied to interpreting research. What is needed is detailed study of separate components, followed by reintegration of research results into a larger model.

3. Memory

Such a larger model will undoubtedly feature a memory component to account for both long-term and shorter-term retention and recall of knowledge and procedures in all forms of interpreting. Studies on the anatomical, biochemical and neurofunctional bases of memory and on its organization and functioning are numerous (for a review see Squire 1987; Tulving 1987; Schacter et al. 1993), but only few have so far been devoted to the implications of memory in interpretation (Gerver 1974; Lambert 1989a; Darò 1989; Isham & Lane 1993; Darò & Fabbro 1994).

3.1 *The state of the art of human memory*

Memory is the capacity of an organism to adapt or change as a result of events and of external stimuli. Owing to this capacity, the experience of an organism can modify its nervous system and lead to different behavior (Squire 1987). Lasting changes in behavior resulting from prior experience can be characterized as the result of learning, memory and retrieval processes (Thompson 1986).

3.2 *Dualistic models of memory*

About 100 years ago William James (1890) was the first to theorize the distinction between *primary* and *secondary memory*, suggesting that there were two related forms of memory storage: one for the information forming the focus of current attention and occupying the stream of thought, and the other for knowledge of events or facts belonging to former states of mind.

The same dualistic approach forms the basis of the modal model by Atkinson and Shiffrin (1984), according to which *short term memory (STM)* retains information only temporarily so as to allow it to be transferred into a more stable, potentially permanent *long term memory (LTM)* store (Fig. 2). Clinical memory syndromes provided clear examples of double dissociations between STM and LTM, which corroborated the hypothesis of the existence of two main memory systems. However, it appeared that certain STM syndromes required additional explanation and that Atkinson and Shiffrin's (1984) model had to be revisited, since integrity of STM was apparently not absolutely necessary for storing information in LTM.

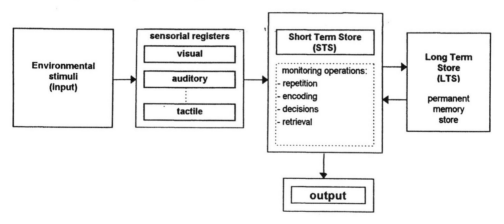

Figure 2. *The modal model adapted from Atkinson and Shiffrin (1984)*

3.3 *The concept of working memory*

The question of limited STM capacity which had been observed during neuropsychological experiments (e.g. Miller 1956) led to the concept of *working memory*, which is supposed to be a memory buffer in which information is maintained while it is being processed (Baddeley & Hitch 1974). Baddeley (1990; 1991) suggested a model based on working memory systems, which presupposes the existence of a *central executive system* controlling the attentional systems connected to a number of *slave systems*, each one processing information according to its own specific modality. One of these systems is the *visuospatial sketch pad*, which processes visual images, another is the *phonological loop*, which accounts for speech-based information. Memory traces of acoustically perceived verbal material that are temporarily processed within the phonological store generally decay and thus become unretrievable after about 1.5 to 2 seconds, unless they are refreshed by the process of *subvocal rehearsal*. By this process the traces are fed back into the articulatory control processes, thus prolonging their presence within the working memory. Similarly, visuospatial images are temporarily set up and maintained on a sort of scratch pad to enhance their presence in the working memory; this accounts for the processing of visual stimuli (Fig. 3).

Visuospatial   phonological
sketch pad   loop

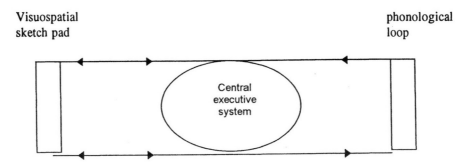

Two main slave systems are represented:
- the visuospatial sketch pad (visual images)
- the phonological loop (speech-based information)

Figure 3. *Baddeley's working memory model (1990)*

3.4 Long term memory systems

LTM should not be viewed as a unitary function, but rather as a multifaceted system with several components (or subsystems), each one representing one modality of information storage that can be functionally independent from the others. Thus, according to Cohen & Squire (1980) a first distinction between *declarative* and *procedural* memory should be made: the former referring to events and facts that are directly accessible to conscious recollection (knowing that), the latter being intrinsically contained within learned skills or cognitive operations (knowing how). Shacter (1987) rightly points out that declarative memory should be better defined as *explicit memory*, since it implies conscious awareness and its contents can be represented or verbalized on demand, whereas procedural memory is a form of *implicit memory* in that it lacks this kind of awareness and is not overt and susceptible to conscious recollection. Explicit (declarative) memory comprises two further subsystems: *semantic memory*, through which individuals store their encyclopedic knowledge of the world, and *episodic memory* which refers to autobiographical recall of one's own experiences. *Implicit (procedural) memory* includes motor, cognitive and perceptual *skills, priming, conditioning* and *habituation* (Kinsbourne 1987; Weiskrantz 1987; Fabbro 1995).

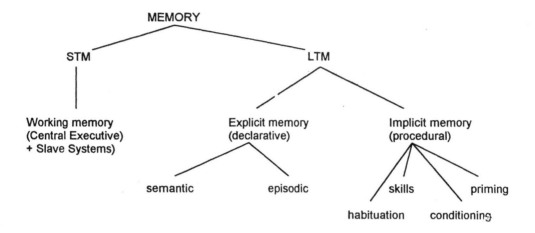

Figure 4. *A schematic representation of memory (adapted from: Mayes 1988)*

Paradis (1994) underlines how this kind of memory classification can be applied to language acquisition, learning and use. When acquiring a language, a child unconsciously and automatically applies rules which have been stored in his implicit memory, and the same happens when an adult acquires a second language by repeated and prolonged exposure in an informal setting, thus acquiring communicative competence. If a language is learned within a formal context (e.g. in class) through the conscious interiorization and application of grammatical rules, this is thought to require the activation of explicit memory strategies.

3.5 Working memory and interpretation

Some parallel, independent studies have shown that after SI the ability to recall what is being heard is severely impaired. In a serial study Isham (1994) noticed that verbatim recall of the final clause of a given passage was worse in SI from French into English as opposed to SI from English into sign language. The main difference between these two performances is that sign language interpreters were dealing with only one spoken language at a time. Isham suggested that there might have been phonological interference caused by the two concurrent speech streams in spoken interpretation.

In a recent experimental study Darò and Fabbro (1994) pointed out that reduced recall after SI as opposed to mere listening and shadowing is most probably due to an effect of articulatory suppression which hinders the normal functioning of the subvocal rehearsal mechanisms within the phonological loop of working memory (Fig. 5). Listening and concurrent speaking apparently prevents the phonological loop from working properly, thus impeding the normal functioning of the working memory for auditory verbal material, which in turn is thought to be a necessary step for consolidation in LTM.

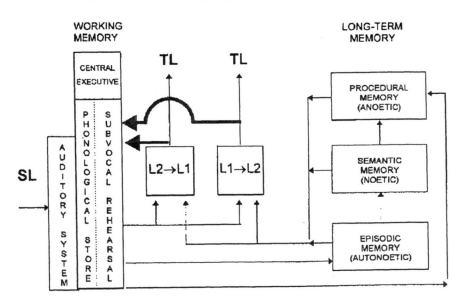

Figure 5. *A general model of memory during simultaneous interpretation (Darò and Fabbro 1994)*

In the mid-seventies Gerver (1974) had already observed reduced recall abilities among interpreters after SI as opposed to listening and shadowing. Further research by Lambert (1989a) has shown that free recall of verbal material was significantly better after consecutive interpretation as opposed to simultaneous interpretation. Lambert suggested that during SI the verbal material was not processed as deeply as in CI and that a less deep processing reduced LTM storage, as theorized by Craik and Lockhart (1972). However, Darò & Fabbro (1994) believe that another possible complementary explanation could be that during consecutive interpretation there may be far less interference to the phonological loop of working memory than during SI, since in CI no articulatory suppression takes place.

3.6 LTM and interpretation

Simultaneous interpreters have thus been found to perform poorly in memory tasks concerning material that they have just translated. Apart from the idea of an impingement on working memory, two other hypotheses can be formulated to account for reduced LTM abilities: the need to divide one's attention among many different concurring tasks may interfere with the normal activity of the central executive system of working memory, in such a way that it becomes somehow overwhelmed by all these tasks. Second, since professional interpreters are exposed to a huge amount of (new) information daily, much of which is not particularly relevant to their personal lives, they might have unconsciously developed a strategy which allows them to censor all this redundant material.

Spiller-Bosatra, Darò, Fabbro & Bosatra (1990) found that the practice of interpretation does not improve one's LTM abilities concerning verbal material stored in semantic memory, as opposed to other skill components of interpretation which do improve with training (e.g. concurrent listening and speaking, divided attention, speaking speed). This could be partially due to the fact that a large proportion of the interpretation process is related to implicit, highly automatized strategies, which, as underlined by Paradis (1994), cannot be enhanced through explicit strategies, since practice does not convert explicit knowledge into implicit competence.

Although no specific studies have been carried out yet, it is reasonable to assume that semantic memory in interpreters increases continually, as is the case for most other professionals who acquire new knowledge through exposure and practice. Implicit strategies of procedural memory systems, however, which are necessary for interpreting, are subject to a slow decay due to ageing, and this may become far more detrimental for an interpreter than for other professionals. For example, a philosopher suffering from Parkinson's disease, a degenerative neurological disorder that destroys subcortical structures subserving implicit memory, may still continue his professional activity, albeit much more slowly, whereas an interpreter loses the most precious abilities related to automatized procedural skills (see Aglioti & Fabbro 1993).

3.7 *Memory and consecutive interpretation*

Memory as a skill component of CI has been less studied than in SI. Even though in CI there might not be any phonological overlapping between two different linguistic codes, it is reasonable to suggest that concurrent listening and writing of notes might well cause interference[3]. In particular, by following Baddeley's (1990) model of working memory, this could also impinge upon the process of transformation of orally presented phonological material into written material. Baddeley (1990) found a significant reduction in working memory in subjects who were asked to read and memorize English words during articulatory suppression (i.e. concurrent overt production of irrelevant syllables, like *the, the, the*). It may be suggested that if words or syntagmatic units are noted in CI as symbols and not in letters, the phonological interference between oral and written material would be reduced, because symbolic representations of verbal utterances may not require an inner articulation of their phonological form while they are being noted. By reducing phonological interference, the mechanisms of working memory may function with fewer constraints, thus facilitating LTM storage of the acoustically perceived verbal màterial.

It is also suggested that during CI, episodic memory should be more involved, since during the reconstruction phase of the message in the TL, interpreters may try to support their memory for content by recalling and again going over the episode which marked the presentation of that particular piece of information.

The development and use of a particular note-taking technique (irrespective of its specific nature, i.e. with or without symbols) leads to the organization of a new cerebral language representation, which relies both on implicit and explicit memorization strategies, but which deserves further research to be properly analyzed.

4. Conclusions

Drawing on research results and methodologies from neighboring disciplines obviously has significant potential for further analyzing the skill components involved in simultaneous interpreting. Perception, comprehension, retrieval, production, and memory can all be studied within a variety of frameworks: as part of general information processing, i.e. processing within an ideal situation; of performance, i.e. processing within an actual situation taking into consideration the effect of variable factors such as stress, fatigue, etc.; as part of quality control, thus focussing on the acceptability of the product; and within the framework of training. It would certainly further research in interpreting if individual studies were clearly positioned within one of the above frameworks as it would allow for comparability of research results.

A number of cognitive issues must be considered in interpreting research. These relate mainly to access to representations, whether lexical or conceptual; to the time lag between the speaker's input and the interpreter's output, as a measure of processing within and between components, the relationship between sufficient context and memory constraints, whether the time lag is voluntary, imposed or caused by access problems; to simultaneity, the interplay between automaticity and attention; and to the precision and comprehensibility of the interpretation for the listener.

The information processing approach mentioned at the beginning of this paper provides interpreting research with an excellent paradigm within which to study the cognitive issues highlighted in this workshop and within which to position studies that attempt to shed light on the skill components involved in interpreting. If the notion of skill components is to be useful in interpreting research, a clear delineation of these components is required, although this may vary somewhat from one study to the next. Without such unequivocal identification research results from different studies, and from different disciplines, would no longer be comparable. This would augur ill for the future of this exciting research domain.

Editors'notes

1.   This assumption is corroborated by the findings of Thiéry's study on "true bilingualism". See *inter alia* Thiéry 1975.

2.   An empirical study on interpreting students (Gile 1987) suggest it does.

3.   As postulated in the Effort Model of consecutive. See Gile 1995a.

Intercultural Communication, Negotiation, and Interpreting

Masaomi Kondo, *Daito Bunka University, Tokyo* (Convenor)
Helen Tebble, *Deakin University, Melbourne* (Rapporteur)
Bistra Alexieva, *University of Sofia*
Helle v. Dam, *Aarhus Business School*
David Katan, *SSLMIT, Trieste*
Akira Mizuno, *Tokyo*
Robin Setton, *Fu Jen University, Hongkong*
Ilona Zalka, *Endskede, Sweden*

1. Introduction

The following is an attempt to give both a brief summary of the views expressed by the six panelists and to report the salient points raised by the audience during the discussion. In composing this synopsis as the convenor, I have tried to arrange the wealth of material provided during the session in a logical sequence while giving due credit to the panelists for the views expressed, and also incorporating the comments made during the discussion. The result is a compromise on many fronts, as is apparent below, and in particular does little justice to the substantial work the panelists had done. Many interesting details as well as important reservations and subtleties may have been omitted. Nevertheless I hope this synopsis will give the reader a sufficient glimpse into the state of research and the views of the researchers as well as practitioners on the subject of the workshop. I gratefully acknowledge all the contributions and the assistance of the panelists in compiling this compiling this synopsis. I am deeply indebted to the rapporteur in finalising the text, both linguistically and substantively.

This synopsis is divided broadly into three parts. In the first part, the concept of culture is delineated in the light of some recent thinking on the topic. This provides perspectives for discussion of the basic relationship between culture and interpreter-mediated communication settings. In the second part, some of the acute problems that arise in such settings are explained. In the final part, we try to define what the role of the interpreter is, and should be, in dealing with (if not solving) these problems. One point of debate is whether the interpreter should be a cultural mediator or a more neutral, pure language transmitter. The general view tends to be that the interpreter should aspire to be a cultural mediator rather than a mere "mouthpiece" for the actual speaker.

Throughout this synopsis, the word *intercultural* was substituted for *cross-cultural* and *transcultural communication*, except in direct quotes, because they basically designate the same form of interaction (Samovar & Porter, 1991: 70) and no points requiring a distinction between these terms were raised during the session.

Perhaps it would be useful first to establish, as Dam does in this workshop, that the communication situation involving the interpreter is always and by necessity an instance of intercultural communication, although not all instances of intercultural communication need involve interpreters. Where linguistic and cultural borders do not coincide (as in the case of English being spoken as a mother tongue by a number of culturally distinct groups), even monolingual communication may be affected by intercultural factors. Where two or more languages are involved, such intercultural factors are invariably involved, even when the participants come from the same country and therefore have a close cultural affinity. This holds true at least to the extent that the language is an important component of culture and that it influences the thoughts and behaviour of its user (however minimal that influence might be). Furthermore, if one can talk of culture at the level of individuals (although this could invite confusion, as seen below), then indeed "all communication is more or less cross-cultural" (Tannen 1986: 8).

2. What is Culture?

Culture is defined in many ways, and has been likened to an onion (Hofstede 1991:9), a series of layers (Trompenaars 1993: 18), to an iceberg, or to a triad made up of technical, formal, and informal components (Hall 1990: 59-93). In his attempt to sort out this confusion, Katan synthesises a number of recent analyses of culture in six levels, borrowed from neurolinguistic programming research.

1) Culture can be defined at the environmental level, i.e., what can be seen, heard and felt, and includes various social institutions, such as visual art, literature, architecture, and food, as well as the impact of climate.

2) Culture can also be defined in terms of behaviour. This includes practice, rituals and customs.

3) Then we can define culture in terms of capabilities, strategies, i.e., those patterns of behaviour that determine how we carry out these practices. We do the same thing, e.g. negotiate, in different cultures, but the way we do it, the accepted sequence of events, depends on culture. In one culture's negotiating strategy, direct business matters may precede the building up of a mutual rapport, while in another, the process may start indirectly and lead slowly to the actual business to be accomplished.

4) This set of strategies depends on a series of beliefs about why we do things.

5) There is the level of basic core values. Recent empirical research through questionnaire surveys and face-to-face interviews has analysed these values and found that there is a great deal of agreement as to what are the priority values in each culture, while there are also differences between cultures. Hofstede (1991), for instance, tabled 116,000 employees of IBM in 72 different countries with a long questionnaire. He reduced the statistical data to four cultural dimensions, or central tendencies: power distance, uncertainty avoidance, collectivism, and masculinity. Each country analysed tended towards or away from each of these dimensions. The Tropenaars Data Bank is almost as large as the empirical evidence amassed by Hofstede, and shows, for instance, that 90 percent of the Americans saw profit as the main motive of business corporations while only 11 percent of the

Japanese did (Tropenaars 1993: 183). In Kondo's eyes, this is food for
thought for those espousing neo-classical micro-economics, because the
allegedly universal archetype of utility-maximising man and
profit-maximising business may not be as widely applicable as is
assumed.

6)   Lastly, there is the level of individual identity.

Katan sees close correspondence between these six levels of culture and the
visible and invisible levels identified by Hofstede, and with the explicit and
implicit levels suggested by Hall as early as the 1950s, and later by
Tropenaars (1993).

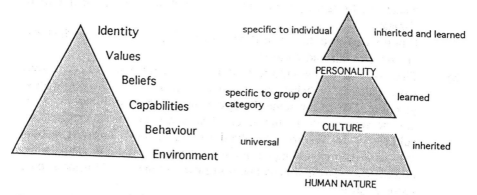

Figure 1. *Six levels of culture*   Figure 2. *Three levels of analysis*
    (adapted from O'Connor &   (Hofstede 1991: 6)
    Seymour 1990: 89)

David Katan also points out that it is useful to bear in mind that culture is but
one of the filters affecting successful communication. Again following
Hofstede (1991: 6), obviously the first level is human nature itself, which is
universal. Then there is culture, which is a filter which restricts the way we
perceive, what we see, hear, or feel. Then there is the individual layer, where
every individual is different from another even with the same cultural
background. To be culturally aware and flexible is to realise the presence of
cultural *and* individual factors, as well as the danger of stereotyping them in
negative and prejudicial ways. Zalka says that "assuming that the habitual
ways of one's own society have universal application" will not do, and that "it
is only through bitter experience that we learn that methods which work best
at home are not necessarily the most appropriate in another cultural context."

A related concept which may prove useful for the analysis of intercultural challenges in interpretation is suggested by Robin Setton. It is the concept of speech community, "a community sharing rules for the conduct and interpretation of discourse." (Hymes 1974a). Intercultural communication then involves more than one speech community.

3. How Do Different Cultures Affect Communication?

Intercultural communication is by definition the communication between persons of different cultural backgrounds. The language which is spoken by a group of people belonging to one culture is different from that spoken by other groups on the levels of semantic fields, syntax, and discourse, reflecting and influencing the entire experience of a cultural community. Not only that, the way they use the language is different. Indeed, the way they communicate is an important aspect of cultural identity. The interpreter stands between two or more of these cultural communities.

The interpreter's task, according to Zalka, is to help the parties perceive and decode, i.e. understand the meaning of the message that is being sent. What is involved here is a complex, multi-layered, dynamic process through which meaning is exchanged. The information is often expressed in the tone of voice, facial expression, behaviour, and physical lay out. How should the informal and colloquial "Yeah!" in an answer of a young American to a question posed in a more formal style be rendered into another language? "Linguistic fidelity" may cause misunderstanding and serious distortions of meaning. The verbosity and the use of flowery expressions characteristic of Hispanic and Arab speakers may sound superficial or as an attempt at avoiding the issue to the receiver from a different culture.

Zalka then offers a synopsis of the communication barriers (/) that intercultural noise creates in the flow of effective communication.

message sent -> message received ->   understanding & action

message sent / problem of equivalence   = message received

message sent / dependance on reasonable   = misunderstanding or in-
         similarity   complete message received

message sent / stereotypes flawing   = more combativeness and
         judgement   less mutual understanding

message sent / projecting one's own   = verbal and nonverbal
         frame of reference   messages get in the way

message sent / attribution of motive   = both sides operate on
                                              different "wavelengths"

Figure 3. *How Intercultural Noise Poses Communication Barriers*

Zalka gives several concrete situations where she becomes involved in an intercultural situation as a practising interpreter. It is always of great help when the organisers of the interpreting event are aware of various intercultural factors and are able to tell how much they want the interpreter to handle. The situation is more complex when the primary parties are unaware of the difficulties and the interpreter has to estimate how far s/he can go in conveying the non-verbal and/or intercultural meanings without jeopardising the intentions of the speaker.

Situations such as a short study visit in some technical or scientific area, fieldwork for an aid organisation, and a workshop with international participants normally present fewer problems. In these situations both parties have essentially the same educational and professional background. "Corporation managers or diplomats would share more professional culture with their international counterparts than these same groups would share within their own societies with college professors or factory workers" (Fisher 1980: 12, quoted by Zalka). When persons in the same profession meet, the emphasis often is on the exchange of information and experiences in a specific field. Zalka finds international business and political negotiations most sensitive and challenging to the interpreter (See below).

4. Lexical Difficulties Faced by Broadcast Interpreters in Japan

Mizuno, a practising broadcast interpreter in Japan, describes one of the many difficulties he and his colleagues face in interpreting English TV news and other programs for general Japanese TV viewers - lexical elements that reflect cultural peculiarities of the source language.

Dozens of news programs produced in other countries are broadcast regularly and are translated into Japanese, not just subtitled. More than one hundred broadcast interpreters work daily in such programs.

The challenges faced by Japanese broadcast interpreters who interpret American TV news programs, for instance, are obvious, even when these are not "live" in the strict sense of the term (Normally they have 60 to 90 minutes to prepare for eight minutes of broadcast). Japanese TV viewers do not share social, cultural, historical, and religious traditions and values with the United States. Nor do Japanese broadcast interpreters. Yet these interpreters must span the divide between Japanese viewers and programs designed for a totally different society. In the constrained situation in which they work, any attempt to add the explanation to a culturally bound lexical item only puts an extra burden on the interpreter's processing capacity.

Mizuno cites the discussion of cultural literacy, where three layers of English vocabulary are mentioned.

> The first is international. Basic literacy in the contemporary world requires knowledge of certain terms known by literate people everywhere in the world, no matter what language they speak... (These are) basic words from world history, world cultures, geography, and the physical and biological sciences... The second layer consists of vocabulary needed for literacy in English, no matter what country the language is used in.
>
> (Hirsh 1988: 75).

Words in the second layer would include Scrooge, Falstaff, and Cinderella. Lying beyond these two layers is the vocabulary "that is special to his or her own country. A literate Briton has to know more about the game of cricket and the Corn Law than an American. An American has to know more about baseball and the Bill of Rights than Britons." (Hirsh 1988: 75).

Mizuno would add another layer of vocabulary that is needed for broadcast interpreters in Japan: the vocabulary of popular culture. Hirsch excludes current events and proper nouns in the field of sports from cultural literacy, because, as he puts it, they are transient. But the American news programs include many words from these areas. Mizuno maintains that the vocabulary that presents the greatest challenges to Japanese broadcast interpreters comprises not only that of the second and third layers but also the vocabulary of popular culture. Popular culture vocabulary is easily understood by the ordinary American people as part of a collective memory, forming a network of shared associations. Examples abound: Superman, Clark Kent, Kryptonite, the Daily Planet, the tooth fairy, the Brooklyn Bridge, "Kilroy was here," "I saw Elvis (Elvis sightings)," "As Sergeant Joe Friday used to say, 'Just the facts, Ma'am,'" the Checkers speech, *Gilligan's Island*... Some of these expressions may well evade even native speakers of English if they are from non-American backgrounds. Mizuno insists that the lexical aspects of intercultural communication should not be relegated to the backseat in its studies, and should be incorporated into the interpreter training curriculum.

5. Proto-typology of Intercultural Events with Interpreting

If we can categorise various intercultural encounters and identify their characteristics, it will help greatly in dealing with them. Alexieva suggests just such a method. However, since an interpreter-mediated communicative act involves contact between (at least) two languages and cultures, and is characterised by a very large number of variables, she posits the box-like approach of categorisation as inapplicable here and that, instead of a rigid typology, one should employ a prototypical approach, thus taking care of the peripheral cases. She argues that a subtler distinction within the variety of interpreting events in an intercultural perspective can be attained if we discuss them in terms of their position along the "*universal - culture specific*" scale, with the further elaboration of a number of sub-scales depending on:

a.   the mode of delivery (non-stop and microphone-mediated in simultaneous interpreting; direct contact and chunked speech in consecutive interpreting);

b.   the elements of the communicative situation (*who* speaks to *whom* about *what* and via *what texts*, or the *how* of the communicative strategy, and the *where*, the *when* and the *why*); and

c.   the complementary use of language and non-language codes.

Alexieva delineates the major sub-scales as:

a.   *Distance - proximity* between Speaker and Addressee(s). CI, for example, involves co-presence of Speaker, Addressee(s), and Interpreter(s), hence all issues related to non-verbal means of expression and proxemics acquire great importance (the proxemic dimensions, posture, kinesthetic factors, touch code, etc.).

b.   *Non-involvement - involvement* of Speaker as an entity (or "voice") in the text. The conference participants - themselves or the institutions they represent - are usually involved as textual entities in socio-economic and political forums, while this is not necessarily the case in scientific and technical symposia.

c.   *Equals - non-equals.* This is related to the role and status of Speaker and Addressee(s) and the power-relationship between them, crucial to whether the communicative situation will be one of equilibrium or tension.

d.   *Formal setting - informal setting.* This is relevant to the extent to which participants can allow themselves the liberty of making greater or lesser use of culture-specific modes of behaviour.

e.   *Objectivity - subjectivity.* This is relevant to the subject matter discussed at a conference. For example, scientific conferences will be closer to the *objectivity* end of the scale, since here the subject of research (the analyser) is different from the object of research (the analysed), which can hardly be the case with socio-political forums.

f.   *Direct negotiation strategy - indirect (covert) negotiation strategy.* This is relevant to the culture-specific ways Grice's conversational maxims (Grice 1975) are observed, i.e, whether the Speaker will be as informative as required, or will withhold information; whether s/he will say only that for which s/he has adequate evidence; whether s/he will avoid ambiguity and be brief and orderly, etc.

g.   *Shared goals - conflicting goals.* This is relevant to the culture-specific ways problems can be handled depending on whether participants have similar goals which can diminish in-group tension and make it easier to arrive at a solution, or whether substantial compromises may be required on the part of some of the participants.

Alexieva maintains that the most powerful among these sub-scales is *distance - proximity*, which is relevant to the distinction between simultaneous and consecutive, followed by *non-involvement - involvement*, *equals - non-equals*, and *shared - conflicting goals*, since the remaining ones may, in some cases, be derived from them. For example, the sub-scale *direct - indirect communicative strategy* is intimately related to *shared - conflicting goals*, and the *objectivity - subjectivity* one is highly dependent on the *non-involvement - involvement* sub-scale.

Alexieva's contention is that the "scale" approach can help us determine more precisely the "family" an interpreting event belongs to in terms of *universality* or *cultural specificity*. We can then predict whether the realisation of the interpreted communicative act will be threatened or not. She reminds us that this exercise in prototypology may have didactic implications since interpreter trainees, as future interlingual and intercultural mediators, do need such procedural knowledge.

6. Intercultural Noise and Cultural Mediation

In her effort to identify the role of the interpreter in instances of intercultural communication, Helle Dam examines the two existing models of conference interpreting that are constructed within a communicative framework, one proposed by Kirchhoff (1976) and the other by Stenzl (1983). These models suggest that a person's cultural perspective is reflected in his text production and linguistic output in general as well as in his expectations as a text receiver. The co-presence of two or several different cultural systems in interpreted communication is supposed to give rise to divergences between, on the one hand, the receiver's textual and linguistic expectations and, on the other hand, the way the sender actually presents his message. The intercultural factor is thus viewed as a source of potential noise (Kirchhoff 1976: 26). If the ideal function of the interpreter is to ensure smooth communication between the primary parties, then his role is to remedy this potential *cultural noise* on the channel by adjusting the culturally determined peculiarities of the source text to the culturally determined expectations of the receiver (Kirchhoff 1976: 24). Thus, the ideal role of the interpreter is to serve not only as a linguistic but also as a cultural mediator.

Dam notes that these models are inspired by translation studies, where the principle of cultural mediation has been advocated for years. One of the most recent attempts to consolidate this principle is the German *skopos* theory whose main claim is that the translator's output should be fully functional (or autonomous) within the target culture (Reiss & Vermeer 1984: 115).

In examining the place of intercultural factors in interpreting, Dam suggests possible lessons to be derived from translation studies. But caution is necessary in doing so because of the different parameters relevant in interpreted communication as opposed to translated communication. She points to two main differences. First, since the target-text receivers in interpreted communication are normally part of the primary audience of the sender (the primary audience being the audience the sender addresses directly in order to get a message across), senders are better aware of the different cultural background of the audience (at least they should be, and if not, the interpreter's task is to make them aware of important cultural differences between them and their audience). Dam thus maintains that in interpreted communication "cultural mediation" is taken care of, at least to some extent, by the sender himself, and is therefore partly removed from the interpreter's task.

The second significant difference between interpreted and translated communication situations arises out of the difference in the medium involved in interpretation and translation as well as the position of the communication parties at the time of the communicative act. The most important implication of these differences is that the interpreter, as opposed to the translator, normally does not have time to adapt the incoming message to the expectations of the target-text receivers.

Dam also emphasises another level where the culture-specificity manifests itself, i.e. the conventions of text structuring, particularly the structuring of argumentation. Hatim (1993) cites the cases of the Arabic and European language users; textual strategies adopted by these two groups are so different that complete structural reorganisation is recommended in translation. The same point is made for Chinese-English (Setton 1993a), Japanese-English (Kondo 1980; Wakabayashi 1991a; Wakabayashi 1991b), and Finnish-German (Koistinen 1992). However, this obviously is not possible in simultaneous interpreting. While Dam feels that even in the consecutive mode of conference interpretation, time pressure does not allow the interpreter to perform the kind of re-structuring and extensive decision-making required in this type of cultural mediation, some feel that restructuring is possible in consecutive and calls for specific training.

The gap is even larger, Dam points out, between discourses produced by members of high-context cultures and those produced by members of low-context cultures. In a high-context culture, the parties to communication tend to rely a great deal on the context for the encoding and decoding of information. She asks: Should the interpreter mediating between persons of these differing cultures undertake the task of adding words to the text produced by the "high-context person" or deleting text in a message from the "low-context person"?

7. What Roles Should Interpreters Play in Intercultural Communication?

Robin Setton explains that the role of the interpreter can be clarified by extending the known definition of the interpreter's competence, and by applying existing principles. Here the interpreter's competence refers not just to the linguistic ability to *translate* a text but more broadly to communicative competence, which he defines as the ability to recognise a full range of communicative intentions from surface signs in at least one source language and to realise expressive procedures for a range of intentions (meanings) in at least one target language. The widely accepted task of the interpreter of providing *equivalent effect* can thus be extended to embrace the intercultural plane.

Setton then points out that Hymes'simple hierarchy of communication contexts (Hymes 1974a), in which speech *acts* make up a speech *event* (e.g., a lecture) within an overall speech *situation*, offers a rough framework for exploring the interpreter's control at different levels. The interpreter can do little to reconcile two different conceptions of an entire speech situation. At the event level, there is room for far greater exploitation of the potential of consecutive interpretation (resequencing, compression, etc.), while simultaneous interpreting offers more limited possibilities of re-packaging, and enhancement or suppression of features of the text. At the speech act level, communicative competence and the principle of equivalent effect come into their own.

Setton gives an example of the speech act level: the Chinese phrase 考慮考慮 *kaolu kaolu*, "I/we (implied) will (implied) think it over", when used in response to a proposal, is generally understood to signify polite refusal, since in this culture politeness is realised as the taboo against an explicit negative, and refusal as the absence of an explicit affirmative. The next step is to realise 'polite refusal' in the target language, regardless of prejudices about rendering the 'logical' value of propositions, which would block translation of an affirmative by a negative: "we'll think about it" would be too blunt, but "your proposal needs further thought" falls short, suggesting mere postponement. Certainly the negative can be politely attenuated: "I am afraid we cannot agree at this time"; but in trying to avoid it altogether there is the risk of giving a different message to the foreigner than what is conveyed by these words to a Chinese.

Kondo (1991) had pointed out certain dangers involved in such a rendition, however: In the case of an interpreter mediating a similar Japanese phrase into English, he may be censored and accused of *mis-translation*. If the speaker's intention was to deceive his counterpart, such a rendition may indeed constitute a case of over-translation. An interesting case was mentioned by a sign language specialist in the audience. Since in the sign language community reference to age and weight even with a female counterpart is totally accepted, a friendly opener of a conversation can be interpreted as "My goodness, you've gained weight!" This phrase has a *bonding* function to the deaf in the United States.

Finally, Setton emphasises that the emerging prominence of non-European conference languages/cultures will have important knowledge as well as processing implications. This will require more study of other cultures and new elements will need to be introduced in the training of interpreters. Fundamental cultural and linguistic differences in the logical presentation of speeches greatly increase the temptation for the interpreter to fall back on surface equivalences. The operations required, especially when interpreters attempt to adjust to the different discoursal structures, will in some cases challenge acquired processing skills. This will mean, for example, altering the balance of the trade-offs used when allocating attention strategies.

8. The Interpreter in the Business Environment

Katan takes up an important area in which interpreter services are provided: international business negotiations. He also asserts that the interpreter should become a cultural mediator.

Katan cites S. Hagen (1994), who says: "Companies are cynical about the use of university trained interpreters, and increasingly they are becoming more confident about handing over interpreting and translating tasks to their own department". A recent University of Nottingham research report echoes the same idea: "Business respondents were very much in favour of independence from interpreters" (Arijoki 1994: 20). Katan himself has heard many Italian business managers claim that interpreters are the least desirable option.

Katan has found that there are two basic reasons for this view of the interpreter on the part of corporations. First, the interpreter is viewed as an intruder, both physically and psychologically. The interpreter is considered as a person who deflects communication between the parties. Secondly, the interpreter is seen as a non-specialist, a generalist, above all with little understanding of corporate culture. In the words of a member of the audience, the interpreter in Europe is seen as an expensive walking dictionary, and never specialised enough, Katan would add. In the discussion, another reason for the reluctance to employ interpreters for business negotiations was pointed out: The client is not sure of the loyalty of the interpreter. Thus, at least in Europe, interpreters in the business environment do not altogether find themselves in a happy situation.

Yet, Katan points out, 50 to 75 per cent of international ventures (joint ventures and mergers) are failing through problems in intercultural communication in today's increasingly globalised business world (Frank 1990; Breuer & de Bertha 1990). Hofstede stresses that "managers chronically underestimate cultural factors in the case of mergers and acquisitions" (Hofstede 1991:239). And cultural factors are possibly the single most important factor in business communication. A dilemma thus surrounds the interpreter in the business environment: The interpreter is an endangered species at least in the European business environment, while the global market is leading to an increasing need for individuals who are capable of mediating between languages and cultures, and this need is not being met.

Katan urges the interpreter to try to close this gap by changing her/his roles, i.e. s/he should become a higher-profile participant in business negotiations, or a cultural mediator. Katan refers to Brislin (1981) who suggests that 1) the interpreter should work with the participants before an event, and prepare them for any intercultural problems that might emerge; 2) the interpreter be given explicit permission to stop a conference if s/he feels a misunderstanding is causing difficulty; and 3) s/he should prepare materials on intercultural meetings to brief clients and, in general, to raise awareness of the cultural factors in communication. For this to happen, however, the business environment must become, and is becoming, more sensitive to cultural issues. Also the interpreter must become both more aware of the possibility of playing such a role and better trained to handle these tasks.

Zalka also points to the need to enlighten the client: "Most of the problems interpreters face should be solved by increasing the intercultural awareness of the participants in the theatre of international relations. Then the interpreters could really concentrate on what their task is: transmitting the message."

9. Should the Interpreter be a Cultural Mediator?

A number of contributions from the audience provided some answer to the question: should the interpreter really be a cultural mediator? Some members of the audience felt that the person adopting such roles as Brislin outlined would be of an entirely new species of interpreter, with different basic skills from those of today's free lance conference interpreters. Today some European business clients would not want to assign to interpreters the role of cultural mediators either. However, more of the audience seemed enthusiastic about playing such roles. In the words of a member of the audience, the twenty-first century interpreter cannot be *a walking dictionary plus*.

A sign language researcher in the audience pointed out that in the sign language community it has been firmly established that the sign language interpreter has to act as a cultural mediator, rather than be a "mechanical" translator. Because of the wide *cultural* gap between the hearing and the deaf, he is bound to end up *mediating*. In fact, one of the issues being debated is the meaning of mediation: should the interpreter "mask" cultural differences or should s/he reveal them?

In the sign language community it has also been found that the interpreter cannot achieve the goal of *neutrality* because s/he stands between the "empowered" and "disempowered" communities. The sign language interpreter is confronted with the ethical issue of deciding whether or not to be an advocate for the deaf community.

A related point was raised by a member of the audience: The interpreter must be sufficiently flexible to adjust to her/his target audience, especially when the audience are non-native speakers of English. With English having become an effective *lingua franca,* those with English as an acquired language often struggle to express themselves, and may find it difficult to understand the refined English of educated native English speakers. This has a bearing on the question of the quality of interpreting: quality for whom? Should quality be judged from the viewpoint of the listeners, the party paying for the service, the speaker, or some other entity?

10. Intercultural Meetings as Real-Life Sessions

As a practising interpreter, Zalka emphasised the point that intercultural encounters which are not set in sophisticated environments such as international conferences or high-level political meetings are the ones that present the real-life intercultural communication tasks interpreters have to deal with. She even humorously urges conference interpreters to "come out of their ivory tower." Consecutive interpreting is still very much used when so-called small or rare languages are concerned. Interpreting into the B language is a non-issue: it has to be done, and is done.

Zalka also says something most practicing colleagues would sympathise with:

> If the interpreter is a full member of a working team and her/his knowledge of the culture is relied on, it is a positive situation...The other variant is where the interpreter is being used as a mere mouthpiece, and is expected to render what is being said *faithfully*. In this case *faithful* refers to linguistically exact transmission. All the cultural nuances would be left out.... From the point of view of executing the job, the second situation is the "easier" one, where the headache of solving very delicate transformations is not the interpreter's task... The first situation is more complex, more difficult and even involves risks. But it is the more rewarding one, as it is actually the really faithful and effective transmission of the message the interpreter must achieve.

Zalka concludes that the interpreter should be empathetic to the parties involved, find out about the situation, and exercise a lot of common sense until more is known on the most desirable role of the interpreter.

11. Conclusion - M.Kondo

Despite the various perspectives from research on culture that can have a significant bearing on the conduct of the profession, more precise knowledge needs to be acquired through empirical and other methods of investigation about the relationship between culture and interpreting, the difficulties encountered by interpreters as well as primary participants in intercultural settings, and above all possible solutions to these difficulties. Perhaps one could go a step further than simply advocating greater awareness of and sensitization to intercultural factors. If no general rules can be established, perhaps a relevant typology or proto-typology can be hypothesised and tested regarding the role of the interpreter in different intercultural settings.

While more needs to be known, we know a number of things sufficiently well. Both practising and would-be interpreters should be instilled with a greater awareness of intercultural factors at play in the exercise of their profession. In the training of interpreters, more emphasis should be placed on their understanding of specific areas of human activity so that they can have a higher profile as cultural mediators. In particular, greater knowledge of corporate culture seems useful both because of its known potentialities as a relatively new locale for the profession and because of its intrinsic needs for intercultural communication and business negotiation in today's global economy.

Even though many points of importance related to the subject of the interpreter, intercultural communication, and negotiation were covered, a number of points still remained unexplored. They include: Are there differences in the roles the interpreter can (and is expected to) play depending on the culture in which s/he finds her/himself performing? Are there differences between male and female interpreters in this context? How is our service related to the non-verbal behaviour of different cultural groups? Are there some substantive and qualitative differences in the nature of intercultural communication and the role of the interpreter in communication settings involving two extremely divergent cultures, such as those of the hearing and the deaf, and Indo-European and non-Indo-European?

This brings me to my last point. The process of rendering *kaolu kaolu* as "We regret we cannot agree at this time" fascinates me. So does a friendly opener rendered into sign language as: "My goodness, you've gained weight!" If Adler is right in saying that "the greater the differences between the sender's and the receiver's cultures, the greater the chance for cross-cultural miscommunication" (Adler 1986: 52-3, cited by Zalka), then it should perhaps be recognised that the task of trying to minimise that chance may involve much longer processes of much greater complexity.

Robin Setton makes a perceptive observation that

> Delegates attending international conferences acquiesce in a mode of debate and decision making in a tradition established by the world's last great empire; even if caucusing, political alignments and so on are defined by the real power relationships of our age, the procedure, and thus the language, are a product of the English-speaking world, and to function effectively in this

mode, delegates are usually prepared to forget their local customs and to behave and frame their statements in internationalese of either British parliamentary or European (Marxist or Protestant) dialectic ancestry, whatever language they may be using. (Setton 1993b:5)

However, it would be insensitive to suggest that this effectively puts an end to the problem. Here I am reminded of one of the most important features of culture that was only alluded to in the workshop or in the conference: Culture is relative, i.e. there is no such thing as a superior or inferior culture in relation to other cultures. Eurocentrism has no place, nor does Japano-centrism. Imperialism in any form should be condemned, and so should cultural and linguistic imperialism.

The concept of cultural relativity is of Western origin. It is an idea that emerged as Western anthropologists examined various cultures that are often described as primitive. They found that they were not primitive: they have complex sets of rules for social behaviour and customs to govern their society; they have as valid a social system, a system of technology, a language, as our contemporary societies; and they naturally try to modernise but in their own way. It is not only ironic but inherently and profoundly tragic that non-Western cultures must rely on a concept of Western origin to assert themselves. I recognise the essential superiority of the specifically modern civilisation (possibly more than those who have lived in it and tend to take it for granted), and it did originate in the West. But thoughtless imposition of it on the non-Western world can only backfire.

If the process of cross-fertilisation and integration of differing perspectives can contribute to a better knowledge ultimately leading us by small steps toward the real *truth*, then incorporation of *very* divergent viewpoints should surely benefit the entire scientific and professional community of conference interpreters. Cultural differences can and should be made a blessing in disguise. And this calls for a large dose of empathy on the part of the dominant, "empowered" community. If that sounds a little too humanistic, then what we need is a vigorous methodological awareness to be able to take into account differing viewpoints.

Linguistics, Discourse Analysis and Interpretation

Carol Taylor Torsello, *SSLMIT, Trieste* (Convenor)
Sandra Gallina, *EU interpreter, Brussels*
Maria Sidiropoulou, *University of Athens*
Christopher Taylor, *SSLMIT, Trieste*
Helen Tebble, *Deakin University, Melbourne*
A. R. Vuorikoski, *University of Tampere*

1. Introduction

Since interpretation is a language-based activity, as are, for example, language teaching, translation and psycho-therapeutic conversation, it seems logical to expect there to be important relationships between interpretation and linguistics. In some circles, there is a tendency to think of linguistics as the study of *linguistics*, i.e. of what linguists have written about what other linguists have written about what other linguists etc. It is important to stress that linguistics is the study of *language*, hence its relevance to interpretation. Any language-based activity which wants to become introspective, to gain awareness of its own workings so as to be able to talk about them, to write about them, to help other people to get into these workings, will need to refer to the discipline (or perhaps better, the disciplines, since we can speak of linguistics, but also of psycholinguistics, sociolinguistics, neurolinguistics and so on) of the study of language.

It is only natural that not all linguistic theory is equally relevant to the particular activity one is interested in. First of all, interpretation is an activity involving spoken rather than written language, so, even if much can be learned from the study of written language that is valid for spoken language as well, a linguistics based on written language will be insufficient for interpretation studies, and it will not have the right focus. In the presentation at 7 below it is held that a dynamic perspective is needed in linguistics for interpretation studies rather than a synoptic perspective, with an orientation toward the process rather than the product. There are, indeed, aspects of spoken language, such as intonation (so important for the type of analysis discussed at 5 below), which are left out completely if one's sole reference point is the written medium. Speakers use intonation to carry out six very important functions: 1) to organize and control the interaction, 2) to structure the message into units, 3) to indicate relationships between parts of their message, 4) to structure the information, signalling relative informativity, 5) to indicate their attitudes toward the message and the listeners and 6) to distinguish the type of speech act involved (Taylor Torsello 1992:91-130).

Furthermore, since what an interpreter works with is a text, it is text-based linguistics that is needed. Linguistics for interpreters will be based on meaning and on language in context. Linguistics based on invented sentences is of little use to interpretation, whereas text-based linguistic activities such as discourse analysis are extremely relevant.

And finally, the linguistics an interpreter needs is interlingual. This does not of course mean that the linguistics of a single language will not be useful. On the contrary, the linguistics of each single language that the interpreter uses will be useful, especially when the focus is appropriate, but it will not be sufficient, since the interpreter will also need to go into the contrastive aspects related to the languages being used, and to the translingual aspects involved in his or her job.

Interpreters and people working on interpretation, then, have every right to demand the linguistics they need; but they must also be willing to accept the challenge of offering a laboratory for experimentation and for the development of that linguistic theory. They must be ready to work with it, apply it, help to develop it, change it and, if need be, discard it. The Turku workshop on "Linguistics, Discourse Analysis and Interpretation" has offered an opportunity to take a step forward in developing this sort of interactive relationship between interpretation and linguistics.

2. Reasoning in Interpreting - Maria Sidiropoulou, University of Athens

Maria Sidiropoulou has applied recent text-linguistic theory on cohesion and studies on contrastive rhetoric in her work on cultural differences between English people and Greeks regarding the explicitation of causal cohesive links. She places a preference for a different persuasion strategy (Lakoff 1990:216) and the tendency to accept a denial attitude (Hatim 1991) at the basis of the Greek tendency to make causal links explicit, as well as relating this tendency to a high degree of speaker responsibility for specifying relations between ideas - higher even than that found in American English, in which the speaker is said to take responsibility, as opposed to Korean, Japanese, Chinese and Athapaskan, which tend to place the responsibility on the listener for understanding these relations (Tyler 1992:15). The corpus at the basis of her study is a 12,000 word sample of the Greek versions of news articles in the Greek press, contrasted with the corresponding source texts in the English press. Her results are of interest to media interpreters in particular and to interpreters in general, since they seem to indicate the expectation of more explicit causal linking in Greek than in English.

Sidiropoulou finds that explicit cause-and-effect relationships in the English source text (ST) are almost always transferred intact in the Greek target text (TT). She says that the translator does not seem to be willing to leave any one of them out unless there is some local constraint disallowing its use.

Furthermore, the Greek TTs often give explicit expression to links which are implicit in the English STs. These modifications are exemplified through the following formulae:

STs	TTs
1. x.	--> x. <u>So</u> y
2. x. y	--> x so...that y
3. x. y	--> x with the result that y
4. x, and y	--> x. Y was the answer.
5. x. y. z	--> x, z, Of course y
6. x...y	--> x with the result that y
7. y. x	--> y. The reason is x
8. y. x	--> y because x
9. y. x	--> y since x
10a. y: x	--> y since x'
10b. y, x	--> y given that x
11. x. That means y.	--> Given x', y
12. z. But y. x	--> z. However, y' given x'. x

In other cases a causal link is added to the target version as the translator's interpretation of the relationship connecting information scattered over various parts of the source text. The numerical result is that an average of 3 cause/effect signs per article are added to the TT, and this in spite of the fact that the TT is always shorter than the ST due to omissions, sometimes of whole paragraphs, made necessary by space limitations. It is clear that the translator considers cause-and-effect relationships a device contributing to target text processibility and, therefore, makes every effort to signal them.

Maria Sidiropoulou was also interested in finding out in what part or parts of the news article such intervention on the part of the translator was most likely to occur. Using van Dijk's (1985:86) superstructure schema for news discourse, she found that in her corpus the translator added explicit cause-effect links in the 'comment' part. In fact, most of the points where such interference occurs relate to some kind of estimation or evaluation on the part of the author. Sidiropoulou's conclusion is that the Greek reader must be rather particular about the way comments are made, requiring that at points of evaluation there should be some overt expression of the reasoning involved.

Points of contact can be found between these results and the results of two other studies, one on the Greek versions and source texts of EEC informative discourses (Sidiropoulou 1993) and one on the Greek versions and source texts of argumentative news articles (Sidiropoulou 1994). Greek translators of EEC informative discourses were found to add markers of evaluative texture in creating their target texts, with the overall result of making the Greek versions seem more argumentative. A 20,300 word sample of translated articles in the Greek press was contrasted with the source versions in the English press with respect to the use of contrastive devices. It was found that Greek translators typically intervened where there were implicit contrastive relationships in the source texts so as to make these explicit in the target texts. The explanations advanced for such intervention are, firstly, that the translators were catering for the Greek readership, which is inclined to take up such social roles as those of denier and detractor (there were added evaluative and intensifying elements in the target version supporting this idea), and secondly, that the translators were following a tendency of Greek text producers to present an oppositional view of the world which gives rise to a stronger version of any particular ideological stance found in the source text. In this case, too, the overall result is to make the Greek text seem more argumentative than the source text.

Sidiropoulou relates her results on the explicitation of cause-and-effect relationships in news reporting to an overt interest of the Greek readership in reasoning which, in its turn, can be accounted for in terms of the acceptance of the role of detractor/denier. She argues that, since Greek readers are more or less reluctant to accept the validity of what is being reported, they need explicit reasoning about cause and effect, at least at points where the author is making estimations, comments and evaluations rather than simply supplying information.

Although the research corpus regards translation, the results seem to have clear implications for the training of interpreters (cf. Renfer 1992). Making trainee English-Greek interpreters aware that their Greek listeners are likely to expect more explicitation of cohesive links than English listeners should help them to 1) avoid interference from English, 2) anticipate the sort of text cohesion that each source language text is likely to offer (Kalina 1992:254), and possibly also 3) use the ability to interpret relationships between parts of texts as a device for text condensing (Dam 1993:297).

3. Discourse Analysis and Dialogue Interpreting - Helen Tebble, Deakin University, Melbourne

As an applied linguist working in a university-level school for interpreting in Australia, Helen Tebble has been able to contribute to the development of a theory of dialogue interpreting. The interpreting she has focussed on - known also as community interpreting, liaison interpreting and three-cornered situation interpreting - is that of consultations between a professional, an interpreter, and a client or patient. The community domains involved are health, the law, education, welfare and the bureaucracies; and dialogue interpreters - and therefore also students preparing for the job - need to be familiar with the registers of all these domains. Since the perspective on the problem is linguistic, the starting point must be recognition of the fact that the study of languages for specific purposes and the work on the discourse of the professions has not yet gone far enough to offer descriptions or models of all these different types of consultation. Given the absence of sufficient monolingual descriptions of these consultations, let alone bilingual ones, Helen Tebble has developed a prototype model, that is to say, a generalized professional consultation (Tebble 1991, 1993), which, although needing further empirical support, seems to hold for the data analysed so far. To do this she has examined real interpreted consultations and role-plays. The model she has created has been given to interpreter trainees, and has been seen to help them make their way through the various parts of the structure of the consultation they are enacting in role-plays, activating proper expectations about the function of each new element, and weighing the amount of energy to give to each part according to its importance in the overall structure.

Working within genre theory, and in Australia where systemic functional linguistics has had such a strong influence, Helen Tebble has followed the work of Halliday and Hasan (1985/1989) in outlining the contextual configuration for interpreted consultations. Her generalized contextual configuration for interpreted professional consultations across the domains of community interpreting is outlined as follows:

FIELD   Presenting with a problem that may need to be defined and for which a solution is required.

TENOR   Role Relationships - Hierarchical:

Professional:	Superordinate
Client/Patient:	Subordinate
Interpreter:	Independent

Social Distance   - Maximum

MODE   Constituted by two languages

The process of creating the discourse is via

- spoken medium
- written medium
- non-verbal communication

Channel   - phonic

- graphic
- signed

The field has to do with the nature of the social activity, its topics, goals and activities. In the case of the interpreted professional consultation it has to do with a client or patient presenting a para/professional with a problem that may need to be defined or at least for which a solution is required. Examples are seeking legal advice on the purchase of a house, or medical advice on an ailment, or advice on how to obtain welfare support.

The tenor has to do with the nature of the relationships of the people participating in the consultation (typically three), that is the institutional roles they play (e.g. a professional such as a solicitor, doctor, or social worker, the client or patient, and the interpreter). Tenor also has to do with the nature of the social distance between them. In professional consultations the role relationships will be hierarchical, with the professional being superordinate and the client being subordinate. The role of the interpreter will be independent. The social distance between all participants will be maximum if measured on a scale of maximum to minimum social distance.

The mode of discourse refers to the roles that both language and the channels of communication play in the context of the professional consultation. The discourse will be constituted in two languages, English (in the Australian context) and a community language. It will be created through the spoken medium, the written medium, and through non-verbal communication. The channels of communication will be phonic, graphic and where appropriate signed. The process of creating the text is between the professional and the client, between the interpreter and the professional and between the interpreter and the client. They will use the spoken medium mainly, but also the written medium for some purposes: e.g. the professional will typically create a written record of the consultation for his/her files, the interpreter may occasionally make notes as an aide memoire, the client may choose to make personal notes, and some written documents may be shared between the client and the professional but mediated through the spoken interpretation of the interpreter. Non-verbal communication between the client and the professional may not necessarily be understood unless it is interpreted, and non-verbal communication will provide feedback between professional and interpreter and client and interpreter.

The contextual configuration can be used to predict the obligatory and optional elements of the structure of the discourse, their sequence, and their iterative nature. The basic stages of a prototypical interpreted professional consultation are Greetings (G), Introductions (IN), Stating/Eliciting Problem (SP), Ascertaining Facts (AF), Diagnosing Facts (DF), Stating Resolution (SR), Client's Decision (CD), Clarifying Residual Matters (RM), Conclusion (C), Farewell (F).

These stages can be described as follows:

Greetings (G)	An obligatory stage which defines the start of the speech event and involves greetings between the interpreter and professional and the interpreter and client.
Introductions (IN)	An obligatory stage in which typically the interpreter introduces the client to the professional, but the professional may introduce him/herself first.

The stages of G and IN may be intermixed. It is at this stage that the interpreter can make clear to the other interlocutors his/her role concerning faithful, complete and confidential interpreting of what each speaker says.

Stating/Eliciting the Problem (SP)

An obligatory stage since, although the client may not always be able to state accurately the nature of the problem, he/she will at least proffer some reason for being there at the consultation. It may even be the professional who states the problem when the client or patient has been referred to him/her, or else the professional may ask for or elicit the reason for the consultation. This serves as the topic for the consultation, and its duration will vary.

Ascertaining the facts (AF) An obligatory stage which may have the longest duration of all stages, it involves the use of appropriate communication strategies on the part of the professional to establish all the relevant facts.

Diagnosis of Facts (DF) An optional stage since, although the diagnosis made by the professional is critical to the consultation, it is not necessarily spoken aloud.

Stating the Resolution (SR) An obligatory stage and a very important one which the interpreter must handle very well. It is at this point that the professional rises to the occasion and demonstrates his/her expertise. Having potentially identified the problem, analysed it and found a solution, he/she now announces it.

Client's Decision (CD) An optional stage, since the client may or may not need to make a decision after the professional has stated his/her judgment.

Clarifying any Residual Matters (RM)

The last opportunity the professional has of ensuring that all relevant information has been provided, it seems that this stage may be obligatory.

Conclusion (C) This obligatory stage marks the end of the contribution to the field of the consultation, and also offers the interpreter an opportunity to reassure both client and professional that confidentiality will be maintained.

Farewell (F)   An obligatory stage which marks the end of the consultation in terms of tenor and mode.

With the above stages of a prototypical interpreted professional consultation determined, Helen Tebble has been able to model the genre, proposing its structure potential. The conventions used are those proposed by Hasan (1985:64): indicating sequence of elements from left to right, ( ) indicating that the enclosed element is optional, < > indicating element(s) whose lexico-grammatical realisation may be interspersed with that of some other stages and [ ] to restrain the mobility of such elements; the capital letters indicate the stages of the consultation. The structure potential proposed for the genre of interpreted professional consultation is:

[<G IN>] SP AF (DF) SR (CD) [<RM C F>]

Greetings and Introductions may be interlinked as people are introduced to each other, but the sequence of the other elements is fixed up until after the optional Client's Decision, which is followed by three obligatory stages which may be intermixed or overlap.

Helen Tebble is now working on combining the above top-down approach, starting with the stages of the genre, inspired by Hasan (1978, Halliday & Hasan 1985/1989), with a bottom-up approach after Sinclair and Coulthard (1975), utilising a rank scale of discourse structures from "speech act" to "move" to "exchange" and up to "transaction". She says that, since each genre element, or stage in the generic structure potential, comprises at least one or a series of transactions (Tebble 1991, 1992), the genre element and finally the genre can represent the next two higher stages in a ranked scale of units comprising the discourse structure after the four taken from Sinclair and Coulthard. It is this integrated model that she plans to use to realise more detailed analyses of interpreted consultations in the future.

4. Cohesion in Political Speeches: Implications for Simultaneous Interpretation - Sandra Gallina, EU Interpreter, Brussels

The results achieved through the application of Halliday and Hasan's (1976)

systemic-functional approach to cohesion in some political speeches are shown by Sandra Gallina to cast light on the on-line process of simultaneous interpretation.

The systemic-functional model has dealt with the issue of text studies from two directions, reflecting complementary traits of textness: structure and texture. The property of structure can be seen illustrated in Helen Tebble's analysis of the generic structure of the professional consultation (see section 3 above). Sandra Gallina's focus is on texture, which is created in the text through cohesion, or the "relations of meaning that exist within the text and that define it as a text" (Halliday and Hasan 1976:6). The fundamental principle is that of a tie, i.e. "one occurrence of a pair of related items", whose salient feature is directionality. The relationship between two elements may be either anaphoric or cataphoric, depending on whether the presupposed item precedes or follows the presupposing one. The two elements may be found in immediately adjoining sentences (immediate tie) or in sentences that are far removed (remote tie), and in this latter instance even through some other intermediate cohesive item (mediated tie), thus leading to ties that are both remote and mediated.

Since text cohesion is basically texture created through ties that link sentences together, the study of oral texts requires a decision about "sentencehood" which, rather than being based on punctuation, involves the division of a text into syntactic units following criteria such as completeness, continuity and intonation.

In her study of the speeches delivered by UK and Italian Members of the European Parliament between September 1985 and January 1986, Sandra Gallina analysed cohesive resources grouping them into four types: reference, substitution (by a substitution item, or by zero, which is ellipsis), conjunctions and lexical cohesion. Reference designates the property that some items display in making reference to "something else" for their interpretation. It fosters continuity in meaning either anaphorically or cataphorically and can be classified as "personal" (mainly realized by pronouns and possessive adjectives), "demonstrative" (realized by demonstrative pronouns and adjectives, the definite article, and the demonstrative adverbs *here, there, now* and *then*), and "comparative" (realized by comparative adjectives and other words of comparison such as *similar, different, more* and *less*). While reference is a relation at the semantic level, through which meanings are retrieved, substitution and ellipsis are mainly relations at the lexicogrammatical level, through which wordings are retrieved. Conjunction is not a 'search instruction' as reference, substitution and ellipsis are. The conjunctive item, through its specific meaning, indicates how what follows is systematically related to what has gone before, whether additively, adversatively, temporally or by some sort of cause relation (see Sidiropoulou's study, 2 above). Lexical cohesion is the tie created in a text when a second word (e.g. the same word repeated, a synonym or a hyperonym) is used to refer to the same referent as an earlier word (reiteration), or the tie created through the association of words that regularly co-occur, such as *law, draft, abrogate, pass* (collocation).

The study showed the peculiar type of referential cohesion the corpus of speeches possessed. Apart from the total absence of instances of possessives as Heads, there was a very low number of "mixed" personal reference items, i.e. where text receivers were included. Instances of ellipsis were negligible. Albeit limited in number, conjunction was significant in that it gave a clue to higher level conceptual structures. While additives followed by causal ties prevailed in the Italian speeches, causal conjunction followed by adversatives prevailed in the English speeches. Temporal conjunctive ties were very limited.

Lexical cohesion was the most important type of cohesion displayed by these texts - both the Italian and the English - and the lexical density created through nominalisations contributed considerably to this type of cohesion.

Sandra Gallina found the different density of cohesive resources within the texts she examined, and between different texts, to be the outcome of two different phenomena: progression and focalization. She describes focalization as rhetorical underlining to ensure that a topic does not go by too fast and finds it to be produced by the insertion of short sentences in an environment of long ones. As far as cohesion is concerned, she finds the effect of focalization to be most striking when remote ties are included in an environment of immediate ones or the number of ties goes up unexpectedly. Progression, on the other hand, is described in her study as concerning stretches of text where the receiver is led onwards from one segment to another. She finds that in sections of text characterised by progression the absence of rhetorical devices is matched by a paucity of cohesive ties, and she considers this situation a corollary to the introduction of ever new elements or predicates. Non-progression, however, may or may not correspond with the phenomenon of focalization as described above, since non-progression may simply be a limited phenomenon of holding up the receiver's attention to allow for "semantic satiation" to occur, for example by means of a paraphrase of a previous stretch of text. In the corpus of political speeches analysed, the highest number of cohesive ties were found to occur in environments of paraphrases of previous stretches of text.

Sandra Gallina suggests that a study combining a typology of speeches in terms of cohesive ties with Gile's effort models (1988) might reveal a link between difficulties experienced by interpreters and differences in cohesion. She believes that simultaneous interpretation is inevitably affected to an extreme degree by the type and density of cohesion displayed in the speeches to be interpreted.

5. Discourse Analysis and Interpreting - Anna-Riitta Vuorikoski, University of Tampere

Anna-Riitta Vuorikoski's approach to the analysis of simultaneous interpretation texts is inspired by ideas developed within computational linguistics and Natural Language Generation. In particular, she makes use of Robert Dale's (1993) definition of a message as "a structure at an intermediate representational level that records the information that is selected to go into an utterance" as an underlying structure for the comparison of the source text with the text the interpreter produces.

The texts interpreters receive for interpreting are spoken discourse, and often they have no advance information of what will be said. Being familiar with the recurrent structures and the syntax of the language they are processing, interpreters develop strategies and tactics for anticipating the structure of the incoming message and, on the basis of their anticipations, create a hypothesis of a plan and a goal for the message they must generate in the target language. Because of this, Anna-Riitta Vuorikoski sees interpreters as being constantly faced with the same problems enumerated by Dale for Natural Language Generation:

1. Deciding how much to say and what not to say
2. Designing text structure
3. Problems in carrying out a detailed text plan once built.

In her own analysis of the interpreter's rendering of an original English text into Finnish, Vuorikoski studies the extent to which the interpreter, in text planning, can be seen to make strategic and tactical decisions of the types listed by Dale: Strategic decisions - 1) the purpose of an utterance, 2) the basic propositional material to be conveyed, 3) the relative importance of the elements in that material; Tactical decisions - 1) the selection of lexical items, 2) the selection of syntactic constructions, and in speech 3) the use of intonation and stress. Her main focus is on the rhetorical structure and the cohesive elements of the discourse sample, which consisted in a recorded version of a speech given by Dr. Eileen Mayers Pasztor at a Seminar on Foster Care held in October 1992, and of the recorded version of the simultaneous interpretation of that speech into Finnish. In her analysis of these spoken texts she found Halliday's (1987) description of the characteristics of spoken language as opposed to written very revealing: the type of complexity these texts displayed consisted in the grammatical intricacy of the sentences or "clause complexes", rather than lexical density (which characterises written texts). Halliday (1987:66-7) says that "The complexity of spoken language is in its flow, the dynamic mobility whereby each figure provides a context for the next one, not only defining its point of departure but also setting the conventions by reference to which it is to be interpreted."

First the whole speech was analysed in order to see what the overall goal of the message was. The next step was to analyse the strategy chosen by the speaker, and the tactical solutions used by the speaker to achieve her goal. The following step was to segment the text into meaning units, applying the principle presented by Halliday (1985:274-288) according to which tone groups (units of intonation) organize spoken discourse into information units. In her presentation of the texts Vuorikoski gives them a layout which reflects their orality, their processual nature, their flow, and the way the listener/interpreter receives them, unit by unit. Intonation was seen to be such an important part of the organization of the information of the text that the suggestion that emerges is that intonation must be a basic part of the training of an interpreter. Here is a sample from the beginning of the speech in the layout proposed:

first of all
  we think
      it is
      important
      to say
      that   <u>family foster care</u> / is essential //

               there always will be
                <u>children/</u>

> who must be separated
> from their <u>parents</u>

and
  how
  important
  it is
      that   we have <u>families</u>
                <u>foster families</u> //
                not institutions for children but
      that   we have / <u>foster families</u> /
                available for the <u>children</u>
                who need them

Vuorikoski found that the strategic decision by the interpreter regarding text planning seemed to be to stay as close as possible to the speaker's structures, probably in order to keep up with the speaker's speed. This strategy, combined with unclear deixis in the source text, has caused some difficulties. The interpreter used repetition of lexical items in the same way as the original speaker, while trying to find the natural collocations and idiomatic expressions in the Finnish language.

    This study is only a beginning attempt at using discourse analysis to see how spoken messages are constructed in the simultaneous interpretation context.

6. Linguistics and interpreting - Christopher Taylor, University of Trieste

Christopher Taylor takes Neubert and Shreve's (1992) concept of "virtual translation" as the starting point for consideration of the impact of linguistics on translation and by extension on interpreting. Where ST is source text, VT is virtual translation, and TT is target text, the model can be stated as: ST > VT > TT. The VT is "a composite of the possible relations between a source text and a range of potential target texts"(p. 14). Taylor believes that in interpreting the virtual text stands as the final one, so he takes a further look at the nature of the virtual text. Neubert and Shreve, who see the mental representation of a virtual translation as a decision-making process, say that de Beaugrande and Dressler's seven parameters are the ones that determine the textual character of a virtual translation as it evolves, and that all of these owe something to linguistics and related disciplines: 1. intentionality (pragmatic: speech acts, illocutionary force), 2. acceptability (style, register), 3. situationality (context of situation), 4. informativity (information structure: theme/rheme, given/new), 5. coherence (logical relations), 6. cohesion (see Halliday and Hasan 1976), 7. intertextuality (genre). Neubert and Shreve see translation studies as related to seven partial theories or approaches: critical, practical, linguistic, text linguistic, socio-cultural, computational and psycholinguistic. In their consideration of the linguistic they say that all source/target differences that occur in translation are traceable to differences in the two language systems, and that, "from this point of view translation studies is nothing but an extension of systemic linguistics". Taylor in fact relates the idea of "virtual translation" to the model proposed by Halliday (1992) for searching for translation equivalences in the target language following the increasing order of the rank scale: morpheme-word group-clause-sentence and then beyond the grammatical ranks into the textual level and to questions of external context.

7. Theme as the interpreter's path indicator through the unfolding text - Carol Taylor Torsello, University of Trieste

In this study a speech given by Bill Clinton during the presidential campaign, and five translations performed by professional simultaneous interpreters, are analysed. The linguistic theory that is most particularly applied and tested in this analysis is indicated by two expressions in the title: "the unfolding text", which is an expression indicative of a dynamic perspective in text linguistics, and "theme", which derives from Prague linguistics and indicates the division of the clause as a message into two parts - a Theme, the starting point of the message, what the speaker or writer is on about, and a Rheme, its development. The dynamic perspective in text linguistics (see, e.g., Martin 1985, Bateman 1989, O'Donnell 1990, Ravelli 1995), which has only begun its development in recent years alongside the more widely practised and firmly established synoptic perspective, would seem to have much to offer for a greater understanding of the mechanisms of simultaneous interpretation and for the promotion of these mechanisms in student interpreters. In a dynamic perspective the syntagmatic ordering of language in text is seen as a flow, or as the unfolding of the text piece by piece, constituent by constituent, with each new constituent contributing to a process of disambiguation of the total meaning. Each new constituent also delimits the range of possible next occurrences, and skews probabilites in one direction rather than in another for how the syntagmatic structure will be completed.

Several studies (e.g. Berry 1992, Ravelli 1995) indicate that, particularly when the text is seen dynamically, as an ongoing process, rather than synoptically, as a finished product, the element which is thematic (Theme in the Theme/Rheme structure), used by the speaker as the starting point for each new message as she/he builds up the text, can serve the hearer as a path indicator to the direction the discourse is taking. Indeed, a recent study by Whittaker (1990) on reading as cognitive processing suggests that writers use Theme to manipulate the reader's reception of the message, indicating the path that is to be followed through the text. Textual studies carried out by Fries (1995) indicate that "Theme functions as an orienter to the message" and that "it orients the listener/reader to the message that is about to be perceived and provides a framework for the interpretation of that message". This implies that, along with the special attention accorded new information, which normally receives end focus, there should also be specific attention paid to the beginnings of sentences and of paratactically linked clauses where, at least in English (but probably also in most European languages), the thematic elements are located. Thematic structuring exists as a type of text-making device. It is a way of organizing the messages that make up a text so that they cohere properly as a text, with each message building upon the previous ones and pointing towards the ones that will follow. Theme is the element which serves as the point of departure of the message (Halliday 1985:38), "the peg on which the message is to hang" (Halliday 1989:73) and functions as a linker by "establishing an anchor point for the clause" (McGregor 1990:31). It is an important part of the message "since it is here that the speaker announces his intentions" (Halliday 1989:73). In English an element of the clause is signalled as thematic by its position at the beginning of the clause (Halliday 1985:38). In a declarative the unmarked theme is the Subject, and if another element (e.g, an Adjunct) is placed at the beginning it constitutes a marked Theme. In Halliday's description of Theme, multiple themes are possible, with textual ("yet", "and", "secondly") and modal ("probably", "perhaps", "fortunately") Themes preceding the constituent of clause structure which functions as topical Theme (in the unmarked case the Subject in declaratives), but the thematic element ends with the topical Theme, and whatever follows this is part of the Rheme. Recently, however, on the basis of the analysis of theme structures in texts, Berry (1992), Matthiessen (1992) and Ravelli (1995) suggest that the boundary of Theme in English needs to be broadened to include the Subject even when this is not topical Theme, so long as it is in pre-verb position. In the study of the Clinton speech and its interpretations this suggestion has been followed and all pre-verb elements have been considered thematic. The analysis, carried out from a dynamic perspective, seems to show that the thematic structure of the text functions in a way that corroborates that theoretical and methodological choice. But to see this it is necessary to consider at least a small portion of the text. Transcriptions of the text and of the interpreters' versions of it are from De Feo (1992-3:118-142). Here sentences have been numbered for ease of reference, and the thematic portion of each sentence has been underlined, while marked themes have also been given bold print. Clinton's speech begins as follows:

> 1. Perhaps **once in a generation,** history presents us with a moment of monumental importance. 2. **In the aftermath of World War I,** our country chose to retreat from the world, with tragic consequences. 3. **After World War II,** we chose instead to lead the world and take responsibility for shaping the post-war era. 4. I am literally a child of the Cold War, born as it was just beginning. 5. My parents' generation wanted nothing more than to return from a world war to the joys of work and home and family. 6. Yet it was no ordinary moment and history would not let them rest. 7. **Overnight,** an expansionist Soviet Union summoned them into a new struggle. 8. **Fortunately,** America had farsighted and courageous leaders like Harry Truman and George Marshall, who recognized the gravity of the moment and roused our battle-weary nation to the challenge. 9. **Under their leadership,** we helped Europe and Japan rebuild their economies, organized a great military coalition of free nations, and defended our democratic principles against yet another totalitarian threat. 10. **Now, we** face our own moment of great change and enormous opportunity. 11. The end of the Cold War and the callapse of the Soviet empire pose an unprecedented opportunity to make our future more prosperous and secure. 12. It reminds us, too, of our duty to prevent the tragedies of the 20th Century - cataclysmic wars and the fear of nuclear annihilation - from recurring in the 21st Century. 13. **Yet at the very moment America's ideas have triumphed and the whole world is rushing to embrace our way of life,** our own leaders have been standing still at home and abroad.

"Thematic" to the text, in the widest, non-structural sense, is the situation that is the speaker's point of departure for his message: in this case, Bill Clinton, as Democratic candidate for the American presidency against the Republican incumbent George Bush, is speaking before the Foreign Policy Association of New York. The listeners can be expected to be interested in hearing what Clinton's foreign policy program is. The speaker will want to show that he has clear ideas in this regard and that what he plans to do is better than what the Republican administrations, both Bush's and Reagan's, have done. This basic situation also functions as the beginning of the interpreter's path through the text.

The first sentence begins with the modal theme, *perhaps*, thus bringing the speaker into the text as evaluator of the possibility/probability of the statement he is about to make. The topical theme, *once in a generation*, being marked, can be expected to be particularly important as a path indicator, but its interpretation is further clarified by the subject history. The marked themes of sentences 2 and 3, *In the aftermath of World War I* and *After World War II*, are interpretable, in the light of the path set up, as two instances of moments of monumental importance which occur once in a generation, and the subjects *our country* and *we* indicate that the comparison between them will regard the political behaviour of the U.S. in those two circumstances. That the behaviour involved is different is clear to the interpreters who, four out of five, add a textual thematic element to sentence 3, the variative conjunctive *invece* (instead).

The theme *I* in sentence 4, and the possessive element of the theme of 5 (*my parents'*), again bring in the speaker's presence with a personal touch, but the path set up in the previous sentences indeed continues, as we see in *generation* as the head of the noun phrase thematized in 5. Two of the interpreters, however, make the subject of 5 *i miei genitori* (my parents), perhaps on the mistaken understanding that the personal path set up by the previous theme was to continue, rather than the historical information path set up by the themes of 1, 2 and 3.

The textual Theme of the first clause of sentence 6, *yet*, is of the type that relates what has gone before, and has set up expectations of one type, to something following which does not fulfil these expectations. At this point in the text it can be interpreted as "Despite Bill Clinton's parents' generations' desire for the private joys of peace time". The meaning (something like "the time and situation faced by the generation of Clinton's parents after World War II") only becomes clear as the Rheme unfolds. One of the interpreters who did not translate *yet* at the beginning of the sentence made the mistake of thinking that the contrast was between the two parts of sentence 6, a contrast which this interpreter expressed with *però* ("...*però la storia*..."). Of course in the original version the whole paratactic clause complex falls within the scope of *yet* and thus is in contrast with the expectations set up previously. History in this text denotes the history of public, international events and contrasts with private joys and desires.

The path of historical events indicates to the interpreter that *overnight* is to be taken in the generic sense of "suddenly", and one of the interpreters translates it very appropriately as *da un giorno all'altro*, while others leave it out. The problem to be faced by the generation of the speaker's parents is introduced in the Subject of 7, *the expansionist Soviet Union*, where the negatively marked adjective *expansionist* makes the speaker's attitude very clear.

The modal theme of 8, *Fortunately*, clearly marks a shift in attitude from negative to positive. This contrast in attitude is underlined by one of the interpreters with the addition of the contrastive conjunctive *Però* (*However*) as textual theme. *America*, as unmarked topical theme, sets the path for a positive situation in the U.S., allowing a positive reaction to the Soviet challenge.

The marked Theme of 9 brings forward the leaders mentioned in the Rheme of 8, and the subject of 9 (*we*) has the same referent as *America* in 8.

With the marked topical theme of sentence 10, the temporal deictic *now*, pointing to the discourse time, and no longer to the past as had previous temporal Themes, there is a shift from recent history as topic to the present. Once the discourse time, the speaker's present, has become marked Theme, the meaning of the Subject *we* is delimited: it is no longer the America of the past but now becomes Clinton, his audience, and their fellow Americans. The topical Theme of 11 is an expression of the moment of great change and enormous opportunity represented by the discourse time. *It* as Theme of 12 must be filled out with its meaning as the Rheme unfolds: "the present situation, with the Cold War over and the Soviet empire collapsed".

Yet, as textual Theme of 13 signalling a contrast with the expectations set up by the previous text, can be interpreted as "Despite the present moment of change, the U.S.'s opportunity to make things better, and its duty to prevent the recurrence of the wars and fear of nuclear annihilation that were the tragedies of this century". One interpreter mistakenly translates this with the dismissive conjunctive *Comunque* (*Anyway*), but clearly this is not the meaning, and what follows is too important simply to be dismissed by the speaker. The long topical Theme of 13 simply reiterates the expectations from the previous text that will not be fulfilled by what will follow in the Rheme. This was difficult to translate and one of the interpreters, who had clearly understood its function, simply said *ora* (*now*). The subject, *our own leaders*, refers to President Bush and the other Republicans in power at the time of discourse. But two of the interpreters did not properly follow the path indicated by thematic Now in 10 and turned these into leaders of the past by using the past tense for the verb, or leaders of too long a time by using the *passato prossimo* tense and adding *sempre* (always).

The analysis shows that theme does seem to serve as path indicator. It also shows that even experienced interpreters sometimes fail to follow the path indicated by theme. These cases of local difficulty often occur where the interpreters do not include thematic material in their own texts. It can also be seen, in the more extensive analysis, that the interpreters who are best at following the path through the whole text also seem to be those who most consistently maintain the thematic material of the original in the thematic portion of their own sentences. The implications for interpreter training would seem to be: 1) that the need for situation as pre-theme should be respected; 2) that a dynamic perspective should be brought into text study from the early stages, perhaps by using audio texts with pauses inserted for testing expectations, or presenting text portions on a computer monitor or overhead projector with the previous text disappearing as a new chunk appears, and the following text appearing only after expectations have been expressed; 3) that the proper chunking for such presentations is the thematic portion of a sentence followed, on command, by the rhematic portion.

8. Conclusion

The studies included under the heading *Linguistics, Discourse Analysis and Interpretation* have confirmed what was said in the "Introduction" to this chapter about the type of linguistics that is useful to interpretation. In fact, the references have all been to functional rather than formal schools. Also, the interest has clearly been in authentic texts and in text and discourse analysis. It is clear that there is much to be done in interpretation studies using the tools offered by linguistics and focussing more closely on spoken texts, on the actual interpretation process, and on the products of this process.

On Media and Court Interpreting

David Snelling, *SSLMIT, Trieste* (Convenor)
Bodil Martinsen, *Aarhus Business School*
Akira Mizuno, *NHK Information Network, Tokyo*
Maria Chiara Russo, *SSLMIT*
Birgit Strolz, *University of Vienna*
Marco Uckmar, *SSLMIT*
Cecilia Wadensjö, *University of Linköping*

1. Introduction

The first question to arise, prompted by a colleague, is, surely, why two apparently disparate subjects are to be dealt with in the same session. I will attempt to answer the question whether court and media interpreting really are such strange bedfellows. Certainly, neither corresponds to the traditional view of conference interpreting, which is why, presumably, they are being discussed together in a separate session to conference interpreting.

My own views of the interpreter's role are familiar. I belong to the minimalist school, maintaining that the interpreter has best done his job when his presence has been barely noticed. Cromwell's definition of the execution of Charles I as "a cruel necessity" reflects to my mind the attitude of those who at a conference are forced to resort to the services of an interpreter and even more so when the event concerned does not see purely verbal communication playing a dominant role. I wish, therefore, to entitle the session "My cue to speak", and invite colleagues to seek an answer to the questions - when, how much and how little the media or court interpreter is required to intervene, and to investigate the circumstances determining the range and intensity of his intervention.

K. Reiss in addition to her three well-known categories of texts for translation purposes - *Inhaltsbetönte, Effektbetönte* and *Stilbetönte* - also proposes a separate category in which the written or spoken text is ancillary to the total or main purpose of the communication exercise - subtitles of films, texts of musicals etc. This would seem to be the dominant feature of interpretation in the two fields under discussion - that in neither case is the purely verbal message the dominating element and that in both cases the verbal message is at the service of a vaster and more deeply involving communicative purpose.

2. Film interpreting: challenges and constraints of a semiotic practice
Mariachiara Russo, SSLMIT, University of Trieste

2.1 *Introduction*

The interpreter of films, especially of silent and fiction movies, is called upon to translate a type of language with a high symbolic and emotional content. Should he/she be the narrating *offstage* voice or a dubber, or rather an improvised actor? Should he try to select meaningful information or repeat whatever is heard at breakneck speed? In other words, which approach ought to prevail: the *minimalist, self-effacing* or the *expressive, interpretative*? Again, how is an interpreter to relate to a film, namely a work of art, without jeopardizing the delicate balance among its various components: music, image, acting, poetry, silence...These are all moot points, challenging, open questions introducing a debate about film interpreting today.

From a theoretical and conceptual perspective, I think that these represent different complementary levels that cut across and structure a triangular problem area: the *first angle of the triangle*, apparently the most prominent, indicates the linguistic solutions to the source language (SL), the *second angle* indicates the supersign 'film' and the *third angle* the interpreter himself (his competence, behaviour, creativity, emotions, sensitivity, etc.). The interaction between these three levels produces the successful performance.

The starting point in facing this challenge is considering the purpose of this multifaceted task, i.e. *enhancing comprehension and doing justice to the film* as a whole, as professional experience in different types of film festivals has revealed. This implies that (Cattrysse, 1992) film translating entails not a simple cross-linguistic task, but an intertextual, semiotic practice.

2.2 Film types and the interpreter's role

Against this backdrop, the role of the interpreter and his emotional participation could be seen as less of an issue because his performance is not the only factor that determines the comprehension and appreciation of a film, since the verbal component is not all there is to it. The supersign "film", indeed, is the synergic outcome of directing, staging, acting, setting, costume, lighting, photography, pictorial representations, music, just to name the main surface features. This proposition must, of course, be duly contextualized since there is a wide range of film types and the performance required of an interpreter varies accordingly.

Silent films. Reiss' classification applied to interpretation (Snelling, 1989) would also appear to lend itself to film classification. In describing this kind of film, I would rename the *Effektbetönte* category *Bildbetönte*, as the image already speaks mainly for itself. The word in the form of written captions is reduced to a minimum and is almost redundant because the musical accompaniment is also extremely expressive. The interpreter is therefore expected to be equally concise and self-effacing just to supplement the esthetic/musical medium. The main challenge of such films lies in the use of archaisms, colloquial expressions, odd syntactic constructions, decontextualized single words, unexpected handwritten messages/letters or one-frame long texts preparing the background for the subsequent scenes.

The second category contains *documentary films* or *Inhaltsbetönte* "texts", where the word is highly informative and densely articulated. The greater his/her experience and knowledge of technical terms, the better the interpreter who must quickly reproduce the highly specialized film content which is invariably read. Here the main challenge lies in the 'world knowledge' implied by this genre, but also in the unremitting and rapid SL flow typical of the written text.

The third category contains *fiction* films (detective, comic, noir, horror, etc.) in two variants: with subtitles or with dialogue. These are typically *Form or Stylbetönte* films. The dialogue is absolutely instrumental to the comprehension of the plot, the humor, the coups de théâtre, the implications, the presuppositions, etc. (this holds true also for subtitles as they already constitute a 25-50% reduction of the original information - cf. Ivarsson, in Brondeel 1994:28). Therefore *synchronism* between the scene and the related sentences becomes of paramount importance, greater than the completeness of the original message (see also Götz & Herbst, in Niemeier 1991:148:

"Translation ought to be more plot-oriented than verbally oriented."). Fiction films are extremely challenging. They are mainly expressed in colloquial language, thus favouring the interpreter, but could also be rich in jargon taken from all walks of life. Furthermore, the difficulties associated with sound films depend on the peculiarities of the dialogues or subtitles. For instance, films with rapid dialogues or quick and complex passages of narration compel the interpreter to speak at a dizzy speed often reaching his/her physical limits of phonation or intelligibility. A useful strategy is to practice in order to speed up one's own articulatory and verbalization ability and prepare the dialogue list thoroughly beforehand, and then try to interpret the film without reading/sight translating the script, but only reacting to the actual screening so as to speak more spontaneously. The successful rendition of this kind of film implies the reproduction of an equivalent dynamic effect on the target language viewers. But considering the impact of variables such as time constraints or the overlapping of voices, it is difficult to strike a balance between what needs to be said and how to say it: here perhaps lies the much-advocated divide between the constituent and the redundant informative channels.

2.3 Relevant and redundant information

In selecting the relevant information the pattern suggested by Brondeel (1994:29) in subtitling films could be followed. This is based on equivalence at three levels - informative, semantic and communicative- to which another two could be added, namely style and mental associations created by words of which the interpreter should be aware (see also Niemeier, 1991).

Turning now to the redundant channel of information in fiction films which could be suppressed under time pressure, the following elements could be included: (1) utterances pronounced by marginal characters; (2) paradigmatic elements (for example, the same ideas repeated literally or expressed differently); (3) connotative items, such as features concerning the characters' way of speaking and (4) musical information (for instance, songs) that is best left untranslated, let alone sung over the original. The definition of point (3) is not always so clearcut; for instance, broken English, an indication of a low social background or a foreign or strong regional accent, are connotative rather than denotative. Yet they could be both, as in the amusing and compelling *Educating Rita* by Lewis Gilbert, where the educating process the hairdresser Rita undergoes is remarkably highlighted by her way of speaking. What is an interpreter expected to do? Time constraints and speed may well force him to opt for a neutral language register even if it implies a loss of information. However, the degree of redundancy and relevance of the informative channels may also be determined also by another important communicative factor: the public's expectations and feedback.

2.4 *Audience types and the interpreter's performance*

The adequacy of the viewers' response is a remarkable external point of reference for the interpreter's strategy. The term "viewers" is used as a blanket word because the target is different, and so is the translation or the style required. The audience can be divided into three categories:

(1)   the general public, which demands participation and emotional involvement expressed through the voice;
(2)   the jury, which expects a minimalist approach, the least possible interference by the interpreter in order to assess the film as a whole and
(3)   critics, journalists and film buffs who often appreciate a minimalist approach too, but who require a faithful, learned and even witty interpretation to be able to catch the in-jokes or cross references to other films and characters.

However, like the viewer, the interpreter is one pole of communication in his own right, which implies that his performance, although to a lesser extent because of his professional role, is bound to respond to the stimuli of the global sign "film". So much so that to his own surprise he might skip or change a passage, shift or stress an emphasis for sheer pragmatic purposes or as an emotional response.

2.5 *Creativity*

A dilemma remains unsolved. An interpreter is not an actor and his performance could be jeopardized by excessive identification. Yet his participation inevitably comes into play (because he likes the story or relates to the characters and by profession, see Kaufmann 1993, he is used to identifying himself with whomever he is interpreting; indeed he always speaks in the first person). So in the final analysis, given the challenges and constraints of this semiotic practice related to the film type, the performance expected from the interpreter and the need to perform certain "text" operations (i.e. the elimination of redundant informative channels), is there room for the interpreter's own creativity in translating such a peculiar form of communication as a film?

3. Broadcast interpreting in Japan. Some theoretical and practical aspects
Akira Mizuno, Bilingual Centre, NHK Information Network, Tokyo

Broadcast interpreting (or *media interpreting*) has become prominent in recent years. Daly (1985) reports on the Eurikon experiment, designed to test the potential appeal of the European Program for satellite television, and Gambier (1994) notes that simultaneous interpreting of voice-over type was extensively used in some European countries during the Gulf War. Kurz (1990) gives a succinct account of media interpreting in Europe. Japan, on the other hand, may be unique in that dozens of news programs that are produced in various countries are being broadcast every day with Japanese translation. More than 200 interpreters are engaged in broadcast interpreting. In NHK (Japanese Public Broadcasting Corporation) alone, about 80 interpreters are working every day as broadcast interpreters, of which English-Japanese interpreters account for approximately 80% (Kisa, 1993). Almost all the programs are recorded on VCR before interpreters prepare their translation. The preparation time for each interpreter ranges from 60 to 90 minutes for about 7 minutes of news broadcast. Live simultaneous interpretation has been used on such occasions as the Gulf War, the Tienanmen Square incident, the coup attempt in Russia, the State of the Union address by the US President, and important press conferences and interviews.

Broadcast interpreters are required to:

1) make their translation aurally intelligible;
2) observe the broadcasting guidelines on speech;
3) finish their translation no later than the original broadcast or at least without lagging too far behind the original;
4) synchronize each of the speech segments in the source language and their translation (not a lipsynch as in dubbing but a loose correspondence);
5) have a voice quality, intonation, and pronunciation close or nearly equivalent to the broadcast standard.

Among these requirements, aural intelligibility or listenability of the utterance of interpreters is considered to be the most important. Because, as Ivor York (1987) puts it, "the newspaper reader can always return to the printed sentence. If necessary he can pore over a dictionary. But words once uttered on television (or radio, of course,) are beyond recall".

One of the ways to enhance the intelligibility of broadcast interpretation in Japanese is to replace *kango* (words and compound words of Chinese origin which more often than not have homonyms) with *wago* (words that are intrinsically Japanese) or rephrase them by using non-confusing words as far as the situation permits.

Some words that are used without further explanation in the source language (SL) must be translated with explanation in the target language (TL). (For example; "Medicare, the program to provide medical care for the elderly".) This procedure of "compensatory translation" becomes necessary because Japanese TV audiences belong to a different socio-cultural context from those of the SL.

In addition to these 'swelling factors' (Setton 1993b) in translation, Japanese broadcast interpreters have to deal with the fast speech tempo of newscasters (anchorpersons, presenters and reporters) and the so-called 'rapid-fire editing', in which speakers alternate very rapidly in the original news item.

Given these constraints, the interpreters, in order to make their translation shorter, must endeavour to

1)   choose shorter TL words than the corresponding SL words;
2)   render redundant expressions in the SL into concise language in the TL;
3)   omit some elements that are essential in the SL in terms of syntax and language conventions but unnecessary in the TL.

When these procedures are not enough to produce aurally intelligible and synchronised interpretation, interpreters have to resort to 'selective reductions' (Hatim and Mason, 1990) of the SL. The criteria for selective reduction may be found in the concept of relevance proposed by Sperber and Wilson (1988). In a paper on subtitle reductions, Kovacic (1994) aptly explains that relevance theory provides a valuable explanatory framework that will account for cases of subtitling reductions. Principles of relevance can also be able to provide a criterion for selective reductions and ellipsis in broadcast interpretation.

Lastly, the voice factor represents another challenge for broadcast interpreters, because "the audience at home is used to television newsreaders and commentators with very good voices, well trained in the fluent delivery of a text and does not understand or appreciate the very different demands made of the interpreter" (Kurz 1990). Thus, broadcast interpreters are required to improve their delivery to near broadcast standards while not losing "the advantages of interpreting spontaneity" (Daly 1985).

Broadcast interpreting in Japan has established itself as a new field of interpreting, providing ample opportunity and an alternative career path for both would-be interpreters and professional interpreters. As broadcast interpreting has much in common with conference interpretation and translation, much can be learned from Interpretation Research and Translation Studies. However, the fact that the audience of broadcast interpreting is the general public, i.e. people of different age groups and with diverse educational and professional backgrounds, and the peculiar constraints imposed on broadcast interpreters suggests that more extensive and interdisciplinary research efforts will be required.

4. Quality of media interpreting - a case study.
Birgit Strolz, University of Vienna

Most interpreters find media interpreting (MI) more stressful than other forms of simultaneous interpreting (SI). This is due to the fact that media interpreters often work under conditions which the International Association of Conference Interpreters (AIIC) would not accept for standard conference interpreting, such as :

- working in front of monitors and not at the site of communication - therefore lacking direct view of speaker and audience, a condition considered a serious disadvantage for the simultaneous interpreter,
- working in a studio instead of an isolated booth, often in the same room with moderators and technicians - thus being subject to all kinds of acoustic and visual inputs not required for information processing and potentially disturbing,
- working for an imaginary audience with no interaction, thus missing an important source of comprehension and knowledge

necessary for anticipation,
- often working for a very short time - thus lacking any possibility of "warming up" as is usual with the paraphernalia of housekeeping, welcomes and introductions usually preceding conference deliberations,
- lacking the possibility of building up a "communication community" between speaker and listener, as is the case in normal communication where interpreters can draw upon co- and context to constitute a relevant knowledge base by progressive activation of cognitive contents,
- knowing that under all circumstances the media interpreter is expected to deliver a formally impeccable product. His performance is judged by the audience against standards set by moderators for a different cognitive product than SI (monolingual, text-supported). The formal rhetorical aspect of the interpreter's discourse is of greater importance in MI than in other forms of SI. This has consequences for the interpreter's priorities as to what he is going to sacrifice when in trouble.
- Knowing that millions of people, amongst them colleagues and students, are listening, is an additional source of uneasiness and stress (Kurz 1990).

All these factors were present in two live interpretations of one and the same speech, broadcast by the media, one on TV and the other on the radio, on the occasion of the celebration of the 30th anniversary of the Austrian State Treaty (see Strolz 1992). A comparison of these two interpretations showed different strategies with consequences on the quality of MI. Clear differences appeared with regard to two parameters: 1. redundancy and 2. pause pattern.

4.1 *Redundancy*

Redundancy is a constituent of language and present in discourse on pragmatic and semantic levels. It can be either intentional or accidental. Intentional redundancy is a rhetorical device used by speakers when they repeat sentence elements or use paraphrases. Accidental redundancy is everything that comes in the form of involuntary repetitions due to false starts, mispronunciations, slips of the tongue, meaningless vocalisations while searching for an expression or preparing one's utterance (the famous "uh"). Various authors (Kirchhoff,

Déjean Le Féal, Shlesinger) consider this accidental redundancy a correlate of the interpreter's cognitive effort. It has an important function in spontaneous speech and is the reflexion of the dynamic interaction between thought and verbalisation, structuring the cognitive process and at the same time reducing the information load to a degree adequate to allow immediate understanding of oral communication.

There was a marked difference in the amount of accidental redundancy between the two interpretations studied.

> (1) Original: "We all have a shared interest in security"
> SI1: "Wir alle erkennen ein gemeinsames Interesse an Sicherheit".
> SI2: "Wir alle erkennen, das wir alle ein Interesse an Sicherheit haben".

The same idea is expressed once in a single translation segment, and once in two segments. Despite the fact that the second version is longer (11 words against 8), it requires less processing capacity, since the two translation segments in the second version are shorter than the one segment in interpretation 1. Since the interpreter can dismiss what has already been processed, his memory load in the second version is smaller than in the first.

The smaller the translation units, the lower the demand in processing capacity, but also the flatter the style. Using lots of subordinate clauses in a German text is not a sign of elegant language and may not constitute the appropriate register for a solemn political address like the one under study.

In German, denser style is more literate but requires more planning and storage effort and can easily lead to unfinished or ungrammatical sentences.

The only error of substance contained in the two interpretations studied happened to the interpreter with greater ambition for literacy, when he miscalculated his capacity reserves and got submerged in non-processed information.

Success in interpretation thus depends on a successful trade-off between language-specific processing requirements and interpreter-specific quality aspirations. With regard to redundancy, interpreters occasionally use a trick, transforming accidental redundancy into rhetorical redundancy.

> (2) Original: "Have we anything to learn from the success of our predecessors?"
> SI 1: "Können wir daraus etwas lernen ? Können wir aus dem Erfolg unserer Vorgänger etwas lernen?"

Because of early segmentation the interpreter had grammatically closed his German translation segment by adding "daraus", which prohibits him from bringing the following information "from the success of our predecessors" into the same sentence. So he transformed the clause into a new translation segment, repeating the idea of the preceding one to make it sound like a rhetorical confirmation of the two preceding elements. He thus found an elegant way of redressing a grammatical impasse due to an early start.

4.2 *Pause pattern*

SI literature (Déjean Le Féal, Gile, Shlesinger) is unanimous in acknowledging the importance of pauses of all kinds: hesitation pauses, syntagmatic and rhetorical pauses.

Interpreter 2 - whose interpretation is less stylish, with language register choice nearer to orality than literacy and segmentation into more numerous translation segments than Interpreter 1 - has a tendency to skip pauses by joining separate sentences without sound interruption, and often without even modifying her intonation or by transforming full stops into "and"s. This makes her sound rushed.

When listeners complain about interpreters speaking too fast, this impression is probably more often due to the absence of pauses at clause ends than to the actual articulation rate of the interpreter. Confronted with such complaints it would be worthwile for the simultaneous interpreter to try and modify his/her pause strategy, deliberately stopping at the end of a sentence or at least marking a change in intonation.

4.3 *Concluding remark*

Redundancy and pause patterns are individual speech characteristics influencing the quality of media interpretation. Both features can, to a certain extent, be controlled by the quality-conscious interpreter. Rhetorical redundancy can be transformed into intentional redundancy. Pause patterns respecting syntactical boundaries in intonation as well as in speech flow can help avoid the impression of hastiness and information overload, which easily raises doubts in the listener about the quality of interpretation.

5. Court Interpreting. Interlingual, intercultural and intersocial communication. Plans for a project.
Bodil Martinsen, Aarhus Business School, Faculty of Modern Languages

The following contribution deals with court interpreting in general and with my own project in this field in particular. From observing interpreters in Danish courts I know that there is a great need for improving the quality of court interpreting. This need concerns in particular the interpreter's understanding of his/her role and his/her mastery of legal terminology. This project, of which I shall here provide only a bare outline, deals with interpreting between Danish and French only, but it is hoped that its results will apply in general and that it may thus contribute to the improvement of court interpreting as such.

The court interpreter has to mediate communication between the court and the defendant or a witness who does not speak the language of the court. This communication can be characterized as an interlingual, intercultural and intersocial communication. That the communication is interlingual is obvious, as it takes place between interlocutors speaking two different languages. The intercultural nature of the communication is also evident from the fact that any language is used within and by a linguistic community that has its own culture. Sometimes, however, the two cultures involved differ immensely. Finally, the communication is intersocial because the defendant often belongs to a social class that differs greatly from that of his/her interlocutors.

The question raised by this project is to what extent these characteristics affect communication in court and pose problems to the interpreter. How do they affect the role and the behaviour of the interpreter? If they make his/her task more difficult, what can then be done to remedy this?

In order to answer these questions, I shall approach communication in court from two different angles: the linguistic angle and the pragmatic angle.

As far as *the linguistic angle* is concerned, I shall use two different but interrelated parameters. One is the "planned discourse-unplanned discourse" dichotomy, and the other is the "oral-literate continuum". According to Ochs (1979), "unplanned discourse" can be defined as "discourse that lacks forethought and organizational preparation", and "planned discourse" can be defined as "discourse that has been thought out and organized (designed) prior to its expression". As far as "the oral-literate continuum" is concerned, pieces of language can be placed somewhere along this continuum at the ends of which you have the oral pole and the literate pole, respectively. You can establish a relation between these two parameters - as Shlesinger (1989a, 1990) has already done - by collapsing the two sets of parameters with planned discourse at the literate pole because of its high degree of literacy, and unplanned discourse at the oral pole because of its high degree of orality.

By applying these two parameters to communication in court, I intend to describe the language used with particular attention given to planned discourse. I assume that the communicative acts performed by the court can, to a large extent, be characterized as "planned discourse" and as such be located close to the literate pole of the continuum in question. This discourse will often be related to or reproduce written language, and will thus be close to legal language. We may therefore define such "planned discourse" as "institutional language", as does Jansen (1995). On the other hand, communicative acts performed by the defendant can be characterized as "spoken language" or "everyday language" and as such be located close to the oral pole of the continuum.

As far as *the pragmatic angle* is concerned, I shall use the "speech-act theory" or rather "the communicative-acts theory" as described by Linell et al. (1993), thus emphasizing that we are dealing with an interaction between two or more persons. In this respect, I shall use the terms "perlocutionary acts" and "perlocutionary effects" and I want to examine whether or not the communicative acts performed by one or the other of the interlocutors change character by passing through the interpreter. If the answer is yes, I should like to see to what extent, in what manner and who/what is to blame.

Still regarding the pragmatic angle, the importance of the extra-linguistic, non-verbal aspects of court interpreting and the problems inherent to the fact that a court interpreter has to alternate between dialogue interpreting, "real" consecutive, simultaneous (whispering) and sight translation will also be discussed in the project.

6. Interpreting between the Slovene and Italian languages in Italian Courts of Law. Marco Uckmar, Slovene Interpreter, Trieste Court of Justice

6.1 Introduction

In Italy the use of interpreters in Courts of Law is limited almost exclusively to criminal cases, as the "Criminal Law Code" recognises, in certain cases, the right of the defendant to be questioned with the aid of an interpreter, while the

"Civil Law Code" only envisages the use of an interpreter if a judge considers it necessary.

Court interpreters for the Slovene language in Italy operate only in the two provinces of Trieste and Gorizia. These two provinces border on Slovenia, and until recently Slovene citizens seldom went beyond these two provinces when coming to Italy. Furthermore, a recognised Slovene linguistic minority, whose members have an acknowledged right to use their own language in their dealings with public authorities, live in this particular area. Thus, Slovene interpreters are called upon to represent two main client groups: 1) citizens of the Republic of Slovenia and 2) members of the Slovene minority in Italy. These two groups present two very different sets of problems.

6.2 *Interpreting for Slovene citizens*

In the case of Slovene citizens, the interpreter has to face problems common to all translation and interpretation work in the legal field, problems associated with the differences between the legal systems, which are the points of reference for the two legal languages the interpreter has to mediate. The fundamental difference between the Italian and Slovene legal systems, as far as criminal law is concerned, lies in the two different ways in which the idea of a crime is conceived in them and which is, in turn, the expression of the two underlying philosophies. Italian legal philosophy, deriving from Roman law, conceives of a crime chiefly as an action whereby a law has been violated (formal conception), while the Slovene system in its recent development introduces a conception which is a compromise between the formal conception and the old Marxist materialistic conception, that is of a crime being an action which is dangerous or harmful to society. This new compromise is very similar to the traditional formal conception but with a particular stress on the fact that the law is there to protect such rights and interests of individuals or of society in general as are endangered by a certain crime. And this is very close to popular opinion, which is usually shared by the interpreter's clients, who are quite ready to accept law as a warranty against arbitrary judgement (possible in the Marxist system), but want to see the rationale behind it. The result is sometimes extreme difficulty, for defendants from Slovenia, in understanding the meaning of their charges and even more so the seriousness of such charges. This, for example, is particularly frequent in cases of "favouring illegal immigration". The Immigration law, and respect for it, is of course necessary for practical reasons, but, as in Slovenia these are not yet strongly felt and also as neither the text of the law nor the statements of the charges make any mention of these reasons, it is the task of the interpreter to explain them to the defendant. Otherwise s/he will not even be able to understand why s/he should be tried at all or even why s/he should be threatened with such severe punishment for an offence which, in her/his own country, is considered trivial.

6.3 *Interpreting for members of the Slovene minority*

The other main source of work for the interpreter of the Slovene language in Italy is constituted by members of the Slovene minority. Here we meet two sets of very particular institutional problems, besides a whole range of linguistic issues.

The first of these problems lies in the fact that Slovene-speaking Italian citizens do not belong to the legal tradition which is the reference background for official Slovene legal language (that used in Slovenia) and they speak a language which is very different from the official language of the legal system to which they belong. Hence the need to create a brand new legal language for the purpose; this is by no means complete yet and that requires the interpreter (and indeed the translator) to take a substantial and active role in the formation process. There must be frequent contacts and discussion both with fellow interpreters and translators and with users, be they members of the legal profession or any member of the Slovene minority who has frequent contacts with the public authorities in general.

The second great problem is associated with role conflicts. The difficulty of remaining impartial, for example, is here felt with particular keenness, as the interpreter himself is usually a member of the Slovene minority and quite positively expected to be "on the side of the Slovene-speaking party." Sometimes the magistrates even seem to take this for granted. But there is a problem which is peculiar to this particular situation. In cases involving members of the minority, the interpreter's function is not to ensure the best possible communication between the public authority and a party who does not know the official language, but to provide the legal right of the members of the minority to use their own language in their dealings with the public authorities. Therefore, what may and frequently does happen is that the person for whom the interpreter has been called knows the official language perfectly well, although s/he would insist on using his/her own language. This leads to a series of anomalous interpreting situations, which may be of help to the interpreter or, on the contrary, be rather embarrassing. In fact, when translating for the Slovene-speaking party, as the party has already understood at least the general sense of what has been said, the interpreter has the advantage of not having to translate everything, and thus having more time, if necessary, to explain with more accuracy any part of the discourse that might prove difficult to understand. On the other hand, there is a potentially dangerous situation: the Slovene-speaking party understands everything, or almost everything, of what is said in court, while the other parties cannot understand what the Slovene-speaking party says without the help of the interpreter. This means, using Agar's terminology (quoted by H.Niska 1995), that a "client" takes complete control of the communication, while the "institutional representative" has imperfect control. It follows that the order principle of communication in Court is partially suspended and it is the interpreter who is expected to prevent anarchy from breaking out. The main danger in such cases is that much depends on the client's willingness to collaborate, while he might well be tempted to take advantage of the situation, with disastrous consequences for communication.

Finally, there are the aforementioned linguistic problems, which frequently emerge and have to be solved by recourse to discussion with colleagues and users. A very frequent problem is that of one term in one of the two languages having two or even more functional equivalents in the other language, according to what the term refers to, what context it is set in etc., and requiring a perfect understanding of the actual situation in question. For example: the Italian verb *rimettere* and its corresponding noun *rimessione*, which means *to transfer* and *transfer*, may be translated into Slovene either as *premestiti* and *premestitev*, when referring to a process (a trial or other legal proceeding) or as *predati* and *predaja*, when referring to documents.

The foregoing is, of course, only one example of such problems, which are many, but the effort of solving these problems, working together with the users, is very worthwhile as the result is the best possible agreement between the interpreter and those benefiting from his services.

7. The Right to Lie: On Interpreter-Mediated Police Interrogations.
Cecilia Wadensjö, University of Linköping

7.1 *Interpreting as Interaction*

"Should only Swedes have the right to lie?". The latter is the title of an article debating the professional dilemma of interpreting for people who are cheating and lying. This article was an answer to another in the same Swedish magazine, where the author raised the question more in terms of: "Should interpreters help people fool the authorities?" In his mind, social workers and police officers sometimes have no chance to see through clients' lies if interpreters stick to just translating. His claim was that this would be the same as being co-responsible for the lies. The interpreter should not only have the right to intervene, but be obliged to do so in certain cases.

The second debater, writing under the catchy title "Should only Swedes have the right to lie?" took the opposite position. Interpreters must not take on a responsibility for revealing what they believe is a lie. Their task is to just to translate whatever is said as closely as possible and do nothing more. The responsibility for revealing lies must be with the representative of the authorities. People not speaking Swedish should be given the same treatment as those who do, and interpreters should not get involved in either doing the police officer's job or being a suspect's advocate.

It is typical of the genre of debating to counterpose positions. I would like to broaden the debate by looking at some of its preconditions. Arguably, when two people interact via an interpreter, this is different from speaking eye to eye in a common language. Yet it seems to be taken for granted that these two situations are comparable, at least when it comes to the conditions for telling (un)truthful stories and catching people telling lies. Debates such as "Should only Swedes have the right to lie?" versus "Should the interpreter help foreigners fool Swedish authorities?" seem to be founded on somewhat simplified conceptions of interpreter-mediated talk as a social activity.

If we look at interpreting as interaction, as I have suggested elsewhere (Wadensjö, 1992), it is evident that interpreter-mediated talk forms a particular type of encounter, with its own specific organisational principles. The question is not then "if?", but "how?" conditions for interaction differ from monolingual situations. Following from an interactionist perspective on language and language use (cf. Linell, in this volume), the interpreter's work can be seen as combining two central functions: *translating* and *co-ordinating* talk. The divide is of course merely theoretical. In practice translating and co-ordinating must be seen as intimately intertwined aspects of what interpreters do in and by interaction. The translating function is obvious for those taking part in interpreted talk (even if the actual translating work of the interpreter's contributions can be transparent only to those understanding both languages involved). The co-ordinating function is obvious in the sense that the interpreter is expected to take every second turn at talking. Answers to the question "how?" above can be related to either of these functions.

7.2 *The difference an interpreter makes - seen from two perspectives*

From the point of view of translation, the interpreter's influence can inevitably be described not only in terms of lexical choice, accent and prosody but also by such things as the presence or absence of hesitation markers, false starts, etc. in the primary parties' originals and the interpreter's renditions respectively. Berk-Seligson (1990) provides rich descriptions of the impact of these aspects of the interpreter's work in courtroom interaction. From the point of view of co-ordination, the interpreter's influence must be traced in other ways. Through detailed discourse analysis, by looking at longer sequences of talk, it is possible to see the impact of such features as feedback, silence, simultaneous talk and other interactively significant communicative actions, as these are performed by primary interlocutors and by the interpreter. Analyses of recorded and transcribed interpreted police interrogations indicate that questioning techniques designed to elicit information from the suspect do not work in the same way as is typically expected in monolingual interaction. For instance, in a case where a Russian shop lifter is heard by a Swedish police officer, it is demonstrated that the officer's efforts to repeat words and expressions from immediately preceding utterances (what is popularly called "catching on words") repeatedly fail to prompt the explanations he needs from the suspect. On the other hand, it is by the interpreter's presence that the suspect can be made to answer at all. In this connection it is interesting to compare how the suspect is addressed by the police officer and by the interpreter respectively. In the half-hour long encounter the policeman addresses the suspect by her name or by "you" 27 times. The interpreter in turn, voicing the police officer, explicitly addresses her 72 times. This can partly be explained by the interpreter's need to make clear the *participation framework* (Goffman, 1981) at hand, in other words, to avoid confusion about who is talking to whom and who is supposed to answer when. Explicit addressing also fulfils another important function in interpreter-mediated talk, namely that of keeping the two parties included in the ongoing activity of common talk. This would indicate that suspects, who in principle have the right to stay silent, to avoid testifying against themselves, are more easily prompted to talk by the interpreter than they hypothetically would be by the police.

From a legal point of view, police interrogation with or without interpretation are regarded as similar cases. But in practice these situations represent different systems of social activity. Police interrogation has some typical organisational principles of its own, basically tied to questioning techniques and strategies of answering and avoiding answering. The interpreter-mediated interaction has yet other characteristic organisational features, which still remain to be systematically explored.

8. Questions and Answers

In reply to comments on media interpreting, the chairman invited those interested in following up the media interpreting debate to get in touch with Mariachiara Russo or Miriam Shlesinger to do so.

In response to a question from Karla Déjean Le Féal, Akira Mizuno replied that for pedagogical purposes, the aspiring interpreter is encouraged to eliminate no significant elements of the speech.

Sergio Viaggio felt that media interpreting was the most demanding task the interpreter is called upon to perform. He also suggested that s/he should be remunerated accordingly, meeting with unanimous approval. The difficulty of synchronization of films was also raised from the floor.

Franz Pöchhacker expressed the hope that sponsors might be prepared to finance research in this field.

Miriam Shlesinger raised the issue of the difference between courtroom interpreting and conference interpreting, stressing the need for a summary and the protection of the defendant in courtroom interpreting.

Sergio Viaggio from the floor introduced the issue of what the speaker is trying *not* to say and therefore hesitations and rhetorical errors become themselves significant in distinguishing between the surface message and the in-depth message transmitted by the speaker.

Karla Déjean Le Féal asked how it was possible for an interpreter to tell whether the speaker is actually lying. Cecilia Wadensjö replied that it was in any case a highly subjective decision.

Nancy Schweda Nicholson mentioned accommodation strategies and regretted that US legal procedures take little account of the presence of the interpreter. She also commented on whether the interpreter is entitled to embellish upon the original. She felt that ideally the defendant should receive the impression that the trial was being held in his/her native language.

Monique Corvington wondered whether listeners might have the impression that the interpreter was actually interfering with the rendering of the statement. Bodil Martinsen replied that it is possible to avoid ambiguities if the interpreter, unaware of the correct legal term, resorts to a reformulation of the original.

9. Conclusion

Having heard our colleagues' views on the interpreter's intervention in court and for the media, the relevance of our initial premise becomes clear. What is the interpreter's "cue to speak"? The original quotation comes, of course, from *Othello*. Othello has been summoned before the Senate to justify his supposed seduction and enchantment of Desdemona and his friends and side-kicks are howling at him to intervene, when he knows that it is neither the time nor the place for him to do so. He waves them contemptuously aside and, majestic above the din, expresses his conviction. "Had it been my cue to speak, I should have known it without a prompter". Colleagues, so must we.

Postscript: After Turku

Daniel Gile, *Université Lumière, Lyon 2 & ISIT, Paris*

At the time these proceedings are ready for print, more than two years have elapsed since the Turku conference "What do we know and how ?", and it is tempting to try to make the best of this lag by reflecting upon the aftermath of the conference with the benefit of some hindsight.

A word of caution may be appropriate here. Since the usual time interval between actual research work and its publication can vary between a few months and several years, the literature that has been published since August 1994 (see *IRTIN Bulletin* issues n°10 to n°13) can scarcely be attributed to the influence of the Turku meeting, but does make it possible to corroborate or weaken hypotheses that were made around that period, in particular as presented in the *Introduction* to this volume. On the other hand, the most recent initiatives such as symposia, training courses and other events could well be the direct or indirect consequence of this meeting, but demonstrating such an influence is difficult, unless the organizers explicitly mention it. It would therefore be presumptuous to postulate any causal relationship between the Turku conference and recent developments in interpretation research, and the following analysis is to be taken as a review of developments and trends more than anything else.

The two years following the Turku conference, 1995 and 1996, proved to be quantitatively productive: the *IRTIN Bulletin* reports a total of 105 publications for 1995 including 4 books devoted exclusively to interpretation and a special issue of *Target* (7:1) on interpreting research, and 56 items had been added for 1996 to the bibliographical lists by the end of October of the same year, including several from the first issue of a new interpretation journal, *Interpreting*, edited by Barbara Moser-Mercer and Dominic Massaro - experience shows that a significant proportion of references for a given year are identified after a lag of several months, and sometimes much longer, so that many more items could be added for 1996 in the months to come. Qualitatively speaking, there has been a steady increase in the number of empirical studies, or at least reports on empirical studies (several were reported more than once), from 9 items in 1991 to 17 in 1992, then on to 22 in 1993 and 1994, 41 in 1995 and to 15 by the end of October 1996. There are no signs in the literature indicating the existence of major new research ventures. Experienced investigators have been either publishing the results of new small-scale studies or continuing to report on on-going research. On the other hand, besides two doctoral theses from Denmark, there have been numerous new graduation theses, especially from Finland (7), but also from Taiwan (2), Belgium (2), Mexico (2), and the UK (1). It does seem that the empirical graduation thesis pattern, which was strongest in Trieste and Heidelberg in past years, is gaining ground geographically to include new countries, which is rather encouraging. These small-scale studies of varying methodological quality are beginning to provide replication and quasi-replication case studies, in particular on issues such as quality perception, language-pair related transformations in interpreting, notes in consecutive and cerebral lateralization. However, three phenomena reduce their potential impact:

- Many of them are not disseminated beyond the institution in which they were prepared. The problem is partly legal (intellectual property issues seem to be involved) and financial, but partly (and significantly) motivational: only a small number of these graduation theses are reported in the literature or summarized and developed into papers, except those completed at the SSLMIT in Trieste, where the will to welcome graduating students into the research community is explicit, while the others rest in the peace of their alma mater's libraries or archives until, in rare cases, an outside investigator learns about their existence and shows enough interest to have them exhumed. This issue has recently been taken up by Mary Snell-Hornby of the EST (European Society for Translation Studies), as regards both translation and interpretation theses, with a proposal to try to collect both information about such theses and the theses themselves so as to make them available to investigators. A positive change in this respect may be in the offing.

- Upon graduation, students still tend to devote all their efforts to building their professional career and to leave research altogether, even though they may have enjoyed the work on their graduation thesis. In this respect, they are not very different from their elders. Neither does there seem to be any reason for this to change.

- Methodological weaknesses are still found in some of these theses and obviously limit further their impact upon interpretation research.

   One of the most efficient means to remedy the situation as regards this last item is clearly research training, and one of the most salient weaknesses of the present interpretation research environment is its conspicuous absence in the very institutions where interpreters are trained and where research comes from. Some interesting efforts are made in this direction, mostly on an individual basis, and very discreetly (while visiting foreign universities and translation and interpretation departments and schools, one sometimes hears about individual courses and action), while institutional initiatives are rare. Interestingly, a spectacular institutional move comes from the Czech Republic: after a long and difficult struggle to obtain academic recognition, the University Charles of Prague has launched in the autumn of 1996 a PhD "translatology" training programme. One might add that in the Hungarian Academy of Sciences, there is an official Working Committee for Translation Theory. In most research training initiatives, interpreting is still bundled into *Translation*, its superordinate concept. However, a few interpretation-specific programmes are also being developed: an Interpreting trainer's training course with a major research component was organized by the E.T.I. in Geneva in January 1996, and two one-week training courses in research methods in interpreting are organized by the E.T.I. and by the Aarhus school of business respectively in January 1997. While the actual knowledge and knowhow gained during such short courses are certainly limited, they could have a major motivational and sociological impact, as has been demonstrated repeatedly through the CE(T)RA summer training programme in Leuven, Belgium, which has proved to be an important gateway into the Translation Studies research community for young researchers. Incidentally, in spite of the differences in the foci and methods between translation research and interpretation research, the two seem to be interacting more strongly than in the past, at least institutionally, with the increasingly regular presence of members of the interpretation research community and of their work in national and international bodies, meetings and publications devoted to translation.

As to the interpretation research community per se, it seems to have evolved to some extent, but perhaps not as much as might have been expected. There is no doubt that through a number of Translation symposia, collective Translation and Interpretation volumes and organizations such as EST, information is disseminated more extensively than in the past. Except for some countries which are still communication-locked for political and linguistic reasons, unlike the situation in the sixties, the seventies and the early eighties, it is now becoming more difficult for an interpretation investigator not to be aware of the existence of other investigators outside his/her own country and outside his/her own school of thought. The scope of interpreting research has also crossed several trade boundaries, such as those separating conference interpreting from court interpreting, sign-language interpreting and community interpreting. A small number of symposia and publications now have representatives from those four sub-disciplines. As a result, the cognitive and sociological issues involved in interpreting have become more salient. However, true cross-fertilisation between the researchers from these horizons is still apparently a long way off, as the foci of attention, theoretical models and research methods differ widely (with a few exceptions, however, such as the involvement of conference interpreters Morris and Shlesinger in court interpreting, and the study on community interpreting completed recently in Vienna by conference interpreter Franz Pöchhacker). Similarly, inter-disciplinary co-presence in publications and in some symposia has been achieved (inter alia in a meeting between psychologists, linguists and translation and interpretation investigators at Kent State University in May 1995 and in an upcoming meeting of linguists, cognitive psychologists and interpreters in Stockholm in February 1997), but there are few signs of significant cross-fertilisation. In particular, as the cognitive psychology and neurophysiological paradigms have gained ground over recent years with the crystallization of a group around an Italian kernel from Trieste, the result may have amounted to further polarization of the community, with members of the group continuing to pay little attention to relevant work done by interpreters on the very subject they were interested in (e.g. bilingualism). Last but not least, the relative solidarity which came out of the Trieste school initiative in the community of conference interpreting investigators in the second half of the eighties may be coming under pressure from the inevitable, but in this case somewhat premature competition and territory-carving exercises.

In concrete terms, interpreting research is still driven mainly by individuals, as opposed to institutions. The only active productive centers so far remain the Trieste school and (interestingly) the non-academic Interpreting Research Association of Japan, with its regular monthly meetings and its journal, *Tsûyakurironkenkyû* (*Interpreting Research*), which publishes almost exclusively papers in Japanese without an English abstract. The graduate interpreting course cum thesis which started last year at *Daito bunka university* thanks to Masaomi Kondo's efforts and under his leadership may provide a foundation for an academically based regular source of research, but this remains to be seen, as the fundamental motivational issue as outlined above for other countries also exists in Japan.

On the whole, it is too early to determine whether the trends detected during the Turku conference are deep and long-lasting or whether whatever headway has been made is still fragile and unstable. We still do not know much *from research*, and are still not quite sure about *how* we should be able to gain further knowledge in view of the existing methodological, institutional and motivational obstacles and other limitations. But the fact that interpeting research is still groping in semi-darkness is what makes it interesting, with much potential for discoveries and innovation, and the undisputable excitement that was felt by participants in the Turku conference should be a positive stimulus for further work.

REFERENCES

Adler, Nancy J. 1986. *International Dimensions of Organizational Behavior*, Boston, Mass.: Kent Publishing Co.

Aglioti, S. & Fabbro, Franco. 1993. "Paradoxical selective recovery in a bilingual aphasic following subcortical lesions". *NeuroReport* 4: 1359-1362.

Agosti, R. 1995. *Stress e interpretazione simultanea: uno studi sperimentale*. SSLMIT, University of Trieste. Unpublished Thesis.

Albert, Martin L. and Obler, L.K. 1978. *The Bilingual Brain*. New York: Academic Press.

Alexieva, Bistra. 1992. "The Optimum Text in Simultaneous Interpreting: A Cognitive Approach to Interpreter Training". In Dollerup C. & A. Loddegard (eds), 221-229.

Anderson, J.R. 1991. "The adaptive nature of Human Categorization". *Psychological Review* 3: 409-429.

Arijoki, C. 1993. "Foreign Language Awareness in the Business Community". *ENCoDe*: 13-33.

Armengaud, Françoise. 1990. *La Pragmatique*. Paris: Presses Universitaires de France. Collection Que sais-je?

Atkinson, R.C. & Shiffrin, R.M. 1984. "Il controllo della memoria a breve termine". *Le Scienze. Quaderni* 19: 19-26.

Baddeley, A.D. 1990. *Human Memory. Theory and Practice*. Hove and London: Lawrence Erlbaum Associates.

Baddeley, A.D. 1991. "The development of the concept of working memory: Implications and contributions of neuropsychology". In Vallar G. & T. Shallice (eds), *Neuropsychological Impairments of Short-term Meeory*. Cambridge: Cambridge University Press.

Baddeley, A.D. & Hitch, G. 1974. "Working memory". In Bower G.A.(ed), *Recent Advances in Learning and Motivation*. Vol. 8. New York: Academic Press, 54-73.

Barik, Henrik C. 1971. "A description of various types of omissions, additions and errors encountered in simultaneous interpretation". *Meta* 16(4): 199-210.

Barik, Henrik C. 1973. Simultaneous Interpretation: Temporal and Quantitative Data. *Language and Speech* 16: 237-271.

Barik, Henrik C. 1975. "Simultaneous interpretation: Qualitative and linguistic data". *Language and Speech* 18: 272-297.

Bateman, J. A. 1989. "Dynamic Systemic-functional Grammar: A New Frontier". *Word* 40(1-2): 263-286.

Bates, E. & MacWhinney, B. 1989. "Functionalism and the Competition Model". In MacWhinney B. & E. Bates (eds), *The Crosslinguistic Study of Sentence Processing*. Cambridge: Cambridge University Press.

Berk-Seligson, Susan. 1990. *The bilingual courtroom: Court interpreters in the judicial process.* Chicago: University of Chicago Press.

Berry, M. 1992. "Bringing Systems Back into a Discussion of Theme". Plenary address to the 19th International Systemic Functional Congress, Macquarie University, July 13-18, 1992, Macquarie (Sydney), Australia.

Bialystock, E. & Sharwood Smith, M. 1985. "Interlanguage is not a state of mind: an evaluation of the construct for second language acquisition". *Applied Linguistics* 6: 101-107.

Botero-Browning, Socorro 1995. "Label of Quality". *AIIC Bulletin* 23(3): 23-24.

Bowen, David & Bowen, Margareta (eds). 1990. *Interpreting - Yesterday, Today and Tomorrow: American Translators Association Scholarly Monograph Series Volume IV.* New York: the State University of New York at Binghamton.

Breuer, J.P. & de Bertha, P. 1990. "Etude sur Le Management Franco-Allemand". In *Le Vesinet* (Unpublished Study, quoted in Harper, J. 1993, "Cross-National Mergers and Joint Ventures: The Cross-Cultural Issues and the Role of Training". *ENCoDe*: 75-82.

Brislin, Richard W. (ed). 1981. *Cross-cultural Encounters, Face-to-face Interaction,* New York: Pergamon Press.

Brislin, W.P. (ed). 1976. *Translation: Applications and Research.* New York: Gardner.

Broca, P.P. 1861. "Remarques sur le siège de la faculté du langage articulé, suivies d'une observation d'aphémie (perte de la parole)". *Bulletin de la Société Anatomique* 6: 330-357.

Brondeel, Hermann. 1994. "Teaching Subtitling Routines". *Meta* 39(1): 26-33.

Bühler, Hildegund. 1984. "Pragmatic Criteria for the Evaluation of Professional Translation and Interpretation". In den Haese J. & J. Nivette (eds) *AILA '84 Proceedings*, Vol.4: 1560, Brussels.

Bühler, Hildegund. 1986. "Linguistic (semantic) and extra-linguistic (pragmatic) criteria for the evaluation of conference interpretation and interpreters". *Multilingua* 5(4): 232-235.

Bühler, Hildegund. 1989. "Discourse Analysis and the Spoken Text - a Critical Analysis of the Performance of Advanced Interpretation Students". In Gran L. & J.Dodds (eds), 131-136.

Cacciary, C. & Glucksberg, S. 1991. "Understanding idiomatic expressions: The contribution of word meanings". In Simpson G.B. (ed), *Understanding word and sentence.* Amsterdam: Elsevier, 217-240.

Caplan, D. 1990. *Neurolinguistics and linguistic aphasiology. An Introduction.* Cambridge: Cambridge University Press.

Cartellieri, Claus. 1983. "The inescapable dilemma: Quality and/or Quantity in Interpreting". *Babel* 29(4): 209-213.

Catrysse, Patrick. 1992. "Film (Adaptation) As Translation: Some Methodological Proposals". *Target: International Journal of Translation Studies* 4 (1): 53-70.

Cenkova, Ivana. 1988. *Teoretické aspekty procesu simultanniho tlumoceni*. Prague: Acta Universitatis Carolinae Philologica XIX, published version of a PhD dissertation defended in 1985.

Chernov, Ghelly. 1978. *Teoriya i praktika sinkhronnogo perevoda*. Moscow: Mezhdunarodnie otnoshenia.

Clark, Herbert H. & Gerrig, R. 1990. "Quotations as demonstrations". *Language* 66: 764-805.

Cohen, N.J. & Squire, L.R. 1980. "Preserved learning and retention of pattern analyzing skill in amnesia: Dissociation of knowing how and knowing what". *Science* 210: 207-210.

Collins, A.M. & Loftus, E.F. 1975. "A spreading-activation theory of semantic processing". *Psychological Review* 82: 407-428.

Collins, A.M. & Quillian, M.R. 1969. "Retrieval Time from Semantic Memory". *Journal of Verbal Learning and Verbal Behavior* 8: 240-247.

Cori, M. & Marandin, J.M. 1994. "Preference in Natural Language Syntax". *Vème conférence Internationale "Information Processing And Management of Uncertainty In Knowledge-Based Systems"*. Paris. 4-8 Juillet 1994.

Craik, F.I.M. & Lockhart, R.S. 1972. "Levels of processing: A framework for memory research." *Journal of Verbal Learning and Verbal Behavior* 11: 671-684.

Criomhthain, Martin O. 1985. "Terms of Address in Translation". *Babel* 31: 138-145.

Cubelli, R. 1991. "A selective deficit for writing vowels in acquired dysgraphia". *Nature* 353: 258-260.

Dale, R. 1993. "Natural Language Generation. Fifth European Summer School in Logic, Language and Information," August 16-27, 1993, Faculdade de Letras, Universidade de Lisboa.

Daly, Albert. 1985. "Interpreting for International Satellite Television". *Meta* 30(1): 91-96.

Dam, Vrønning Helle. 1993. "Text condensing in consecutive interpreting". In Y. Gambier & J. Tommola (eds), 297-313.

Darò, Valeria. 1989. "The Role of Memory and Attention in Simultaneous Interpretation: A Neurolinguistic Approach". *The Interpreters' Newsletter* 2: 50-56.

Darò, Valeria. 1994. "Effects of simultaneous interpretation on the phonological loop". *4th International Congress of the International Society of Applied Psycholinguistics*. June 23-27, 1994, Bologna, Italy.

Darò, Valeria & Fabbro, Franco. 1994. "Verbal memory during simultaneous interpretation: Effects of phonological interference". *Applied Linguistics* 15: 365-381.

De Feo, N. 1992-3. *Strategie di riformulazione sintetica nell'interpretazione simultanea dall'inglese in italiano: un contributo sperimentale*. Graduation Thesis. University of Trieste, SSLMIT.

Déjean Le Féal, Karla. 1978. *Lectures et improvisations. Incidences de la forme de l'énonciation sur la traduction simultanée*. Thèse de doctorat de 3ème cycle. Université Paris III.

Déjean Le Féal, Karla. 1990. "Some Thoughts on the Evaluation of Simultaneous Interpretation". In Bowen D.& M. (eds), 154-160.

Detienne, M. 1967. *Les maîtres de vérité dans la Grèce archaïque*. Paris: Libraire François Maspero.

Dodds, John. M. 1989. "Linguistic Theory Construction as a Premise to a Methodology of Teaching Interpretation". In L. Gran & J. M. Dodds (eds), 17-20.

Dollerup, Cay & Loddegaard, Annette (eds). 1992. *Teaching Translation and Interpreting. Training, Talent and Experience*. Amsterdam and Philadelphia: Benjamins.

Dollerup, Cay & Lindegaard, Annette (eds). 1994. *Teaching Translation and Interpreting 2: Insights, Aims and Visions*. Amsterdam & Philadelphia: Benjamins.

ENCoDe 1993. Language and Culture Bridges to International Trade: The Proceedings of ENCODE 5th International Seminar, 4-6 February 1993, Lancaster Business School, University of Central Lancashire.

Ericsson, K.A. & Simon, H.A. 1980. "Verbal Reports as Data". *Psychological Review* 3: 215-251.

Fabbro, Franco. 1993. "Neuropsicologia dell'interpretazione simultanea". *Giornale di Psicologia, Neurologia e Psichiatria* 53: 108-125.

Fabbro, Franco. 1994. *Il cervello dei bilingui. Neurolinguistica del bilinguismo*. Milano: Mondadori.

Fabbro, Franco & Darò, Valeria. 1994. "Delayed auditory feedback in polyglot simultaneous interpreters". *Brain and Language* 48: 309-319.

Fabbro F., Gran B.& Gran L. 1991. "Hemispheric specialization for semantic and syntactic components of language in simultaneous interpretation". *Brain and Language* 41: 1-42.

Fabbro, Franco & Gran, Laura. 1994. "Neurological and neuropsychological aspects of polyglossia and simultaneous interpretation". In Lambert S.& Moser-Mercer B. (eds), 273-317.

Fabbro Franco, Gran Laura, Basso G. & Bava A. 1990. "Cerebral lateralization in simultaneous interpretation". *Brain and Language* 39: 69-89.

Fabbro Franco, Gran Laura & Bava A. 1987. "Modifications in cerebral lateralization during the acquisition of a second language (English) in adult Italian-speaking females". *Neuroscience* (Suppl. 22): S748.

Fabbro, Franco & Paradis, Michel. 1995. "Differential impairments in four multilingual patients with subcortical lesions". In Paradis M. (ed), *Aspects of Bilingual Aphasia*. London: Pergamon Press (in press).

Fisher, Glen 1980. *International Negotiation: A Cross-Cultural Perspective*, Intercultural Press Inc.

Frank, G. 1990. "Mergers and Acquisitions: Competitive Advantages and Cultural Fit". *European Management Journal* 8(1).

Fries, Peter H. 1995. "Themes, Methods of Development, and Texts". In Hasan, R. & P. H. Fries (eds), 317-359.

Fusco, Maria Antonietta. 1990. "Quality in Conference Interpreting between Cognate Languages: A Preliminary Approach to the Spanish-Italian Case". *The Interpreters' Newsletter* 3: 93-97.

Gambier, Yves. 1994. "Audio-Visual Communication: Typological Detour". In Dollerup, Cay & Annette Lindegaard (eds), 275-283.

Gambier, Yves & Tommola, Jorma (eds). 1993. *Translation and Knowledge*. (Fourth Scandinavian Symposium on Translation Theory, Turku, June 1992). University of Turku: Centre for Translation and Interpreting.

Gastaldi G. 1951. "Osservazioni su un afasico bilingue". *Sistema Nervoso* 2: 175-180.

Gelman, S.A. 1988. "The development of induction within Natural Kind and Artifact Categories". *Cognitive Psychology* 20: 65-95.

Gerver, David. 1972. "Simultaneous and consecutive interpretation and human information processing". *Social Science Research Council Report*, London, HR 566/1.

Gerver, David. 1974. "Simultaneous listening and speaking and retention of prose". *Quarterly Journal of Experimental Psychology* 26: 337-342.

Gerver, David. 1976. "Empirical studies of simultaneous interpretation: A review and a model". In Brislin R.W. (ed), 165-207.

Gerver, David & H. Wallace Sinaiko (eds). 1978. *Language Interpretation and Communication*. New York and London: Plenum Press.

Giambagli, A. 1990. "Transformations grammaticales syntaxiques et structurales dans l'interprétation consécutive vers l'italien d'une langue latine et d'une langue germanique". *The Interpreters' Newsletter* 3: 98-111.

Gile, Daniel. 1983. "Aspects méthodologiques de l'évaluation de la qualité du travail en interprétation simultanée". *Meta* 28(3): 236-243.

Gile, Daniel. 1984. "Les noms propres en interprétation simultanée". *Multilingua* 3(2): 79-85.

Gile, Daniel. 1985. "Le modèle d'efforts et l'équilibre d'interprétation en interprétation simultanée". *Meta* 30(1): 44-48.

Gile, Daniel. 1987. "Les exercices d'interprétation et la dégradation du français: une étude de cas". *Meta* 32(4): 420-428

Gile, Daniel. 1988. "Le partage de l'attention et le *modèle d'efforts* en interprétation simultanée". *The Interpreters' Newsletter* 1: 4-22.

Gile, Daniel. 1989. "Perspectives de la recherche dans l'enseignement de l'interprétation". In Gran L. & J. M. Dodds (eds), 27-34.

Gile, Daniel. 1990a. "Research Proposals for Interpreters". In Gran L. & C. Taylor (eds), 226-236.

Gile, Daniel. 1990b. "Scientific Research vs. Personal Theories in the Investigation of Interpretation". In Gran L. & C. Taylor (eds), 28-41.

Gile, Daniel. 1990c. "L'évaluation de la qualité de l'interpretation par les délégués: une étude de cas". *The Interpreters' Newsletter* 3: 66-71.

Gile, Daniel. 1991a. "Methodological Aspects of Interpretation (and Translation) Research". *Target* 3(2): 153-174.

Gile, Daniel.1991b. "The processing capacity issue in conference interpretation". *Babel* 37(1): 15-27.

Gile, Daniel. 1991c. "Prise de notes et attention en début d'apprentissage de l'interprétation consécutive - une expérience-démonstration de sensibilisation". *Meta* 36(2): 432-441.

Gile, Daniel. 1992. "Predictable Sentence Endings in Japanese and Conference Interpretation". *The Interpreters' Newsletter.* Special Issue 1: 12-23.

Gile, Daniel. 1995a. *Basic Concepts and Models for Interpreter and Translator Training.* Amsterdam and Philadelphia: Benjamins.

Gile, Daniel. 1995b. *Regards sur la recherche en interprétation de conférence.* Lille: Presses Universitaires de Lille.

Gile, Daniel. 1995c. "Interpretation Research - A New Impetus?". *Hermes* 14: 15-29.

Goffman, Erving. 1981. *Forms of talk.* Philadelphia: University of Pennsylvania Press.

Gold, David. 1973. "On Quality in Interpretation". *Babel* 19(4): 154-155.

Goldman-Eisler, Frieda. 1958. The Predictability of Words in the Context of the Length of Pauses in Speech. *Language and Speech* 1. Hampton Hill, Middlesex.

Goldman-Eisler, Frieda. 1964. Hesitations, Information and Levels of Speech Production. In Reuck & O'Connors (eds), *Disorders of Language.* London.

Goldmann-Eisler, Frieda. 1972. "Segmentation of input in Simultaneous Interpretation". *Psycholinguistic Research* 1: 127-140.

Graesser A.C., Singer M. & Trabasso T. 1994. "Constructing Inferences During Text Comprehension". *Psychological Review* 101(3): 371-395.

Graf, P.& Masson, M.E.J. (eds). 1993. *Implicit Memory.* Hillsdale: Erlbaum.

Gran, Laura. 1992. *Aspetti dell'organizzazione cerebrale del linguaggio: dal monolinguismo all'interpretazione simultanea.* Udine: Campanotto.

Gran, Laura. & Dodds, John (eds). 1989. *The Theoretical and Practical Aspects of Teaching Conference Interpretation*. Udine: Campanotto.

Gran, Laura & Fabbro, Franco. 1991. "A dichotic-listening study on error recognition among professional-interpreters". In Jovanovic M.(ed), *Proceedings of the XII World Congress of FIT*. Belgrade: Prevodilac, 564-572.

Gran, Laura & Taylor, Christopher (eds). 1990. *Aspects of Applied and Experimental Research on Conference Interpretation*. Udine: Campanotto.

Gravier, Maurice. 1978. Preface to: Seleskovitch, Danica. *Interpreting for International Conferences: Problems of Language and Communication*. Washington: Pen and Booth.

Green, D.W. 1986. "Control, activation and resource: A framework and a model for the control of speech in bilinguals". *Brain and Language* 27: 210-223.

Green, A., Schweda-Nicholson N., Vaid J., White N. & Steiner R. 1990. "Hemispheric involvement in shadowing vs. interpretation: a time-sharing study of simultaneous interpreters with matched bilingual controls". *Brain and Language* 39: 107-133.

Grice, H. Paul. 1975. "Logic and Conversation". In Cole P. & Morgan J. L.(eds), 1975, *Syntax and Semantics* vol. 3, New York: Academic Press, 41-58.

Hagen, S. 1994. Director of Language Project, Open University Centre for Modern Languages, Milner Keynes, personal communication.

Hall, Edward T. 1990. *Silent Language*, New York: Anchor Books (Doubleday).

Halliday, Michael Alexander Kirkwood. 1973. *Explorations in the Functions of Language*. London: Edward Arnold.

Halliday, M.A.K. 1985. *An Introduction to Functional Grammar*. London: Edward Arnold.

Halliday, M.A.K. 1985/1994. *An Introduction to Functional Grammar*. London: Edward Arnold. Second edition 1994.

Halliday, M.A.K. 1987. "Spoken and written modes of meaning." In Horowitz R. & S.J. Samuels (eds) *Comprehending Oral and Written Language*. San Diego: California Academic Press, 55-81.

Halliday, M.A.K. 1989. *Spoken and Written Language*. Oxford: Oxford University Press.

Halliday, M.A.K. 1992. "Language theory and translation practice". *Rivista Internazionale di Tecnica della Traduzione* 0: 15-25.

Halliday, M.A.K. & Hasan, R. 1976. *Cohesion in English*. London: Longman.

Halliday, M.A.K. & Hasan, R. 1985/1989. *Language, context and text: Aspects of language in a social-semiotic perspective*. Geelong: Deakin University Press 1985; also Oxford: Oxford University Press 1989.

Harris, Brian. 1990. "Norms in Interpretation". *Target* 2(1): 115-119.

Harris, Brian. 1994. "A taxonomic survey of professional interpreting"..Paper presented at poster session at ICI conference, Turku, August 1994.

Hasan, Ruqaiya. 1978. "Text in the systemic-functional model". In Dressler W.U. (ed), *Current Trends in Textlinguistics*. Berlin: de Gruyter, 228-246.

Hasan, Ruqaiya. & Fries, Peter H. (eds). 1995. *On Subject and Theme: A Discourse Functional Perspective*. Amsterdam: Benjamins.

Hatim, Basil. 1991. "The pragmatics of argumentation in Arabic". *Text* 11(2):189-199.

Hatim, Basil. 1993. "Discovering Method in the Madness of Texts: A Text-Type Approach". In Gambier Y. & Tommola J. (eds), 351-361.

Hatim, Basil & Mason, Ian. 1990. *Discourse and the Translator*. London: Longman.

Herbert, Jean. 1952. *Manuel de l'interprète: comment on devient interprète de conférence*. Genève: Librairie de l'Université.

Hieranta, Pertti. 1993. "Framing languages: towards a frame-theoretical view of translation". In Gambier Y. & Tommola J. (eds), 115-127.

Hirsh, E.D. Jr. 1988. *Cultural Literacy*, New York: Vintage Books.

Hirst W., Spelke E.S., Reaves C.C, Caharack G.& Neisser U. 1980. "Dividing attention without alternation or automaticity". *Journal of Experimental Psychology* 109: 98-117.

Hofstede, G. 1991. *Cultures and Organizations: Software of the Mind*. London: McGraw Hill.

Hönig, Hans. 1988. "Wissen Übersetzer eigentlich was sie tun ?". *Lebende Sprachen* 33(1): 10-14.

Huber W., Poeck K., Weniger D.& Willmes K. 1983. *Der Aachener Aphasie Test (AAT)*. Göttingen: Hogrefe.

Hunt, R.R. & McDaniel, M.A. 1993. "The Enigma of Organization and Distinctiveness". *Journal of Memory and Language* 32: 421-445.

Hymes, Dell. 1972. "Models of the Interaction of Language and Social Life". In Gumperz John J. & Hymes Dell H. (eds), *Directions in Sociolinguistics*. New York: Holt Rhinehart and Winston, 35-71

Hymes, Dell (ed). 1974a. *Foundations in Sociolinguistics: An Ethnographic Approach*. Philadelphia: University of Pennsylvania Press.

Hymes, Dell. 1974b. "Why linguistics needs the sociologist". In Hymes D. (ed), 69-82.

Ilg, Gérard. 1980. "L'interprétation consécutive - les fondements". *Parallèles* 3: 109-136. Université de Genève.

Ilg, Gérard. 1989. "Outillage linguistique". In Gran L. & J. Dodds (eds), 147-150.

IRAJ, 1991-1994. *Interpreting Research Association of Japan: Journal of the IRAJ*. 1-7. Tokyo: IRAJ.

Isham, William P. 1994. "Memory for sentence form after simultaneous interpretation: Evidence both for and against deverbalization". In Lambert S.& Moser B. (eds), 191-211.

Isham, W.P.& Lane, H. 1993. "Simultaneous interpretation and the recall of source-language sentences". *Language and Cognitive Processes* 8: 241-264.

Jakobson Roman. 1971. *Studies on Child Language and Aphasia*. The Hague: Mouton de Gruyter.

James, William. 1890. *Principles of Psychology*. New York: Holt.

Jansen, Peter. 1995. "The Role of the Interpreter in Dutch Courtroom Interaction and the Impact of the Situation on Translational Norms". In Jansen P. (ed), *Translation and the Manipulation of Discourse*. Selected Papers of the CERA Research Seminars in Translation Studies 1992-1993. Leuven: K. U. Leuven, 133-156.

Jönsson, L. Forthcoming. "Accommodating to dialogue interpreting: specific features of interpreted and non-interpreted courtroom discourse". (Ms.). Linköping: Department of Communication Studies.

Jumpelt, R. Walter. 1985. "The Conference Interpreter's Working Environment Under the New ISO and IEC Standards". *Meta* 30(1): 82-90.

Kalina, Sylvia. 1992. "Discourse processing and interpreting strategies - an approach to the teaching of interpreting". In Dollerup C. & A. Loddegaard (eds), 251-258.

Kalina, Sylvia. 1994. "Analyzing Interpreters' Performance: Methods and Problems". In: Dollerup C. & A. Lindegaard (eds), 217-224.

Kauders, O. 1929. "Über polyglotte Reaktionen bei einer sensorischen Aphasie". *Zeitschrift für die gesamte Neurologie und Psychiatrie* 122: 651-666.

Kaufmann, Francine. 1993. "Interview et interprétation consécutive dans le film *Shoah* de Claude Lanzmann. *Meta* 38(4): 665-673.

Kinsbourne, M. 1987. "Brain mechanisms and memory". *Human Neurobiology* 6: 81-92.

Kintsch, Walter & van Dijk, Teun Adrianus. 1978. "Towards a Model of Text Comprehension and Production". *Psychological Review* 85(5): 363-394.

Kirchhoff, Hella. 1974. *Eine Didaktik des Dolmetschens*. Heidelberg. Unpublished manuscript.

Kirchhoff, Hella. 1976a. "Das dreigliedrige, zweisprachige Kommunikations-System Dolmetschen". *Le langage et l'homme* 31: 21-27.

Kirchhoff, Hella. 1976b. "Das Simultandolmetschen: Interdependenz der Variablen im Dolmetschprozess, Dolmetschmodelle und Dolmetschstrategien". In H.W. Drescher & S. Scheffzek (eds), *Theorie und Praxis des Übersetzens und Dolmetschens*. Bern: Lang, 59-71.

Kisa, T. 1993. "Doujituuyaku no Nihongo: Shichousha ha dou Uketomete Iruka" (Japanese Language in Simultaneous Interpreting on TV: A Survey on Reception). *Housou Kenkyu to Chousa (Broadcasing Research)* 3: 28-39.

Klonowicz, Tatiana. 1994. "Putting one's heart into simultaneous interpretation". In Lambert S. & B.Moser- Mercer (eds), 213-224.

Koistinen, Liisa. 1992. "Asking for Information. Differences in the Interactional Structure of Openings in Finnish and German Telephone Calls". In Nyyssonen, Heikki & Kuure, Leena (eds), *AFinLA Yearbook 1992*. Publications de l'Association finlandaise de linguistique appliquée 50: 203-223.

Kondo, Masaomi. 1980. "Ibunkakan Komiyunikeeshon no mezasumono (What does Cross-Cultural Communication Aspire to Achieve?) (in Japanese)". *Daito Bunka Daigaku Kiyo* 18: 1-14.

Kondo, Masaomi. 1986. "Eigo ni okeru museibutsu shugo no youhou to shakai kagaku no houhouron". (Inanimate Subjects in English and the Methodology of Social Science). *Daito Bunka Daigaku Kiyo* 24: 1-21.

Kondo, Masaomi. 1990. "What Conference Interpreters Should Not Be Expected To Do". *The Interpreters' Newsletter* 3: 59-65.

Kondo, Masaomi. 1992. " 'Cassette Effect' in Japanese translation words". *The Interpreters' Newsletter*. Special Issue 1: 24-34.

Kopczyński, Andrzej. 1994. "Quality in Conference Interpreting: Some Pragmatic Problems". In Snell-Hornby, Mary, Franz Pöchhacker & Klaus Kaindl, eds. *Translation Studies: An Interdiscipline*. Amsterdam and Philadelphia: Benjamins, 189-198.

Kovacic, Irena. 1994. "Relevance as as factor in Subtitling Reductions". In Dollerup C. & A. Loddegard (eds), 245-251.

Krings, Hans P. 1986. *Was in den Köpfen von Übersetzen vorgeht. Eine empirische Untersuchung zur Struktur des Übersetzungsprozesses an fortgeschrittenen Französischlernern*. Tübingen: Gunter Narr.

Kuhn Thomas S. 1970. *The Structure of Scientific Revolutions*. Chicago: The University of Chicago.

Kurz, Ingrid. 1990. "Overcoming Language Barriers in European Television". In Bowen D. & Bowen M. (eds), 168-175.

Kurz, Ingrid. 1992. "'Shadowing' Exercises in Interpreter Training". In Dollerup C. & A. Loddegaard (eds), 245-250.

Kurz, Ingrid. 1993. "Conference Interpretation: Expectations of Different User Groups". *The Interpreters' Newsletter* 5: 13-21.

Kurz, Ingrid. 1994. "What Do Different User Groups Expect from a Conference Interpreter?" *Jerome Quarterly* 9(2): 3-7.

Lakoff Tolmack, R. 1990. *Talking Power*. New York: Basic Books.

Lambert, José. 1993. "History, historiography and the discipline. A programme". In Gambier Y. & Tommola J. (eds), 3-25.

Lambert, Sylvie. 1989a. "Information processing among conference interpreters: A test of the depth-of-processing hypothesis". In Gran L. & J. Dodds (eds), 83-91.
Lambert, Sylvie. 1989b. "La formation d'interprète: la méthode cognitive". *Meta* 34(4): 736-744.
Lambert, Sylvie. 1992. "Shadowing". *The Interpreters' Newsletter* 4: 15-24.
Lambert, Sylvie. 1993. "The Effect of Ear of Information Reception on the Proficiency of Simultaneous Interpretation". *The Interpreters' Newsletter* 5: 22-34.
Lambert Sylvie, Darò Valeria & Fabbro Franco. 1993. "Focalized attention on input vs output during simultaneous interpretation: possibly a waste of effort". In C.Picken (ed), *Proceedings - XIII FIT World Congress. Translation - the vital link*. Brighton, 381-388.
Lambert, Sylvie & Lambert, Wallace E. 1985. Physiology: a Questionnaire. *Meta* 30: 68-72.
Lambert Sylvie & Barbara Moser-Mercer (eds). 1994. *Bridging the Gap. Empirical Research on Simultaneous Interpretation*. Amsterdam and Philadelphia: Benjamins.
Lawson, Everdina A. 1967. "Attention and simultaneous translation". *Language and Speech* 10: 29-35.
Lebrun, Yves. 1991. "Polyglotte Reaktionen". *Neurolinguistik* 5: 1-9.
Levelt, Willem. 1989. *Speaking*. Cambridge, Mass.: Bradford.
Linell, Per. 1992. "The embeddedness of decontextualization in the contexts of social practices". In Heen Wold A. (ed), *The Dialogical Alternative: Towards a Theory of Language and Mind*. Oslo: Scandinavian University Press, 253-271.
Linell, Per. 1995a. "Troubles with mutuality: towards a dialogical theory of misunderstanding and miscommunication". In Marková I., Graumann C.F. & Koppa K. (eds), *Mutualities in Dialogue*. Cambridge: Cambridge University Press, 176-213.
Linell, Per. 1995b. "The dynamics of contexts in discourse". In Millar Sh. & J.Mey (eds), *Form and Function in Language. RASK* Supplement, vol.2. Odense: University Press, 41-67.
Linell Per, Alemyr L. and Jönsson L. 1993. "Admission of guilt as a communicative project in judicial settings". *Journal of Pragmatics* 19: 153-176.
Linell, Per & Jönsson, L. 1991. "Suspect stories: perspective-setting in an asymmetrical situation". In Marková I. & Foppa K. (eds), *Asymmetries in Dialogue*. Hemel Hempstead: Harvester, Wheatsheaf, 75-100.
Linell, Per & Marková, I. 1993. "Acts in discourse: From monological speech acts to dialogical inter-acts". *Journal for the Theory of Social Behaviour* 23: 173-195.

Linell Per, Wadensjö Cecilia & Jönsson L. 1992. "Establishing communicative contact through a dialogue interpreter". In Grindsted A. & Wagner J. (eds), *Communication for Specific Purposes / Fachsprachliche Kommunikation.* Tübingen: Günter Narr Verlag, 125-142.

Luria A.R. 1976. *Basic Problems of Neurolinguistics.* The Hague: Mouton de Gruyter.

Mack, Gabriele & Lorella Cattaruzza. 1995. "Users Surveys in Simultaneous Interpretation: a Means of Learning about Quality and/or Raising some Reasonable Doubts". In Tommola J. (ed), 51-68.

Mackintosh, Jennifer. 1995. "Portrait of the 'ideal'interpreter". *AIIC Bulletin* 23(3): 61-63.

Macnamara, J. 1967. "The bilingual's linguistic performance: A psychological overview". *Journal of Social Issues* 23: 59-77.

Mantyla, T. 1986. "Optimizing cue effectiveness: recall of 500 and 600 incidentally learned words". *Journal of Experimental Psychology: Learning, Memory and Cognition* 12: 303-312.

Marr, David. 1982. *Vision,* New York: W.H. Freeman.

Marrone, Stefano. 1993. "Quality: Shared Objective". *The Interpreters' Newsletter* 5: 35-41.

Martin, J. R. 1985. "Process and text: Two aspects of human semiosis". In Benson J. D. & W. S. Greaves (eds), *Systemic Perspectives on Discourse,* Vol. 1, Norwood, N. J.: Ablex, 248-274.

Massaro, Dominic W. 1989. *Experimental Psychology. An Information Processing Approach.* San Diego: Harcourt Brace Jovanovich Publishers.

Matthiessen, C. 1992. "Interpreting the Textual Metafunction". In Davies M. & L. Ravelli (eds), *Advances in Systemic Linguistics: Recent Theory and Practice.* London and New York: Pinter, 37-81.

Mayes, A.R. 1988. *Human Organic Memory Disorders.* Cambridge: Cambridge University Press.

McGregor, W. 1990. "The metafunctional hypothesis and syntagmatic relations". *Occasional Papers in Systemic Linguistics* 4: 5-50.

Meak, Lidia. 1990. "Interprétation simultanée et congrès médical: attentes et commentaires". *The Interpreters' Newsletter* 3: 8-13.

Miller, G.A. 1956. "The magical number seven, plus or minus two: Some limits on our capacity for processing information". *Psychological Review* 63: 81-97.

Mizuno, Akira. 1993. "Doujitsuuyaku no doutaimoderuni mukete" (Towards a Dynamic Model of Simultaneous Interpretation). In the *Proceedings of the Fourth International Japanese/English Translation Conference.* IJET 4. Brisbane: The University of Queensland, 421-447.

Morris, Ruth. 1989a. *The Impact of Court Interpretation on Legal Proceedings*. Communications Institute, Hebrew University of Jerusalem, unpublished M.A. Thesis.

Morris, Ruth. 1989b. "Court Interpretation: The Trial of Ivan John Demjanjuk. A Case Study". *The Interpreters' Newsletter* 2: 27-37.

Neubert, Albrecht & Gregory Shreve. 1992. *Translation as Text*. Kent, Ohio: Kent State University Press.

Newell, A. & Simon, H.A. 1972. *Human Problem Solving*. Englewood-Clifs, N.J.: Prentice-Hall.

Ng, Bee Chin. 1992. "End Users' Subjective Reaction to the Performance of Student Interpreters". *The Interpreters' Newsletter*. Special Issue 1: 35-41.

Nida, Eugene A. 1976. "A framework for the Analysis and Evaluation of Theories of Translation". In R.W. Brislin (ed), 47-91.

Niemeier, S. 1991. "Intercultural Dimensions of Pragmatics in Film Synchronization". *Pragmatics and beyond: new series* 6(3): 145-162 .

Niska, Helge. 1995. "Just interpreting: Role conflicts and discourse types in court interpreting". In Morris Marshall (ed), *Translation and the Law*. (ATA Scholarly Monograph Series VIII). Amsterdam and Philadelphia: Benamins.

Nouss, Alexis. 1993. "Translation: art or science? A hermeneutical reading". In Gambier Y. & Tommola J. (eds), 53-63.

Nowak-Lehmann, Elke. 1989. "Apprendre l'interprétation simultanée: aspects cognitifs". In Gran L. & J. Dodds (eds), 151-154.

O'Connor, J. & Seymour, J. 1990. *Introducing Neuro-Linguistic Programming*, London: Mandula (Harper Collins).

O'Donnell, M. 1990. "A dynamic model of exchange". *Word* 41(3): 293-327.

Obler L.K., Zatorre R.J., Galloway L.& Vaid J. 1982. "Cerebral lateralization in bilinguals: Methodological issues". *Brain and Language* 15: 40-45.

Ochs, Elinor. 1979. "Planned and Unplanned Discourse". *Syntax and Semantics* 12: 51-80.

Oléron Pierre & Nanpon H. 1965. "Recherches sur la traduction simultanée". *Journal de Psychologie normale et Pathologique* 62: 73-94.

Paradis, Michel. 1977. "Bilingualism and aphasia". In Whitaker H. & H. Whitaker (eds), *Studies in Neurolinguistics, vol. 3*. New York: Academic Press.

Paradis, Michel. 1984. "Aphasie et traduction". *Meta* 29(1): 57-67.

Paradis, Michel. 1987. *The Assessment of Bilingual Aphasia*. Hillsdale, N.J.: Erlbaum.

Paradis, Michel. 1990. "Notes and discussion. Language lateralization in bilinguals: enough already". *Brain and Language* 39(4): 576-586.

Paradis, Michel. 1993. "Multilingualism and aphasia". In Blanken G. et al.(eds), *Linguistic Disorders and Pathologies*. Berlin: de Gruyter, 278-288.

Paradis, Michel. 1994. "Neurolinguistic aspects of implicit and explicit memory: Implications for bilingualism". In Ellis N. (ed), *Implicit and Explicit Language Learning*. London: Academic Press, 393-419.

Paradis M., Goldblum M.C.& Abidi R. 1982. "Alternate antagonism with paradoxical translation behavior in two bilingual aphasic patients". *Brain and Language* 15: 55-69.

Penfield, W. & Roberts, L. 1959. *Speech and Brain Mechanisms*. Princeton: Princeton University Press.

Perecman E. 1984. "Spontaneous translation and language mixing in a polyglot aphasic". *Brain and Language* 23: 43-63.

Pinter (Kurz), Ingrid. 1969. *Der Einfluss der Übung und Konzentration auf simultanes Sprechen und Hören*. Unpublished doctoral dissertation, University of Vienna.

Pöchhacker, Franz. 1993a. "From knowledge to text: coherence in simultaneous interpreting". In Gambier Y. & Tommola J. (eds), 87-100.

Pöchhacker, Franz. 1993b. "On the *Science* of Interpretation". *The Interpreters' Newsletter* 5: 52-59.

Pöchhacker, Franz. 1994. "Quality Assurance in Simultaneous Interpreting". In Dollerup C. & A. Lindegaard (eds), 233-242.

Pöchhacker, Franz. 1995. "'Those who do…'; A Profile of Research(ers) in Interpreting". *Target* 7(1): 47-64.

Posner, M. & Warren, R. 1972. "Traces, concepts and conscious constructions". In Melton A. & E.Martin (eds), *Coding processes in human memory* . New York: Halsted Press.

Pym, Anthony. 1995. "Translation as a Transaction Cost". *Meta* 40(4): 594-605.

Ravelli, Louise. 1995. "A dynamic perspective: Implications for metafunctional interaction and an understanding of theme". In Hasan R. & P. H. Fries (eds), 187-234.

Reiss, Katharina. & Vermeer, Hans J. 1984. *Grundlegung einer allgemeinen Translationstheorie*. Tübingen: Niemeyer.

Renfer, Christoph. 1992. "Translator and interpreter training: a case for a two-tier system". In Dollerup C. & A. Loddegaard (eds), 173-184.

Richard, J. F., Poitrenaud S. & Tijus, C. 1993. "Problem-solving restructuration: elimination of implicit constraints". *Cognitive Science* 4: 497-529.

Roditi, Edouard. (s.d.). *Interpreting: Its History in a Nutshell*. Washington: Georgetown University Press.

Romaine, Suzanne. 1989. *Bilingualism*. Oxford: Blackwell.

Rumelhart, D.E. & McClelland, J.L. 1986. *Parallel Distributed Processing: Explorations in the Microstructure of Cognition.* Volume 1: *Foundations*; Volume 2: *Psychological and Biological Models.* Cambridge, Mass.: MIT, ss/Bradford Books.

Salevsky, Heidemarie. 1986. *Probleme des Simultandolmetschens. Eine Studie zur Handlunksspezifk.* Berlin. Linguistische Studien 154.

Salevsky, Heidemarie. 1990. "Interne Abläufe beim Dolmetschen und externe Dolmetschkritik - ein unlösbares Problem der Übersetzungswissenschaft?". *TEXTconTEXT* 5(3-4): 143-165.

Salevsky, Heidemarie. 1992. "Dolmetschen - Objekt der Übersetzungs- oder Dolmetschwissenschaft?". In Salevsky H. (ed), *Wissenschaftliche Grundlagen der Sprachmittlung.* Berliner Beiträge zur Übersetzungswissenschaft. Frankfurt am Main,Berlin,Bern,New York,Paris, Wien: Peter Lang, 85-117.

Salevsky, Heidemarie. 1993. "The Distinctive Nature of Interpreting Studies". *Target* 5(2): 149-167.

Samovar, Larry A. & Porter, Richard E. 1991. *Communication Between Cultures.* Belmont, California: Wadsworth Publishing Company.

Schacter, D.L. 1987. "Implicit expressions of memory in organic amnesia: Learning new facts and associations". *Human Neurobiology* 6: 107-118.

Schacter, D.L., Chiu, C.Y.P. & Ochsner, K.N. 1993. "Implicit memory: A selective review". *Annual Review of Neuroscience* 16:159-182.

Schiffrin, Deborah. 1994. *Approaches to Discourse.* Cambridge: Blackwell.

Schweda-Nicholson, Nancy. 1989a. "Linguistic Perspectives on Courtroom Language and Interpretation Services". In Aguirre A. M. (ed), *Northeast Conference on Legal Interpretation and Translation, May 5 and 6, 1989.* N.J.: The Consortium of Educators in Legal Interpretation and Translation at Jersey State College: 65-74.

Schweda-Nicholson, Nancy. 1989b. "Documentation and Text Preparation for Simultaneous Interpretation". In Hammond D. L. (ed). *Proceedings of the 1989 American Translators Association Conference.* Medford, NJ: Learned Information Inc., 163-182.

Schweda-Nicholson, Nancy. 1990a. "Consecutive Note-Taking for Community Interpretation". In Bowen D. & M. (eds), 136-145.

Schweda-Nicholson, Nancy. 1990b. "The Role of Shadowing in Interpreter Training". *The Interpreters' Newsletter* 3: 33-37.

Schweda-Nicholson, Nancy. 1993. "The Constructive Criticism Model". *The Interpreters' Newsletter* 5: 60-67.

Scoville, W.B. & Milner, B. 1957. "Loss of recent memory after bilateral hippocampal lesions". *Journal of Neurology, Neurosurgery and Psychiatry* 20: 11-21.

Searle, John R. 1977. *Speech Acts. An Essay in the Philosophy of Language*. New York: Cambridge University Press.

Seleskovitch, Danica. 1975. *Langage, langues et mémoire*. Paris:Minard.

Seleskovitch, Danica. 1986. "Who Should Assess an Interpreter's Performance?" *Multilingua* 5-4: 236.

Seliger, H.W. & Vago, R.M. 1991. *First Language Attrition*. Cambridge: Cambridge University Press.

Selinker, Larry. 1972. "Interlanguage". *International Review of Applied Linguistics* 10: 209-230.

Setton, Robin. 1993a. "Is Non-Intra-IE Interpretation Different? European Models and Chinese-English Realities". *Meta* 38(2): 238-256.

Setton, Robin. 1993b. "Speech in Europe and Asia: Levels of evaluation in cross-cultural conference interpretation". *Interpreting Research: Journal of the IRAJ* 3(2): 2-11.

Shallice, T. 1988. *From Neuropsychology to Mental Structure*. Cambridge: Cambridge University Press.

Shiryaev, A. F. 1979. *Sinkhronny perevod.*(Simultaneous Interpretation. The Activity of a Simultaneous Interpreter and Methods of Teaching Simultaneous Interpretation). Moscow: Voiennole izdatelstvo.

Shlesinger, Miriam. 1989a. *Simultaneous Interpretation as a Factor in Effecting Shifts in the Position of Texts on the Oral-Literate Continuum*. Unpublished M.A. Thesis. Tel Aviv University.

Shlesinger, Miriam. 1989b. "Extending the Theory of Translation to Interpretation: Norms as a Case in Point". *Target* 1(1): 111-115.

Shlesinger, Miriam. 1990. "Factors affecting the applicability of the oral-literate continuum to interpretation research". *Hebrew Linguistics* 28-30: 49-56.

Shlesinger, Miriam. 1994. "Intonation in the Production and Perception of Simultaneous Interpretation". In Lambert S. & Moser-Mercer B. (eds), 225-236.

Shlesinger, Miriam. 1995. "Shifts in Cohesion in Simultaneous Interpreting". *The Translator* 1/2: 193-214.

Sidiropoulou, Maria. 1993. "Thematic Organization in Translation". In Kakouriotis A. (ed), *Proceedings of the 7th International Symposium on English and Greek: Description and/or Comparison of the two Languages*. Thessaloniki: Aristotle University, 94-109.

Sidiropoulou, Maria. 1994. "Contrast in English and Greek news reporting: a Translation Perspective". In Kakouriotis A. (ed), *Proceedings of the 8th International Symposium on English and Greek: Description and/or Comparison of the two Languages*. Thessaloniki: Aristotle University, 96-108.

Sinclair, John M. & R. J. Coulthard. 1975. *Towards an Analysis of Discourse: The English used by Teachers and Pupils*. London: Oxford University Press.

Snelling, David. C. 1989. "A Typology of Interpretation for Teaching Purposes". In Gran L. and J. Dodds (eds), 141-142.

Snelling, David C. 1990. "Upon the Simultaneous Translation of Films". *The Interpreters' Newsletter* 3: 14-16.

Snelling, David. 1992. *Strategies for Simultaneous Interpreting from Romance Languages into English.* Udine: Campanotto.

Spelke E., Hirst W.& Neissser U. 1976. "Skills of divided attention". *Cognition* 4: 215-230.

Sperber, David. & Wilson, Deirdre. 1986. *Relevance: Communication and Cognition.* Cambridge: Harvard University Press.

Spiller, Edith & Bosatra, Andrea. 1989. "Role of the auditory sensory modality in simultaneous interpretation". In Gran L. & J. Dodds (eds), 37-38.

Spiller-Bosatra E. & Darò, V. 1992. "Delayed Auditory Feedback Effects on Simultaneous Interpretation". *The Interpreters' Newsletter* 4: 8-14.

Spiller-Bosatra E., Darò V., Fabbro F. & Bosatra, A. 1990. "Audio-phonological and neuropsychological aspects of simultaneous interpretation". *Scandinavian Audiology* 19: 81-87.

Squire, L.R. 1987. "Memory: Neural organization and behavior". In Mountcastle S. et al. (eds), *Handbook of Physiology.* Vol. 5. Bethesda: American Physiological Society, 295-371.

Stenzl, Catherine. 1983. *Simultaneous Interpretation: Groundwork towards a Comprehensive Model.* Unpublished M.A. thesis, University of London.

Stenzl, Catherine. 1989. "From Theory to Practice and from Practice to Theory". In Gran L. & J.M. Dodds (eds), 23-26.

Stenzl, Catherine. 1990. "From Theory to Practice and from Practice to Theory". In Gran L. & J.M. Dodds (eds). 23-26.

Strolz, Birgit. 1992. *Theorie und Praxis des Simultandolmetschens. Argumente für einen kontextuellen Top-down Ansatz der Verarbeitung und Produktion von Sprache.* Unpublished doctoral Thesis, University of Vienna.

Strolz, Birgit. 1995. "Une approche asymptotique de la recherche sur l'interprétation", *Target* 7(1): 65-74.

Supreme Court Task Force on Interpreter and Translation Services - Background Report #22: *A day in the Life of New Jersey's Court Interpreters.* An Evaluation of Current Spanish-English Court Interpreting in New Jersey. March 23, 1984.

Tannen, Deborah. 1986. *That's Not What I Meant!,* New York: Ballantine Books.

Tannen, Deborah. 1989. *Talking Voices.* Cambridge: Cambridge University Press.

Target 7(1) 1995. Special Issue: Interpreting Research, Guest-editor: Gile Daniel.

Tarone, E. 1974. "Speech perception in second language acquisition: A suggested model". *Language Learning* 24: 223-233.

Tarone, E. 1983. "On the variability of interlanguage systems". *Applied Linguistics* 4: 43-163.

Tarone, E. 1985. "Variability in interlanguage use: A study of style-shifting in morphology and syntax". *Language Learning* 35: 375-404.

Taylor, T. 1992. *Mutual Misunderstanding: Scepticism and the theorizing of language and interpretation*. London: Routledge.

Taylor Torsello, Carol. 1992. *English in Discourse: A Course for Language Specialists*, Volume II, Padova: Cleup.

Tebble, Helen. 1991. "Towards a theory of interpreting". In Hellander P. (ed) *Proceedings of the 13th Conference of Interpreter and Translator Educators' Association of Australia*. Adelaide: South Australian College of Advanced Education, 54-59.

Tebble, Helen. 1992. "The Genre Element in the Systems Analyst's Interview". *Australian Review of Applied Linguistics* 15(2): 120-136.

Tebble, Helen. 1993. "A discourse model for dialogue interpreting". In Australian Institute of Interpreters and Translators (AUSIT), *Proceedings of the First Practitioners' Seminar*. Canberra: National Accreditation Authority for Translators and Interpreters, 3-26.

Thiéry, Christopher. 1975. *Le bilinguisme chez les interprètes de conférence professionnels*. Unpublished Doctoral Dissertation. Université Paris III.

Thompson, R.F. 1986. "The neurobiology of learning and memory". *Science* 233: 941-947.

Tijus Charles Albert, Legros D. & Moulin F. 1995. "Semantic memory of verb meaning". *IV European Congress of Psychology*. Athens: July 1995.

Tijus, Charles Albert & Santolini, A. (unpublished paper). "How to Change Mental Constructs: The Cognitive Reconstruction of the Berlin Wall.

Tirkkonen-Condit, Sonja .(ed), 1991. *Empirical Research in Translation and Intercultural Studies*. Tübingen. Gunter Narr Verlag.

Tommola, Jorma (ed), 1995. *Topics in Interpreting Research*. Turku: Center for Translation and Interpreting, University of Turku.

Toury, Gideon. 1980. *In Search of a Theory of Translation*. Tel Aviv: The Porter Institute for Poetics and Semiotics. Tel Aviv University.

Toury, Gideon. 1991. "Experimentation in Translation Studies: Achievements, Prospects and Some Pitfalls". In: Sonja Tirkkonen-Condit (ed), 45-66.

Treisman, A.M. 1965. "The effects of redundancy and familiarity on translating and repeating back a foreign and a native language". *British Journal of Psychology* 4: 369-379.

Trompenaars, Fons. 1993. *Riding the Waves of Culture: Understanding Cultural Diversity in Business*, London: The Economist Books.

Tulving, E. 1987. "Multiple memory systems and consciousness". *Human Neurobiology* 6: 67-80.

Tyler, Andrea. 1992. "Discourse structure and specification of relationships: A cross-linguistic analysis". *Text* 12(1): 1-18.

Uchiyama, Hiromichi. 1991. "Problems caused by word order when Interpreting/Translating from English into Japanese: The Effect of the Use of Inanimate Subjects in English". *Meta* 36(2-3): 405-413.

Ullmann, Stephen. 1977. *Semantics. An Introduction to the Science of Meaning.* Oxford: Basil Blackwell.

Van Dam, Ine Mary. 1989. "Strategies of simultaneous interpretation: a methodology for the training of simultaneous interpreters". In Gran L. & Dodds J.(eds), 167-176.

Van Dam, Ine Mary. 1990. "Letter to the Editor". *The Interpreters' Newsletter* 3: 5-7.

Van Dijk, A.T. 1985. "Structure of news in the press". In van Dijk A.T. (ed), *Discourse and Communication.* Berlin: Mouton de Gruyter, 69-93.

Veyrac G.J. 1931. "A study of aphasia in polyglot subjects". In Paradis M. (ed), *Readings on Aphasia in Bilinguals and Polyglots.* Paris: Didier, 320-338.

Viezzi, Maurizio. 1989. "Information Retention as a Parameter for the Comparison of Sight Translation and Simultaneous Interpretation: An Experimental Study". *The Interpreters' Newsletter* 2: 65-69.

Viezzi, Maurizio. 1990. "Sight Translation, Simultaneous Interpretation and Information Retention." In Gran L. & C.Taylor (eds), *Aspects of Applied and Experimental Research on Conference Interpretation.* Udine: Campanotto, .

Viezzi, Maurizio. 1992. "The translation of Film Subtitles from English into Italian". *The Interpreters'Newsletter* 4: 84-86.

Viezzi, Maurizio. 1993. "Considerations on Interpretation Quality Assessment". In Catriona Picken (ed), *Proceedings - XIII FIT World Congress: Translation - the vital link.* (Brighton, 6-8 August 1993). Volume 1, 389-397.

Vinay, Jean-Paul & Darbelnet, Jean. 1958. *Stylistique comparée du français et de l'anglais.* Paris: Didier (édition revue et corrigée, 1977). Translated in English by J.C.Sager & M.J.Hamel. 1995. *Comparative Stylistics of French and English. A Methodology for Translation.* Amsterdam and Philadelphia: Benjamins.

Vuorikoski, Anna-Riitta. 1993. "Simultaneous Interpretation - User Experience and Expectations". In Picken C. (ed), *Proceedings -XIII FIT World Congress: Translation - the vital link.* (Brighton, 6-8 August 1993). Volume 1. 317-327.

Wadensjö, Cecilia. 1992. *Interpreting as Interaction - On dialogue interpreting in immigration hearings and medical encounters.* Linköping: Linköping University, Department of Communication Studies.

Wakabayashi, Judy. 1991a. "The Translator as Editor: Beginnings and Endings in Japanese-English Translation". In Larson M.L. (ed), *Translation: Theory and Practice - Tension and Interdependence*. (ATA Scholarly Monograph Series V). Amsterdam and Philadelphia: Benjamins: 224-234.

Wakabayashi, Judy. 1991b. "Translation between unrelated languages and cultures, as illustrated by Japanese-English translation". *Meta* 36(2-3): 414-423.

Wakabayashi, Judy. 1992. "Some Characteristics of Japanese Style and the Implications for Japanese-English Translation". *The Interpreters' Newsletter*. Special Issue 1: 60-68.

Weiskrantz, L. 1987. "Neuroanatomy of memory and amnesia: A case for multiple memory systems". *Human Neurobiology* 6: 93-106.

Wernicke C. 1874. *Der aphasische SymptomenKomplex. Eine psychologische Studie auf anatomischer Basis*. Breslau: Max Cohn & Weigert.

Whittaker, R. 1990. "Theme in cognitive processing". Paper delivered at the 7th International Systemic Congress, University of Stirling, U. K, 3-7 July 1990.

Williams, J.N. 1992. "Processing Polysemous Words in Context: Evidence for Interrelated Meanings". *Journal of Psycholinguistic Research* 21(3): 193-218.

Williams, Sarah. 1994. "The application of SLA research to interpreting". *Perspectives: Studies in Translatology* 1: 19-28.

Williams, Sarah. 1995a. "Processes in Simultaneous Interpreting - (PRINS)". HSFR Project Proposal.

Williams, Sarah. 1995b. "Observations on anomalous stress in interpreting". *The Translator: Studies in intercultural communication* 1: 47-64.

Williams, Sarah. 1995c. "Research on Bilingualism and its Relevance for interpreting". *Hermes* 5: 143-154.

Wilss, Wolfram. 1978. "Syntactic Anticipation in German-English Simultaneous Interpreting". In Gerver D. & W. Sinaiko (eds), 343-352.

Yorke, I. 1987. *The Technique of Television News*. London: Focal Press.

Index of authors

List of participants
Turku 25 - 27 August, 1994

Aarup, Hanne, Copenhagen School of Business, Denmark
Ackerman, Dorothea, Leipzig, Germany
Adams, Christine, University of Westminster, UK
Ahron, Thomas, University of Stockholm, Sweden
Alexieva, Bistra, University of Sofia, Bulgaria

Bassa-Korcmáros, Lia, Technical University of Budapest, Hungary
Björk, Kerstin, AB Stockholmstolkarna, Stockholm, Sweden
Blanco, Irma, Mexican Association of Conference Interpreters, Mexico City, Mexico
Bohák-Szabari, Krisztina, Eötvös L. University, Budapest, Hungary
Boronkay, Zsuzsa, Eötvös L. University, Budapest, Hungary

Carlsson, Rune, University of Stockholm, Sweden
Cattaruzza, Lorella, University of Bologna, Trieste, Italy
Cenkova, Ivana, Charles University, Prague, Czech Republic
Cervato, Emanuela, University of Hull, UK
Champoux-Cadoche, Ariane, Lafleur-Brown, Montreal, Canada
Corvington, Monique, United Nations, New York, USA

Dam, Helle, Aarhus School of Business, Denmark
Daró, Valeria, SSLMIT, University of Trieste, Italy
De Ferra, Donatella, University of Hull, UK
Déjean Le Féal, Karla, University of Paris III, ESIT, France
Detthow, Annica, Tolkinterserv, Vintrosa, Sweden
Dodds, John, SSLMIT, University of Trieste, Italy
Dubslaff, Friedel, Aarhus School of Business, Denmark
Durham, Maria, Joszef Attila University, Szeged, Hungary

Englund Dimitrova, Birgitta, University of Stockholm, Sweden

Fabbro, Franco, University of Trieste, Italy

Forstner, Martin, Johannes Gutenberg-Universität Mainz in Germersheim, Germany

Gallina, Sandra, European Commission, Brussels, Belgium

Gambier, Yves, University of Turku, Finland

Gergely-Láng, Zsussa, Eötvös L. University, Budapest, Hungary

Gile, Daniel, ISIT & INALCO, Paris, France

Giordani, Alessandra, Scuola Superiore per Interpreti e Traduttori, Forli, Italy

Gram, Torben, European Parliament, Brussels, Belgium

Gran, Laura, SSLMIT, University of Trieste, Italy

Gringiani, Angela, SSLMIT, University of Trieste, Italy

Haack, Maria Cristina, Johannes Gutenberg-Universität Mainz in Germersheim, Germany

Haaksilahti, Tiina, Turku Christian Institute, Finland

Hammarström, Karin, Tolkcentralen, Stockholm, Sweden

Hermansson, Monica, AB Stockholmstolkarna, Stockholm, Sweden

Hernandéz, Elizabeth, Mexican Association of Cenference Interpreters, Mexico City, Mexico

Hertog, Erik, Katholike Vlaamse Hogeschool, Antwerpen, Belgium

Hiltunen, Sinikka, Toijala, Finland

Hoenig, Hans G., Johannes Gutenberg-Universität Mainz in Germersheim, Germany

Holz-Mänttäri, Justa, Turku, Finland

Huber, Dieter, Johannes Gutenberg-Universität Mainz in Germersheim, Germany

Humphreys, Tuula, University of Turku, Finland

Irsula, Jesus, Cuban Centre for Translation and Interpretation, Havanna, Cuba
Isham, William, University of Mexico, Albuqurque, USA

Jääskeläinen, Riitta, University of Joensuu, Finland
Jänis, Marja, University of Joensuu, Finland
Jansen, Peter, K.U. Leuven, Belgium
Johansson, Anders, Tolkcentralen, Stockholm, Sweden
Johansson, Marjut, University of Tampere, Finland

Kalina, Sylvia, University of Heidelberg, Germany
Katan, David, SSLMIT, University of Trieste, Italy
Klaudy, Kinga, Eötvös L. University, Budapest, Hungary
Kohrs Kegel, Helga, University of Granada, Spain
Kondo, Masaomi, Daito Bunka University, Japan
Konttinen, Kalle, University of Turku, Finland
Kretschmann, Birgit, University of Turku, Finland
Kumpulainen, Tea, Tampere, Finland
Kurz, Ingrid, University of Vienna, Austria

Laakso, Ritva, Nordiska Språk- och Informationscentret, Helsinki, Finland
Lamberger, Heike, University of Graz, Austria
Lambert, Sylvie, School of Translation and Interpretation, Ottawa, Canada
Laukkanen, Johanna, University of Joensuu, Finland
Lemhagen Gunnar, University of Stockholm, Sweden
Levy-Berlowitz, Ruth, AIIC, Ramat Gan, Israel
Liefländer-Koistinen, Luise, University of Joensuu, Finland
Linell, Per, University of Linköping, Sweden
Liu, Minha, Fu Jen University, Taipei, Taiwan, ROC
Lonsdale, Deryle, Carnegie Mellon University, Pittsburgh, USA
Lörscher, Wolfgang, University of Leipzig, Germany
Lozey, Brigitte, University of Graz, Austria

Mack, Gabriele, University of Bologna, Italy
Makarova, Viera, University of Warwick, Coventry, UK
Martinssen, Bodil, Aarhus School of Business, Denmark
Mizuno, Akira, NHK Bilingual Centre, Tokyo, Japan
Moser-Mercer, Barbara, University of Geneva, Switzerland

Natune, Martina, University of Joensuu, Finland
Nicholson, Nancy S., Gaithersburg, Maryland, USA
Nilsson, Anna-Lena, University of Stockholm, Sweden
Niska, Helge, University of Stockholm, Sweden

Örkényi, Rósza, University of Agricultural Sciences, Gödöllö, Hungary
Ozores, Vida, Universitat Autònoma de Barcelona, Spain

Padilla, Presentacion, University of Granada, Spain
Peerless, Aase, Birkerod, Denmark
Petit, Núria, Universitat Pompeu Fabra, Barcelona, Spain
Platter, Monika, University of Innsbrück, Austria
Pöchhacker, Franz, University of Vienna, Austria

Rådahl, Jannice, University of Stockholm, Sweden
Rådahl, Tord, University of Stockholm, Sweden
Raita, Siiri, University of Tartu, Estonia
Riccardi, Alessandra, SSLMIT, University of Trieste, Italy
Roinila, Pauli, University of Joensuu, Finland
Russo, Maria Chiara, SSLMIT, University of Trieste, Italy

Salevsky, Heidemarie, Humboldt-Universität Berlin, Germany
Saluveer, Madis, Folkuniversitet Tartu, Estonia
Sanchez, Maria Mercedes, Johannes Gutenberg-Universität Mainz in Germersheim, Germany

Schaeffner, Christina, Aston University, Birmingham, UK
Schjoldager, Anne, Aarhus School of Business, Denmark
Schweda-Nicholson, Nancy, University of Delaware, Newark, USA
Setton, Robin, Fu Jen niversity, Taipei, Taiwan, ROC
Shlesinger, Miriam, Bar-Ilan University, Ramat An, Israel
Sidiropoulou, Maria, University of Athens, Greece
Sikh, Helena, Tolkcentralen, Örebro, Sweden
Snelling, David, SSLMIT, University of Trieste, Italy
Somos, Csilla Edit, Technical University, Budapest, Hungary
Strolz, Birgit, University of Vienna, Austria
Sunnari, Marianna, University of Turku, Finland
Suomela-Salmi, Eija, University of Turku, Finland
Szomor, Imréné, University of Agricultural Sciences, Gödöllö, Hungary

Tamm, Mall, University of Tartu, Estonia
Taylor, Christopher, SSLMIT, University of Trieste, Italy
Taylor Torsello, Carol,. SSLMIT, University of Trieste, Italy
Tebble, Helen, Deakin University, Melbourne, Australia
Tijus, Charles Albert, University of Paris VIII, France
Tirkkonen-Condit, Sonja, University of Joensuu, Finland
Tommola, Jorma, University of Turku, Finland
Torikka, Gerda, University of Turku, Finland
Tuononen, Jyrki, Joensuu, Finland

Ukmar, Marco, SSLMIT, University of Trieste, Italy

Välimäki, Jacqueline, University of Turku, Finland
Viaggio, Sergio, United Nations, Vienna, Austria
Viezzi, Maurizio, SSLMIT, University of Trieste, Italy
Vik-Tuovinen, Gun-Viol, University of Vaasa, Finland
von Essen, Pia, Intertext Oy, Tampere, Finland

Vuorikoski, Anna-Riitta, University of Tampere, Finland

Wadensjö, Cecilia, University of Linköping, Sweden
Weller, Georganne, Centro De Estudios De Linguistica Aplicada, Mexico City, Mexico
Williams, Sarah, University of Stockholm, Sweden
Wolf, Petra, Pains, Austria

Yánez, Patricia, Mexican Association of Conference Interpreters, Mexico City, Mexico

Zalka, Ilona, Stockholm, Sweden

Benjamins Translation Library

A complete list of titles in this series can be found on *www.benjamins.com*

47   SAWYER, David B.: Fundamental Aspects of Interpreter Education. Curriculum and Assessment. 2004. xviii, 312 pp.

46   BRUNETTE, Louise, Georges BASTIN, Isabelle HEMLIN and Heather CLARKE (eds.): The Critical Link 3. Interpreters in the Community. Selected papers from the Third International Conference on Interpreting in Legal, Health and Social Service Settings, Montréal, Quebec, Canada 22–26 May 2001. 2003. xii, 359 pp.

45   ALVES, Fabio (ed.): Triangulating Translation. Perspectives in process oriented research. 2003. x, 165 pp.

44   SINGERMAN, Robert: Jewish Translation History. A bibliography of bibliographies and studies. With an introductory essay by Gideon Toury. 2002. xxxvi, 420 pp.

43   GARZONE, Giuliana and Maurizio VIEZZI (eds.): Interpreting in the 21st Century. Challenges and opportunities. 2002. x, 337 pp.

42   HUNG, Eva (ed.): Teaching Translation and Interpreting 4. Building bridges. 2002. xii, 243 pp.

41   NIDA, Eugene A.: Contexts in Translating. 2002. x, 127 pp.

40   ENGLUND DIMITROVA, Birgitta and Kenneth HYLTENSTAM (eds.): Language Processing and Simultaneous Interpreting. Interdisciplinary perspectives. 2000. xvi, 164 pp.

39   CHESTERMAN, Andrew, Natividad GALLARDO SAN SALVADOR and Yves GAMBIER (eds.): Translation in Context. Selected papers from the EST Congress, Granada 1998. 2000. x, 393 pp.

38   SCHÄFFNER, Christina and Beverly ADAB (eds.): Developing Translation Competence. 2000. xvi, 244 pp.

37   TIRKKONEN-CONDIT, Sonja and Riitta JÄÄSKELÄINEN (eds.): Tapping and Mapping the Processes of Translation and Interpreting. Outlooks on empirical research. 2000. x, 176 pp.

36   SCHMID, Monika S.: Translating the Elusive. Marked word order and subjectivity in English-German translation. 1999. xii, 174 pp.

35   SOMERS, Harold (ed.): Computers and Translation. A translator's guide. 2003. xvi, 351 pp.

34   GAMBIER, Yves and Henrik GOTTLIEB (eds.): (Multi) Media Translation. Concepts, practices, and research. 2001. xx, 300 pp.

33   GILE, Daniel, Helle V. DAM, Friedel DUBSLAFF, Bodil MARTINSEN and Anne SCHJOLDAGER (eds.): Getting Started in Interpreting Research. Methodological reflections, personal accounts and advice for beginners. 2001. xiv, 255 pp.

32   BEEBY, Allison, Doris ENSINGER and Marisa PRESAS (eds.): Investigating Translation. Selected papers from the 4th International Congress on Translation, Barcelona, 1998. 2000. xiv, 296 pp.

31   ROBERTS, Roda P., Silvana E. CARR, Diana ABRAHAM and Aideen DUFOUR (eds.): The Critical Link 2: Interpreters in the Community. Selected papers from the Second International Conference on Interpreting in legal, health and social service settings, Vancouver, BC, Canada, 19–23 May 1998. 2000. vii, 316 pp.

30   DOLLERUP, Cay: Tales and Translation. The Grimm Tales from Pan-Germanic narratives to shared international fairytales. 1999. xiv, 384 pp.

29   WILSS, Wolfram: Translation and Interpreting in the 20th Century. Focus on German. 1999. xiii, 256 pp.

28   SETTON, Robin: Simultaneous Interpretation. A cognitive-pragmatic analysis. 1999. xvi, 397 pp.

27   BEYLARD-OZEROFF, Ann, Jana KRÁLOVÁ and Barbara MOSER-MERCER (eds.): Translators' Strategies and Creativity. Selected Papers from the 9th International Conference on Translation and Interpreting, Prague, September 1995. In honor of Jiří Levý and Anton Popovič. 1998. xiv, 230 pp.

26   TROSBORG, Anna (ed.): Text Typology and Translation. 1997. xvi, 342 pp.

25   POLLARD, David E. (ed.): Translation and Creation. Readings of Western Literature in Early Modern China, 1840–1918. 1998. vi, 336 pp.

24   ORERO, Pilar and Juan C. SAGER (eds.): The Translator's Dialogue. Giovanni Pontiero. 1997. xiv, 252 pp.

23   GAMBIER, Yves, Daniel GILE and Christopher TAYLOR (eds.): Conference Interpreting: Current Trends in Research. Proceedings of the International Conference on Interpreting: What do we know and how? 1997. iv, 246 pp.

22   CHESTERMAN, Andrew: Memes of Translation. The spread of ideas in translation theory. 1997. vii, 219 pp.

21   BUSH, Peter and Kirsten MALMKJÆR (eds.): Rimbaud's Rainbow. Literary translation in higher education. 1998. x, 200 pp.

20   SNELL-HORNBY, Mary, Zuzana JETTMAROVÁ and Klaus KAINDL (eds.): Translation as Intercultural Communication. Selected papers from the EST Congress, Prague 1995. 1997. x, 354 pp.

19   CARR, Silvana E., Roda P. ROBERTS, Aideen DUFOUR and Dini STEYN (eds.): The Critical Link: Interpreters in the Community. Papers from the 1st international conference on interpreting in legal, health and social service settings, Geneva Park, Canada, 1–4 June 1995. 1997. viii, 322 pp.

18   SOMERS, Harold (ed.): Terminology, LSP and Translation. Studies in language engineering in honour of Juan C. Sager. 1996. xii, 250 pp.

17   POYATOS, Fernando (ed.): Nonverbal Communication and Translation. New perspectives and challenges in literature, interpretation and the media. 1997. xii, 361 pp.

16   DOLLERUP, Cay and Vibeke APPEL (eds.): Teaching Translation and Interpreting 3. New Horizons. Papers from the Third Language International Conference, Elsinore, Denmark, 1995. 1996. viii, 338 pp.

15   WILSS, Wolfram: Knowledge and Skills in Translator Behavior. 1996. xiii, 259 pp.

14   MELBY, Alan K. and Terry WARNER: The Possibility of Language. A discussion of the nature of language, with implications for human and machine translation. 1995. xxvi, 276 pp.

13   DELISLE, Jean and Judith WOODSWORTH (eds.): Translators through History. 1995. xvi, 346 pp.

12   BERGENHOLTZ, Henning and Sven TARP (eds.): Manual of Specialised Lexicography. The preparation of specialised dictionaries. 1995. 256 pp.

11   VINAY, Jean-Paul and Jean DARBELNET: Comparative Stylistics of French and English. A methodology for translation. Translated and edited by Juan C. Sager, M.-J. Hamel. 1995. xx, 359 pp.

10   KUSSMAUL, Paul: Training the Translator. 1995. x, 178 pp.

 9   REY, Alain: Essays on Terminology. Translated by Juan C. Sager. With an introduction by Bruno de Bessé. 1995. xiv, 223 pp.

 8   GILE, Daniel: Basic Concepts and Models for Interpreter and Translator Training. 1995. xvi, 278 pp.

 7   BEAUGRANDE, Robert de, Abdullah SHUNNAQ and Mohamed Helmy HELIEL (eds.): Language, Discourse and Translation in the West and Middle East. 1994. xii, 256 pp.

 6   EDWARDS, Alicia B.: The Practice of Court Interpreting. 1995. xiii, 192 pp.

 5   DOLLERUP, Cay and Annette LINDEGAARD (eds.): Teaching Translation and Interpreting 2. Insights, aims and visions. Papers from the Second Language International Conference Elsinore, 1993. 1994. viii, 358 pp.

 4   TOURY, Gideon: Descriptive Translation Studies – and beyond. 1995. viii, 312 pp.

 3   LAMBERT, Sylvie and Barbara MOSER-MERCER (eds.): Bridging the Gap. Empirical research in simultaneous interpretation. 1994. 362 pp.

 2   SNELL-HORNBY, Mary, Franz PÖCHHACKER and Klaus KAINDL (eds.): Translation Studies: An Interdiscipline. Selected papers from the Translation Studies Congress, Vienna, 1992. 1994. xii, 438 pp.

 1   SAGER, Juan C.: Language Engineering and Translation. Consequences of automation. 1994. xx, 345 pp.